$25 00

10/98

Records of
PLYMOUTH COLONY:
Births, Marriages, Deaths, Burials, and Other Records, 1633-1689

Edited By
NATHANIEL B. SHURTLEFF

Reprinted with
"Plymouth Colony Vital Records,"
a Supplement from *The Mayflower Descendant*
BY GEORGE ERNEST BOWMAN

Originally published as Volume 8 of
Records of the Colony of New Plymouth in
New England: Miscellaneous Records, 1633-1689
Boston, 1857
Reprinted with "Plymouth Colony Vital Records,"
Excerpted from *The Mayflower Descendant*
Vol. XIII, pp. 83-86 (1911)
Vol. XV, pp. 25-29 (1913)
By Genealogical Publishing Co., Inc.
1001 N. Calvert St., Baltimore, Maryland 21202
1976, 1979, 1991, 1997
Reprinted from a volume in the George Peabody Department
Enoch Pratt Free Library
Baltimore, Maryland
Library of Congress Catalogue Card Number 75-34715
International Standard Book Number 0-8063-0701-3
Made in the United States of America

RECORDS

OF THE

COLONY

OF

NEW PLYMOUTH

IN

NEW ENGLAND.

PRINTED BY ORDER OF THE LEGISLATURE OF THE
COMMONWEALTH OF MASSACHUSETTS.

EDITED BY

NATHANIEL B. SHURTLEFF, M.D.,

MEMBER OF THE MASSACHUSETTS HISTORICAL SOCIETY, FELLOW OF THE AMERICAN ACADEMY OF ARTS
AND SCIENCES, MEMBER OF THE AMERICAN ANTIQUARIAN SOCIETY, FELLOW
OF THE SOCIETY OF ANTIQUARIES OF LONDON, ETC.

MISCELLANEOUS RECORDS.

1633—1689.

BOSTON:

FROM THE PRESS OF WILLIAM WHITE,

PRINTER TO THE COMMONWEALTH.

1857.

REMARKS.

THE miscellaneous records appertaining to the Plymouth Colony, originally forming part of the contents of several volumes, have been printed collectively, and are comprised in this volume.

The earliest marriages on record in the colony will be found entered among the Court Orders. All the births, marriages, and deaths which were returned for record anterior to the year 1647, with the above-mentioned exception, have been lost by the decay of the first part of the original volume in which they were recorded at Plymouth.

The Treasurers' Accounts commence in 1658 and terminate in 1686, when the government of the colony was usurped by Andros. They are preserved in very good order, in connection with certain miscellaneous records, and are in the handwriting of many different persons.

The lists of freemen, taken at various times, and of those who were able to bear arms in the year 1643, are among the interesting records preserved in this volume.

Complete indexes have been prepared for the printed volume, to take the place of those in the original volumes, which were comparatively useless on account of their want of minuteness.

N. B. S.

December, 1857.

MARKS AND CONTRACTIONS.

A Dash ‾ (or straight line) over a letter indicates the omission of the letter following the one marked.

A Curved Line ~ indicates the omission of one or more letters next to the one marked.

A Superior Letter indicates the omission of contiguous letters, either preceding or following it.

A Caret ‸ indicates an omission in the original record.

A Cross × indicates a lost or unintelligible word.

All doubtful words supplied by the editor are included between brackets, [ ].

Some redundancies in the original record are printed in Italics.

Some interlineations, that occur in the original record, are put between parallels, ‖ ‖.

Some words and paragraphs, which have been cancelled in the original record, are put between ‡ ‡.

Several characters have special significations, namely: —

@, — annum, anno.

ā, — an, am, — curiā, curiam.

ā̃, — mātrate, magistrate.

ƀ, — ber, — numƀ, number; Roƀt, Robert.

c̃, — ci, ti, — accõn, action.

c̃õ, — tio, — jurisdiccõn, jurisdiction.

ꝺ, — cre, cer, — aꝺs, acres.

đ, — đđ, delivered.

ẽ, — Trẽr, Treasurer.

ē, — committē, committee.

g̃, — g̃ñal, general; Georg̃, George.

h̃, — c̃hr, charter.

ī, — begīg, beginīg, beginning.

ł, — łre, letter.

m̄, — mm, mn, — com̄ittee, committee.

m̃, — recom̃dac̃õn, recommendation.

m̃, — mer, — form̃ly, formerly.

m̊, — month.

ñ, — nn, — Peñ, Penn; año, anno.

ñ, — Dñi, Domini.

ñ, — ner, — manñ, manner.

õ, — on, — mentiõ, mention.

õ, — mõ, month.

p̃, — par, por, — p̃t, part; p̃tion, portion.

p, — per, — pson, person.

ꝑ, — pro, — ꝑporc̃õn, proportion.

ꝑ, — pre, — ꝑsent, present.

q̗, — qstion, question.

q̃ꝑ, — esꝗꝑ, esquire.

r̃, — Apr̃, April.

s̃, — s̃, session; s̃d, said.

s̃, — ser, — s̃vants, servants.

ƭ, — ter, — neuƭ, neuter.

ƭ, — capƭ, captain.

û, — uer, — seûal, seueral.

ū, — aboū, aboue, above.

v̂, — ver, — seŷal, several.

w̃, — w̃n, when.

yᵉ, the; yᵐ, them; yⁿ, then; yʳ, their; yˢ, this; yᵗ, that.

ȝ, — us, — vilibȝ, vilibus.

ℓ — es, et, — statutℓ, statutes.

ℓꝺ, &ꝺ, &cᵃ, — et cætera.

vizℓ, — videlicet, namely.

./ — full point.

CONTENTS.

MISCELLANEOUS RECORDS.

1633—1689.

PLYMOUTH RECORDS.

MISCELLANEOUS RECORDS OF THE COLONY OF NEW PLYMOUTH IN NEW ENGLAND.

[The following pages contain the records of Births, Marriages, Deaths, and Burials, in the several towns of the Colony of New Plymouth, as they were returned by the respective town clerks. The first portion of the manuscript part having been lost, and the first page of what remains being in a tattered condition, the original record commences in a fragmentary manner. The handwriting in the original is that of Secretary Morton. The pages of the manuscript volume are noted in the printed copy by an asterisk in the text, and by Arabic figures in the margin.]

BIRTHS, MARRIAGES, DEATHS, AND BURIALS.

*x   x   x   x   twentyeth of Nouember.   [*1.]

x   x   buried the tenth of Febreary.

Zebx   xeman buried the 23ᵈ of March.

1647. *Yarmouth Regester of the Beirth of theire Children.*   YARMOUTH.

SUSANNA MILLER, daughter of Mᵣ John Miller, was born the 2ᶜᵒⁿᵈ of May.

Elizabeth Hedge, daughter of Mᵣ Wilłam Hedge, was born the twenty ne of May.

Samuell Matthews, the sonn of James Matthews, was born the first of May.

Jonathan Hallot, the sonn of Andrew Hallott, was born the twentyeth f Nouember.

Ruth Tayler, the daughter of Richard Tayler, was born the 29ᵗʰ of July.

Mary Rider, the daughter of Samuell Ryder, was born the sixt of September.

Sara Hull, the daughter of Trustrum Hull, was born the 18ᵗʰ of October.

Beniamin Staare, the sonn of Thõ Staare, was born the sixt of Febreary.

    x   Darby, the sonn of John Darby, was born the last of Febreary.

Josepth, the sonn of Wilłam Nicherson, born the 10 month, 1647.

YARMOUTH.   *1647.   Yarmouth Regester for Marriages and Burialls.*

Hugh Tilby died the twenty eight of January, buried the day follŏing.

Henry Wilden maried to Eedx   ×   the twenty fift of January.

Sara Hull, the   ×   ×   died   ×   ×

×   ×   ×   ×   Winter,   ×   ×   ×   was born on   ×   ×   ×

PLYMOUTH.   *[1647.   Plymouth Register of Births.]*

[*4.]   *THŎ & Hanna Smith, the son & daughter of Richard Smith, being twines, were born on the twenty third of Aprell.

Lidia Barnes, the daughter of John Barnes, was born on the twenty fourth of Aprell.

Samuell Wood, the sonn of Henery Wood, was born the twenty fift of May.

Hanna Glase, the daughter of James Glase, was born the 2^{cond} of June.

Ann Sturtivant, the daughter of Samuell Sturtivant, was born the 4th of June.

Lidia Bartlet, the daughter of Robert Bartlet, was born on the 8th of June.

Rebekah Billington, the daughter of Francis Billington, was born on the 8th of June.

Abigaill Church, the daughter of Richard Church, was born on the 22^{cond} of June.

Hanna Eedy, the daughter of Samuell Eedy, was born on the twenty third of June.

Elizabeth Chipman, the daughter of John Chipman, was born on the 24th of June.

Hester Willet, the daughter of M^r Thŏ Willet, was born on the sixt of July.

Sara Heward, the daughter of John Heward, was born on the twentyeth day of August.

Thomas Paddy, the sonn of Mr Wilłam Paddy, was born the sixt of September.

×   ×   sonn of Wilłam Hoskins, was born the last day of November.

×   ×   ×   John Tompson,   ×   ×   ×

* × Rener, the daughter of M^r × Rener, was born the 26th of December.

Seth Pope, the sonn of Thõ Pope, was born on the 13th of January.

Elizabeth Cook, the daughter of Jakob Cook, was born on the 18th of January.

Samuell & Elizabeth Watson, being twines, the sonn & daughter of Gorḡ Watson, were born the 18th of January.

Ephraim Morton, the sonn of Ephraim Morton, was born on the 27th of January.

Isaak Doty, the sonn of Edward Doty, was born on the 8th of Febrewary.

Isaak Cushman, the sonn of the Elder Cushman, was born the 8th of Febrewary.

Mary Atkins, the daughter of Henery Atkins, was born the 13th of March.

Elizabeth Faunce, the daughter of John Faunce, was born the twenty third of March.

1648. Plym̃ Regester of Mariages & Burialls.

Elizabeth Spooner, the wife of Wiłłam Spooner, died the twenty eight of Aprell.

John Wood, the sonn of Steuen   ×   ×   ×   ×

Thõ Smith, the sonn of Richard Smith,   ×   ×   ×

Hanna Glase, the daughter of James Glase, died the 15th of June.

John Young was mařied vnto   ×   ×   the 13th of December.

Mr Beniamin Vermayes mařied vnto M^ris Mercy Bradford the one and twentyeth of December.

John Barnes, the sonn of John Barnes, died the twenty fift of December.

John Smith, Junĩ, of Plym̃, was mařied vnto Deborah Howland, the 4th of January.

John Tompson, the sonn of John Tompson, died the eleventh of Febrewary.

×

---

*1648. Sandwidg Regester of the Beirths of their Children.

× Boatfish borne the 27th of March.

Mary Willis was born the 14th of Aprell.

Bathshenah Skiffe born the twenty one of Aprell.

SANDWICH.

Meriam Wood was born the 8th of May.

Ezra Bourne was born the 12th of May.

Micaell Blackwell was born the first of June.

Caleb Allen was born the 27th of June.

Patience Butler was born the 14th of August.

Susanna Turner was born the 28th of September.

Debora Wing was born the tenth of October.

Nathaneell Fish was born the 27th of Nouember.

Hester Allen was born the 8th of December.

Sara Wright was born the eleuenth of Febrewary.

Benet Elles was born the 27th of Febrewary.

A sonn of Peeter Wright still born, the 16th of December.

1648. Sanawidg Regester for Mariages & Burials.

Wiltam Wright buried the 2cond of May.

Gorḡ Allen, Senier, buried the 2cond of May.

Gorḡ Knot buried the third of May.

Meream Wood buried the 9th of May.

Wiltam Newland mar̃ied to Rose Holloway the 19th May.

John Presbery buried the 19th of May.

Thõ Burgis mar̃ied to Elizabeth Basset the 8th of Nouember.

× × mar̃ied to Mary Vincent the 8th of Nouember.

× × buried the eleuenth of October.

× × buried the eleuenth of December.

ꝑ me, WILTAM WOOD.

YARMOUTH.

1648. Yarmouth Regester of the Beirth of their Children.

HANNAH, the daughter of Richard Templare, was borne the fift of January, anno Doñ 1642.

Elizabeth, the daughter of Edward Sturgis, was born the twentieth of Aprell.

Mary, the daughter of Robert Dauis, the 28th of the same.

Samuell, the sonn of Francis Baker, the first of May.

Mary, the daughter of John Marchant, the 20th of May.

Ephraim, the sonn of John Wing, the thirtieth of May.

John, the sonne of Roger Elles, the first of December.

Ann, the daughter of Richard Tayler, the 2cond of the same.

Beniamin, the sonne of John Gray, about the 7th of December.

Ann, the daughter of Wilłam Eldred, about the 16th of the same.

Samuell, the sonne of Richard Templer, the 22cond of January.

The daughter of Peeter Worden, Febrewary the tenth.

Mary, the daughter of Wm Hedge, the 24×

   ×   ×   the sonn of Richard Templer,   ×   at Yarmouth.

*1648.   Yarmouth Regester of Burials.   [*7.]

Elizabeth, the daughter of Hugh Norman, of the age of six, was drowned in a well the 28th of May.

Ruth, the daughter of Richard Tayler, was buried.

The sonne of John Winge drowned in the snow about the eleuenth of December.

1649.   Plymouth Regester of the Beirth of theire Children.   PLYMOUTH.

EPHRAIM TINKHAM, the sonne of Ephraim Tinkham, was born the fift of August.

Samuell King, the sonne of Samuell King, was born the twenty ninth of August.

Wybra Glase, the daughter of James Glase, was born the 9th of August.

Sara Warrin, the daughter of Nathaneell Warrin, was born the twenty ninth of August.

Thõ Sheriue, the sonne of Thõ Sheriue, was born on the 2cond of September.

Joseph Paddy, the sonne of Mr Wilłam Paddy, was born the tenth of September.

Daniell Ramsden, the sonne of Josepth Ramsden, was born on the 14th of September.

Hanna Wood, the daughter of Steuen Wood, was born on the 14th of October.

John Young, the sonne of John Young, was born the 9th of Nouember.

Hanna Churchill, the daughter of John Churchill, was born the tweluth of Nouember.

PLYMOUTH.   John Tompson, the sonne of John Tompson, was born on the 24th of
Nouember.

James Willet, the sonne of Mr Thõ Willet, was born the 24th of Nouember.

Sara Bonum, tho daughter of Goorg̃ Bonum, was born the 4th of December.

John Morton, the sonn of John Morton, was born the eleuenth of December.

Hasadiah Smith, the daughter of John Smith, Junĩ, was born the eleuenth of January.

Moses Sauory, the sonne of Thõ Sauory, was born the 22cond of January.

Hester Wright, the daughter of Richard Wright, was born on the ×

Jonathan Wood, the sonne of Henery Wood, was born the first of January.

John Wood, the sonne of John Wood, was born the 4th of March.

× Padduck, the daughter of   ×   ×

[*8.]   *1649.   *Plymouth Regester of Mariages & Burialls.*

Mary Atkins, the daughter of Henery Atkins, died the fifteenth of June.

Samuell Dunham marĩed vnto Martha Falloway the 29th of June.

Wiłłam Browne marĩed vnto Mary Murcock the 16th of July.

Samuell Watson, the sonne of Gorg̃ Watson, died the twentyeth of August.

Christian Finny, the wife of John Finny, died the 9th of September.

Ephraim Hicks marĩed vnto Elizabeth Howland the 13th of September.

Ephraim Hicks died the 12th of December.

John Morton, the sonne of John Morton, died the twentyeth of December.

Wiłłam Harlow marĩed vnto Rebekah Bartlet the twentyeth of December

Eliezer Morton, the sonne of Nathaneell Morton, died the sixteenth of January.

Sara Bonum, the daughter of Gorg̃ Bonum, died the   ×   ×

Josepth Paddy, the sonne of Mr Wiłłam Paddy, died the 18th of Febrewary.

Elizabeth Faunce, the daughter of John Faunce, died the third of March.

SANDWICH.   *1649.   Sandwidge Regester of the Beirth of their Children.*

MARY WOOD born March the 29th.

Ephraim Winge born Aprell the 2cond.

Mary Newland born Aprell the 16th.

Elizabeth Jenkins born Aprell the 30.

Dauid Bessey born May the 23ᵈ.

Samuell Gibbs born June the 22ᶜᵒⁿᵈ.

Mary Dexter born August the 11ᵗʰ.

Caleb Fish born August the 18ᵗʰ.

Mordecay Wright born October the 30.

Jonathan Nye born Nouember the 20ᵗʰ.

Encrease Kirbey,
   ×   Kirbey, } twines, born February.

*Ebenezer Allen born Febrewary the 10ᵗʰ.

[*9.]

1649. *Sandwidge Regester of Marriages and Burialls.*

Wiłłam Allen married to Presilla Browne the 21 of March.

Richard Chadwell married to Katheren Presberry July the 22ᶜᵒⁿᵈ.

Ephraim Wing was buried December the 10ᵗʰ.

John Freeman married to Mary Prence Febrewary the 14ᵈ.

Caleb Fish was buried Febrewary 28ᵗʰ.

Abigaill Kerbey buried the 29ᵗʰ of Febrewary.

Mordecay Wright buried March the 20ᵗʰ.

Jane Kerbey, mother, and Richard Kerbey, sonn, buried March
he 23ᵈ.

Encrease Kerbey buried March the 24ᵗʰ.

ꝑ me,   WIŁŁAM WOOD.

1649. *Yarmouth Regester of the Beirth of theire Children.*

R UTH, the daughter of Richard Tayler, born Aprell the 11ᵗʰ.

    Samuell, the sonne of Samuell Arnoll, born May the 9ᵗʰ.

Thõ and } twines, sonn and daughter of Mʳ Eluerton Crow, born
Elisabeth, }   May the 9ᵗʰ.

Sara, daughter of James Matthewes, born July the 21.

Mary, the daughter of Robert Dennis, born September 19ᵗʰ.

Elizabeth, daughter of Mʳ Miller, born October the 13ᵗʰ.

Jehosaphat, sonn of Mʳ Thõ Starre, born January the 12ᵗʰ.

Mathew, the sonn of John Darbey, born Febrewary the 8ᵗʰ.

YARMOUTH.   *1649.   Yarmouth Regester of Marriages and Burialls.*

Hester Templer, aged fiue yeares and an halfe, was buried September the 13th.

×   ×   sonne of Robert Dennis, died at the   ×   ×

[*10.]   *Ephraim Winge, of the age of one yeare and seauen months, was buried the last of December.

Robert Eldred and Elizabeth Nicarson were married the last week of October.

PLYMOUTH.   *1650.   Plym̃ Regester of the Beirth of theire Children.*

JOHN BRYANT, the sonn of Steuen Bryant, born the 7th of Aprell.

Sara Dunham, the daughter of Samuell Dunham, born the 10th of Aprell.

Mary Browne, the daughter of Wiłłam Browne, born the 14th of May.

Ephraim Little, the sonn of Thõ Little, born the 17th of May.

Mercy Latham, daughter of Robert Latham, born the 2^{cond} of June.

Jonathan Dunham, sonn of John Dunham, Junier, born the 12th of August.

Joseph Rener, sonn of Mr John Rener, born the 15th of August.

Hester Cook, the daughter of John Cook, born the 16th of August.

Wiłłam Harlow, sonn of Wiłłam Harlow, born the fift of October.

See more in the next page of this yeares beirths.

John Sturtivant, sonn of Samuell Sturtivant, born the 17th of October.

John Morton, sonn of John Morton, born the 21 of December.

Sara Bonum, daughter of Gorge Bonum, born the 12th of January.

1650.   Plymouth Regester of Marriages and Burialls.

Ralph James married to Mary Fuller the 17th of Aprell.

Mother Feney, aged fourscore yeares and vpward, died the 22^{cond} of Aprell.

Moses Savory, the sonn of Thõ Savory, died the 9th of June.

[*11.]   *Robert Padduk died the 25th of July.

Mis Sara Holmes died the 18th of August.

Jonathan Dunham, the sonn of John Dunham, died the 26 of August.

Wiłłam Harlow, sonn of Wm Harlow, died the 26 of October.

John Sturtivant, sonn of Samuell Sturtivant, died the 30th of October.

Thõ Lettece, sonn of Thõ Lettice, died the 3ᵈ of Nouember.
Grigory Armstrong died the fift of Nouember.
A daughter of Nathaniell Mortons still born the 23ᵈ of November.
Edward Gray married to Mary Winslow the 16 of January.
Katheren Goulder died the sixteenth of March.
Thõ Roberts mãried to Mary Padduk the 24ᵗʰ of March.

1650. *More Children born at Plyñ, 1650, which were omitted in the last ymediate page.*

Joane Nellson, daughter of Wiłłam Nellson, born the 28ᵗʰ of February.
Baruch Jurdaine, the sonn of John Jurdaine, born the 24ᵗʰ of February.
Hope Warren, the daughter of Nathaniell Warren, born the sixt of March.
Mercy Bartlet, the daughter of Robert Bartlet, born the 10ᵗʰ of March.
Rebeckah Morton, the daughter of Ephraim Morton, born the 15ᵗʰ of March.

1650. *Sandwidge Regester of Beirth of theire Children.*

MERCY WING, the daughter of Steuen Winge, was born the 13ᵗʰ of Nouember.
Nathaniell Fish, the sonn of Jonathan Fish, was born the 18ᵗʰ of December.
Dorithy Butler, the daughter of Thõ Butler, born the 23ᵈ of January.
Judah Allen, the sonn of Gorge Allen, born the 30ᵗʰ of January.
Adam Wright, the sonn of Peter Wright, born the 20ᵗʰ of March.
*Mary Skiffe, the daughter of James Skiffe, born March the 24ᵗʰ.   [*12.]
Mordecay Elles, the sonn of John Elles, born the 24ᵗʰ of March.

1650. *Sandwidge Regester of Marriages.*

Thomas Tobye and Marthay Knott were married the 18ᵗʰ of Nouember.
John Dillingham and Elizabeth Feake were married March the 24ᵗʰ.

N. W.

1650.   Yarmouth Regester of yᵉ Beirthes of Children.

SARA WHILDEN born the twenty one of June.
Nicolas Eldred August the eightoenth.
Daniell Baker September the 2ᶜᵒⁿᵈ.
Josepth Winge about the same time.
William Gray October the fift
Sara Eldred October the tenth.
John Hallot December the eleuenth.
Martha Tayler the eighteenth of the same.
Hester Mathues January the 8ᵗʰ.
Abijah Marchant 10ᵗʰ of the same.

Burialls at Yarmouth.   1650.

Ann Tayler was buried the 29ᵗʰ of March, aged about a yeare and a halfe.

Joseph Sturgis was buried the 16ᵗʰ of Aprell, about ten daies old.

A son of Thomas Gage was drownded in a well, aged about a yeare an an halfe.

[*13.]   **1651.   Plymͫ Regester of the Beirth of their Children.*

THO: POPE, son of Thͦ Pope, born the 25ᵗʰ of March.
Caleb Cook, son of Jacob Cook, born the 29ᵗʰ of March.
Mercy Faunce, daughter of John Faunce, born the 10ᵗʰ of Aprell.
Josepth Dotey, son of Edward Dotey, born the last of Aprell.
Elkanan Cushman, son of the Elder Cushman, born the first of June.
Samuell Sauory, son of Thͦ Sauory, born the 4ᵗʰ of June.
Hezekiah Willet, son of Captain Thͦ Willet, born the 20ᵗʰ of July.
Samuell Knowles, son of Richard Knowles, born the 17ᵗʰ of September
Ebenezer Tinkham, son of Ephraim Tinkham, born the 30ᵗʰ of September
John Smith, the son of John Smith, Junier, born the first of October.
Dauid Wood, the son of Henery Wood, born the 17ᵗʰ of October.
Isack King, the son of Samuell King, born the 24ᵗʰ of October.
Desire Gray, the daughter of Edward Gray, born the sixt of Nouembe

Mary Sturtivant, daughter of Samuell Sturtivant, born the 7th of De- PLYMOUTH.
cember.

Hannah Glasse, daughter of James Glasse, born the 24th of December.

Samuell Dúnham had two sonns born, which were twines, the 29 of December.

Gorge Browne, ye son of Wiltam Browne, was born on the 16th of January.

Dorcas Hickes, the daughter of Samuell Hickes, borne the 14th of Febrewary.

Samuell Atkins, son of Henery Atkins, born the 24th of Febrewary.

Nathaniell Wood, son of John Wood, born the twenty fift of Febrewary.

Samuel Dunham, son of John Dunham, Junier, born the 25 of Febrewary.

Daughter of Francis Billington born the same daie.

Jonathan Watson, the son of Gorge Watson, born the 9th of March.

1651. Plym̄ Regester of Marriages and Burialls. [*14.]

Mis Alice Paddy, wife of Mr Wiltam Paddy, died the 24th of Aprell.

Mary Barnes, the wife of John Barnes, died the 2^{cond} of June.

John Dickarson married to Elizabeth Hickes the 10 of July.

Hezekiah Willet, son of Captain Willet, died the 26th of July.

Richard Foster married to Mary Bartlet the 10th of September.

John Howland married to Mary Lee the 26th of October.

John Rickard married to Hester Barnes the 31 of October.

Gyles Rickard, Junier, married to Hannah Dunham the 31 of October.

A son of Samuell Dunham, being a twine, died soone after the beirth mentioned on the other side, and the other twine died six daies after.

Audey Webb died the 4th of March.

Wiltam Spooner married to Hannah Pratt the 18th of March.

1651. *Sandwidg Regester of Beirths of Children.* SANDWICH.

JOSEPTH, son of Robert Botfish, born the 3^d of Aprell.

John Fish, son of Nathaniell Fish, born the 13th of Aprell.

These bee the names of Leiftenant Joseph Rogers his children, as followeth : —

SANDWICH.   Sarah was borne the sixt of August, 1633, and died the fifteenth of the
same month.

Josepth was born the 19th of July, 1635.
Thomas was born the 29th of March, 1638.
Elizabeth was born the 29th of September, 1639.
John was born the 3^d of Aprill, 1642.
Mary was born the 22^{cond} of September, 1644.
James was borne the 18th of October, 1648.
Hannah was borne the 8th of August, 1652.

———

PLYMOUTH.   *1652.   *Plymouth Regester of the Beirth of theire Children.*
[*15.]

JOSIAH SMITH, son of John Smith, borne the 16th of Aprill.
  Elizabeth, daughter of Andrew Ringe, born the 19th of Aprill.
Eliezer, son of John Churchill, born the 20th of Aprill.
Elizabeth, daughter of Nathaniell Morton, borne the 3^d of May.
Isack Wright, sonne of Richard Wright, born 26th of August.
William, sonne of Mr Willam Paddy, born about the 16th of September.
John, the sonne of Gyles Rickard, Juni̇, borne the   ^   ^
Jane, the daughter of Nathaniell Warren, borne the 31 of December.
Samuell, the sonne of Willam Harlow, borne the 27th of January.
John, the sonne of Mr Willam Bradford, born the twentieth of February.
Jonathan, the sonne of Thomas Sauory, borne the 4th of March.
Mary, the daughter of Richard Foster, borne the 8th of March.
John, the sonne of Thomas Pope, borne the 15th of March.

1652.   Plymouth Regester of Marriages and Burials.

Rebeckah Willett died the 2^{cond} of Aprill.
Arther Hathaway married to Sara Cooke the 20th of Nouember.
Josepth Reyner died the 23^d of Nouember.
James Cole, Junier, married to Mary Tilson the 23^d of December.
James Shaw married to Mary Michell the 24th of December.
Willam Pontus died the 9th of Febrewary.

*Att the Towne of Eastham.

JONATHAN SPARROW married to Rebeckah Banges the 26th of October, 1654.

Marke Snow married vnto Ann Cooke the 18th of January, 1654.

Wilłam Walker married to Sarah Snow the 25th of February, 1654.

Mehitabell, the daughter of Richard Knowles, born the 20th of May, 1652.

Rebeckah, the daughter of Job Cole, born the 26 of August, 1654.

Deborah, the daughter of Ralph Smith, born the 8th of March, 1654.

Bethyah, the daughter of Edward Banges, born the 28th of May, 1650.

Marcye and Apphyah, the daughters of Edwards Banges, which said daughters were born, being twines, *were born* the 15th of October, 1651.

Israell, the son of Daniell Cole, borne the 8th of January, 1653.

Nathaniell, the son of Thomas Williams, born the 24th of Aprill, 1655.

John, the son of Wilłam Walker, born the 24th of Nouember, 1655.

℘ me, DANIELL COLE, Towne Clarke.

---

*1653. Plymouth Regester of the Beirth of theire Children.

JACOB, the sonne of Jacob Cooke, borne the twenty sixt of March.

Josepth, the sonne of John Faunce, born the 14th of May.

Mannasses and Ephraim, twines, the sonns of John Morton, born the 7th of June.

Feare, the daughter of the Elder Cushman, borne the 20th of June.

Beniamine, the sonne of Mr John Winslow, born the 12th day of August.

Josias, the sonne of Ephraim Morton, borne the   ^   ^

John, the sonne of Arther Hathewey, born the 17th of September.

Mary, the daughter of Edward Gray, born the 18th of September.

Sarah, the daughter of Wilłam Spooner, born the fift of October.

Hezekiah, the sonne of Capt Willett, born the 16th of Nouember, or therabouts.

Mary, the daughter of James Cole, Junier, born the 3d of December.

Sarah, the daughter of Gorḡ Bonum, born the 10th of December.

Peter Tinkham, the sonne of Ephraim Tinkham, born the 25 of December.

Isacke, the sonne of John Wood, borne the 27th of February.

PLYMOUTH.   *1654. Plymouth Regester of the Beirthes of theire Children.*

Margerett, the daughter of Samuell Hickes, born the 9th of March.
Willam, the son of Willam Browne, born the first of Aprill.
Mara Sauory, the daughter of Thomas Sauory, born the seauenth of Aprill.
Samuell Sturtivant, the sonne of Samuell Sturtivant, born the 19th of Aprill.
Eliazer Smith, the sonne of John Smith, Junī, born the 20th of Aprill.

[*18.]   **Plymouth Regester of Marriages and Burials.*

Thomas Gray died about the seauenth of June.
John Faunce died the 29th of Nouember.
Susanna Jenings died the 23ᵈ of March.

1654. Plymouth Regester of Beirth of theire Children. 1654.

Mary, the daughter of John Churchill, borne the first of August.
Samuell, the sonne of Willam Hoskins, borne the 8th of August.
Joannah, the daughter of Nathaniell Morton, was born the 9th of Nouember, 1654.
James, the son of James Shaw, born the 6th of December.
William Bradford, the sonne of William Bradford, Junior, was borne the 11 of March, 1654, and was baptized the 25 of March, 1655.
[This last entry is in the handwriting of Governor Bradford.]

Elkanan, the son of Gorḡ Watson, was born the fiue and twentieth day of February, 16⁵⁵⁄₅₆.
Samuell, the son of William Brown, was born att Plymouth, the begīning of March, 165⅚.
Hezkiah, the son of John Smith, Junier, born the 28th of Nouember, 1655.
Samuell, the son of Willam Spooner, born the 14th day of January, 1655.
Hezkiah, the son of Ephraim Tinkham, was borne the eight of February, 1655.
Sarah, the daughter of Arther Hatheway, was born the 28th of February, 1655.
Eliazer, the son of the Elder Cushman, was born the 20th of February, 1656.
Marcye, the daughter of John Cooke, was born the fiue and twentieth of July, ×.

*Mis Ann Atwood died the first of June.

Allice Shaw, the wife of John Shaw, died the sixt of March, 1654.

Rebecka, the daughter of Wiłłam Harlow, was born the 12th of June, 1655.

Wiłłam Shirtley married vnto Elizabeth Lettice the 18th of October, 1655.

Hannah Sturtivant, the daughter of Samuell Sturtivant, was borne the ᵤrth of September, 1656.

Jonathan Dunham was married vnto Mary Delanoy the 29th of Nouem-r, 1655.

Benajah Prat married to Persis Dunham the 29th of Nouember, 1655.

Edward Dotey died the 23^d of August, 1655.

Samuell Rider married to Sarah Bartlett the 23^d of December, 1656.

James Clarke married to Abigaill Laythorp the seauenth of October, 1657.

Jonathan Dunham married to Mary Cobb the fifteenth of October, 1657.

Jonathan Shaw married to Phebe Watson the 22^{cond} of January, 1656.

Wiłłam, the son of Wiłłam Harlow, was born the 2^{cond} day of June, 1657.

Abraham Jackson married to Remember Morton the 18th of Nouem-ː, 1657.

Joseph Dunham married to Mercye Morton the same day.

Samuell, the son of Samuell Ryder, was born the 18th of Nouember, 1657.

John, the son of John Rickard, born the twenty fourth day of Nouem-ː, 1657.

Mary, the daughter of Jacob Cooke, was born the 12th of January, 1657.

John Cobb marryed to Martha Nelson the 28th of Aprill, 1658.

Abigaill, the daughter of Benajah Pratt, born the 21 of Nouember, 1657.

John, the son of Ephraim Tinkham, was born the seauenth of June, 1658.

ᵃmes of those whoe were marryed, recorded by Leiftenant James Torrey, since hee was chosen Towne Clarke of the Towne of Scittuate, the 18th of July, 1653.

ᵃAMES TORREY married to Ann Hach, the daughter of Wiłłam Hatch, the 2^{cond} of Nouember, 1643.

John Bryant married to Mary Lewis, the daughter of Gorge Lewis, of ᵤstable, Nouember 14, 1643.

Ephraim Kemton married to Joanna Rawlins, the daughter of Thomas ᵣlins, January 28, 1645.

Anthony Dodson married to Mary Williams the tweluth of Nouember, 1651.

3

Beirths of Children.

Joseph, the son of Robert Studson, born June, 1639.

Benjamine, the son of Robert Studson, born in the month of August, 1641.

Thomas, the son of Robert Studson, born the 11th of December, 1641.

James, the son of James Torrey, born the 3^d of September, 1644.

Sarah Witherell, the daughter of M^r Wiłłam Witherill, was born the 10th of February, 1644.

Samuell, the son of Robert Studson, born in the month of June, 1646.

Hannah, the daughter of M^r Wiłłam Witherill, born the 20th of February, 1646.

Wiłłam, the son x James Torrey, born March the 15, 1646.

John, the son of Robert Studson, born Aprill, 1648.

Joseph, the son of James Torrey, born the 18th March, 1648.

Eunice, the daughter of Robert Studson, born the 28th of Aprill, 1650.

Damaris, daughter of James Torrey, born the 26th of October, 1651.

Sarah, the daughter of Anthony Dodson, born August the 26, 1652.

Lois, the daughter of Robert Studson, born in the month of February, 1652.

Samuell, the son of Walter Hatch, born December the 22^{cond}, 1653.

Robert, the son of Robert Studson, born the 29th of January, 1653.

Gershom, the son of Anthony Dodson, born February 14th, 1653.

[*21.]   *Joanna, the daughter of Ephraim Kemton, was born the 29th of September, 1647.

Patience, the daughter of Ephraim Kemton, was born the 2^{cond} of October, 1648.

Ephraim Kemton, the son of Ephraim Kemton, was born the first of October, 1649.

Lydia, the daughter of John Turner, was born the 24 of January, 1652.

Mannasses, the son of Ephraim Kemton, was born the first of January, 1651.

Deborah, the daughter of Wiłłam Berstow, born in August, 1650.

Wiłłam, the son of Wiłłam Berstow, born in Sept^r, 1652.

John, the son of Humphrey Johnson, born in March, 1653.

John, the son of John Bryant, born the 17th of August, 1644.

Hannah, the daughter of John Bryant, born the 25 of January, 1645.

Sarah, the daughter of John Bryant, born the 29th of September, 1648.

Mary, the daughter of John Bryant, born the 24th of February, 1649.

Martha, the daughter of John Bryant, born the 26th of February, 1651.

Samuell, the son of John Bryant, born the 6 of February, 1653.

Patience, the daughter of Ephraim Kemton, deceased the first of July, 1648.
Mary, the daughter of John Bryant, dec⁴ the 8ᵗʰ of Aprill, 1652.
Henery Merritt deceased the last of Nouember, 1653.
Katherin Winter deceased the 28ᵗʰ of December, 1653.

P me, JAMES TORREY, Towne Clarke.

A Note of the Pʳsons recorded since June last, pʳ me, James Torrey, Towne Clarke of Scittuate, sent to March Court, 1654.

R ESOLUED WHITE marryed to Judith, the daughter of Mʳ Willam Varssall, Aprill the 8ᵗʰ, 1640.

James Adams marryed to Francis, the daughter of Mʳ Willam Varssall, July the 16ᵗʰ, 1646.

Walter Hatch married to Elizabeth Holbrooke, May the sixt, 1650.

Nathaniell Rawlins maryed to Lydia, the daughter of Richard Siluester, September the 4ᵗʰ, 1652.

*John Damman married to Katherin, the daughter of Henery Merritt,   [*22.]
in June, 1644.

Willam Parker marryed to Mary, the daughter of Thomas Rawlins, in Aprill, 1639.

Willam Parker marryed to Mary, the daughter of Humphry Turner, Nouember the 13ᵗʰ, 1651.

Thomas King marryed to Jane Hatch, widdow, March the 31, 1653.

Beirthes of Children.

Willam, the son of Resolued White, born Aprill the 10ᵗʰ, 1642.
John, the son of Resolued White, born March the 11ᵗʰ, 1644.
Samuell, the son of Resolued White, born the 13ᵗʰ of March, 1646.
Willam, the son of James Adames, born May the 16ᵗʰ, 1647.
Samuell, the son of Willam Wills, born in May, 1640.
Lydia, the daughter of Willam Wills, born in Aprill, 1645.
Resolued, the son of Resolued White, born Nouember 12ᵗʰ, 1647.
Anna, the daughter of Resolued White, born June the 4ᵗʰ, 1649.
Elizabeth, the daughter of Resolued White, born the June 4ᵗʰ, 1652.
Josiah, the son of Resolued White, born September 29, 1654.
Jonathan, the son of James Torry, born September the 20ᵗʰ, 1654.
Anna, the daughter of James Adams, born Aprill the 18ᵗʰ, 1649.

Richard, the son of James Adams, borne Aprill the 19th, 1651, and deceased the 25 of July, 1651.

Mary, the daughter of James Adams, born January the 27, 1653.

Lydia, the daughter of William Hatch, Seni^r, born January the 7th, 1651.

Elizabeth, the daughter of Nathaniell Rawlins, born March the first, 1653.

Jonathan, the son of John Turner, Seni^r, born September 20th, 1646.

Josepth, the son of John Turner, Seni^r, born January the 12th, 1647, and deceased January 15, 1647.

[*23.] *Josepth, the son of John Turner, Seni^r, born January the 12th, 1649.

Ezekiell, the son of John Turner, Seni^r, born January the 7th, 1650.

John, the son of John Turner, Seni^r, born October 30, 1654.

Thomas, the son of Thomas Pinchin, born May the 15, 1640.

Hannah, the daughter of Thomas Pinchin, born December the 4th, 1642.

Hannah, the daughter of Henery Ewill, born June the 22^{cond}, 1649.

Gershom, the son of Henery Ewill, born the Nouember 14, 1650.

Hannah, the daughter of Walter Hatch, born March the 13th, 1650.

Deborah, the daughter of John Damman, born Aprill the 25th, 1645.

John, the son of John Damman, born Nouember the 3^d, 1647.

Mary, the daughter of John Damman, born in July, 1651.

Daniell, the son of John Damman, born in February, 1652.

Zacaryah, the son of John Damman, born in February, 1649, deceased in February, 1649.

William, the son of William Randall, born in December, 1647.

John, the son of William Randall, born in Aprill, 1650.

Elizabeth, the daughter of William Randall, born in October, 1652.

Mary, the daughter of William Parker, born January the first, 1639.

William, the son of William Parker, born in December, 1643.

Patience, the daughter of William Parker, born in February, 1648.

Lydia, the daughter of William Parker, born May the 9th, 1653.

Josepth, the son of William Randall, was born in March, 1642.

Hannah, the daughter of William Randall, born in March, 1644.

Job, the son of William Randall, was born February the 8th, 1654.

[*24.] *Rhode King, the daughter of Thomas Kinge, was born Ootober th 11th, 1639.

Gorg King, the son of Thomas Kinge, born December the 24th, 1642.

Thomas, the son of Thomas Kinge, born June the 21, 1645.

Daniell, the son of Thomas Kinge, was born February the 4th, 1647.

Sarah, the daughter of Thomas King, was born May the 24th, 1650.

John, the son of Thomas Kinge, was born May the 30th, 1652.

Deathes.

Willam Hatch, Senir and elder, deceased Nouember the sixt, 1651.

Mary, the wife of Willam Parker, deceased in August, 1651.

Richard, the son of James Adames, deceased the 25 of July, 1651.

Josepth, the son of John Turner, Senir, deceased January the 15th, 1647.

Zachariah, the son of John Damman, deceased in February, 1649.

Sarah King, the wife of Thomas Kinge, deceased June the sixt, 1652.

John, the son of Thomas Kinge, deceased about July the 26th, 1652.

Jane, the wife of Thomas Kinge, deceased October the 8th, 1653.

Thomas Turner marryed to Sarah Hiland January the sixt, 1651.

Josepth Tilden married to Ellice Twisden Nouember the 20th, 1649.

Beirthes of Children.

Ruth, the daughter of Nathaniell Rawlins, born September the 27th, 1655.

Nathaniell, the son of Thomas Turner, born March the first, 1654.

Jane, the daughter of Walter Hatch, born March the 7th, 1655.

*Joseph, the son of Humphrey Johnson, born June the 24th, 1655.   [*25.]

Nathaneell, the son of Josepth Tilden, born in September, 1650.

John, the son of Josepth Tilden, born in December, 1652.

Rebeckah, the daughter of Josepth Tilden, born in Febrewary, 1654.

Elizabeth, the daughter of Thomas Turner, born in July, 1656.

Sarah, the daughter of Thomas Ingham, born January the 21, 1647.

Josepth, the son of Josepth Tilden, born Febrewary the 12th, 1656.

Mary, the daughter of James Torrey, born February the 14th, 1656.

Elisha, the son of John Turner, Senir, born March the eight, 1656.

Benjamine, the son of Humphrey Johnson, born August the 27, 1657.

P me,   JAMES TORREY, Towne Clarke.

Of the Towne of Plymouth.

WILLAM HARLOW married to Mary Faunce the 15 of July, 1658.

Mr Samuell Hooker married to Mis Mary Willett the 22cond of Sep-ber, 1658.

PLYMOUTH.

Mr Barnabas Laythorpe was married to Susanna Clarke, the 3^d of N uember, 1658.

Mr John Saffin was married vnto Mis Martha Willett, the 2^{cond} of D cember, 1658.

Mary, the daughter of Wiłłam Harlow, was borne the 19 day of May, 165

Jonathan Morrey was married vnto Mary Foster, widdow, the 8th July, 1659.

Lydia, the daughter of Abraham Jackson, was born the 19th of Noue ber, 1658.

John, the son of Samuell Sturtivant, borne the sixt of September, 165!

Samuell, the son of Samuell Jenney, was borne the third of July, 165

Sarah, the daughter of Steuen Bryant, was borne the 28th of Noue ber, 1659.

Wiłłam Clarke married to Sarah Woolcott, on the first of March, 165

[*26.] *Martha, the daughter of Jacob Cooke, was born the sixteenth March, 1659.

Mary, the daughter of Stephen Bryant, was borne the 29th of May, 16!

Stephen, the son of Stephen Bryant, was borne the 2^{cond} day of Febre ary, 1657.

Winnefred Whitney, the wife of Thomas Whitney, died the 23^d July, 1660.

Mr Robert Marshall married to Mary Barnes, the ×   ×   ×

Benajah Dunham married to Elizabeth Tilson the 25 of October, 166C

Edward Cobb maried to Mary Hoskins the 28th of Nouemb^r, 1660.

Benjamine Eaton married to Sarah Hoskins the 4th of December, 166

Lydia, the daughter of Samuell Sturtivant, was born the 13 day of I cember, 1660.

Repentance, the daughter of Wiłłam Harlow, was borne the 22^{cond} Nouember, 1660.

Samuell Eaton married to Martha Billington the 10th of January, 166

Joseph Ramsden married to Mary Sauory the 16 day of October, 166

[*27.] *Elizabeth, the daughter of Edward Gray, was born the eleuenth February, 165x.

Sarah, the daughter of Edward Gray, was born the tweluth of gust, 1659.

Name changed after it was entered. ‡Samuell,‡ ‖John,‖ the son of Edward Gray, was borne the first October, 1661.

John Holmes married to Patience Faunce the twentyeth day of I uember, 1661.

M[r] John Holmes married to Mary Atwood the eleuenth of Decem-
r, 1661.

Daniell Wilcockes was married to Elizabeth Cooke the 28th of Nouem-
r, 1661.

Anthony Sprague was married to Elizabeth Bartlett the 26 of Decem-
r, 1661.

Judith, the wife of Gyles Rickard, Seni[r], died the sixt day of Febrew-
y, 1661.

Gyles Rickard, Seni[r], married to Jone Tilson the twentyeth day of
ay, 1662.

Thomas Leonard married to Mary Watson the 21 of August, 1662.

John, the son of John Cobb, was borne the 24th of August, 1662.

John, the son of Wilłam Harlow, was borne the 19th of October, 1662.

Francis, the son of Jacob Cooke, was borne the fift of January, 1662.

John Churchill died the first of January, 1662.

Mannasses Kemton died the 14th of January, 1662. Hee did much
od in his place the time God lent him.

Edward Doty married to Sarah Faunce the 26 of February, 1662.

Lydia, the daughter of Stephen Bryant, was borne the 23 of Octo-
·, 1662.

Francis Cooke died the seauenth of Aprill, 1663.

*Zachariah Eedey was married to Allice Padduck the seauenth of   [*28.]
·y, 1663.

Samuell Rickard, the son of Gyles Rickard, Juni[r], was borne the 14th of
iary, 1662.

Phebe Watson, the wife of Gorge Watson, died the 22[cond] day of May,
33.

John Lucas, the son of Thomas Lucas, was borne the fifteenth day of
y, 1656.

Mary Lucas, the daughter of Thomas Lucas, was borne the fifteenth day
March, 1658.

Benony Lucas, the son of Thomas Lucas, was borne the 30th day of
ober, 1659.

Samuell Lucas, the son of Thomas Lucas, was borne the fifteenth day of
tember, 1661.

Wilłam Lucas, the son of Thomas Lucas, was borne the 13th of Janu-
, 1662.

John, the son of John Holmes, was borne the 22[cond] of March, 1662.

PLYMOUTH. *A Register of the Age of some of the Children of Nathaniel Warren as followeth : —*

Hope, the daughter of Nathaniel Warren, was borne the seauenth of March, 1651.

Jane, the daughter of Nathaniel Warren, was borne the 10th of Janu ary, 1652.

Elizabeth, the daughter of Nathaniel Warren, was borne the 15 of September, 1654.

Allice, the daughter of Nathaniel Warren, was borne the 2cond of August, 1656.

Mercye, the daughter of Nathaniel Warren, was borne February th 20th, 1657.

Mary, the daughter of Nathaniel Warren, was borne the 9th of March 1660.

Nathaniel, the son of Nathaniel Warren, was borne the 10th of March 1661.

John, the son of Nathaniel Warren, was borne the 23 of October, 166

James, the son of Nathaniel Warren, was borne the 7th of Nouem ber, 1665.

There are two other of his children recorded in this booke, elder the any of thes heer named.

[*29.] *The Regester of the Age of the Children of Mr Wiłłam Paddy is followeth : —*

Elizabeth, the daughter of Mr Wiłłam Paddey, was borne the twelu day of Nouember, 1641.

John, the son of Mr Wiłłam Paddey, was born the twenty fift of N uember, 1643.

Samuell, the son of Mr Wiłłam Paddey, was borne about the first August, 1645.

Robert, the son of Mr Robert Marshall, was borne the fifteenth day August, 1663.

The Register of the Age of some of the Children of Robert Pad-   <small>PLYMOUTH.</small>
docke, deceased.

Imprimis, Willam Palmer, the son in law of the said Robert Paddocke, was borne the 27th of June, 1634.

Zachariah Paddocke, the son of Robert Paddocke, was borne the 20th of March, 1636.

Mary, the daughter of Robert Paddocke, was borne the tenth of March, 1638.

Allis, the daughter of Robert Paddocke, was borne the 7th of March, 1640.

John, the son of Robert Paddocke, was borne the first of Aprill, 1643.

There are two other that are before registered in this booke.

Willam Crow was married to Hannah Winslow the first of Aprill, 1664.

Francis Goulder died the 17th of May, 1664.

James, the son of Samuell Sturtivant, was borne the eleuenth of February, 1663.

Nathaniel, the son of Willam Harlow, was born the 30th of September, 1664.

Mary, the wife of Willam Harlow, dyed the 4th of October, 1664.

Jonathan Pratt was married to Abigaill Wood the 2cond of Nouember, 1664.

Thomas Cushman was married to Ruth Howland the 17th day of Nouember, 1664.

James, the son of Nathaniel Warren, was born the 7th of Nouember, 1665.

Plymouth Register.   [*30.]

Josepth Howland was married to Elizabeth Southworth the seauenth day of December, anno 1664.

Gorge Morton was married to Joanna Kempton the 22cond of December, 1664.

Julian Kempton, widdow, aged fourscore and one yeare, died the 19th day of February, anno Dom 1664, and was buried the 20th of the same; shee was a faithfull servant of God.

Josepth, the sonne of Mr Joseph Bradford, was borne the 18th of Aprill, 1665.

4

PLYMOUTH.   Elizabeth, the daughter of Stephen Bryant, was borne the seauenteenth of October, 1665.

Sacary Eedey, the son of Sacary Eedey, was borne the tenth day of Aprill, 1664.

Wiłłam Harlow married to Mary Shelley the 25 of January, 1665.

Mary, the daughter of Ephraim Tinkham, was borne the fift of August, 1661.

John, the son of Ephraim Tinkham, was borne the 15th of Nouember, 1663.

EASTHAM.   *The Register of Eastham, of their Beirths, Marriages, & Burialls,*
[*31.]   *as they came to my hand.*

JOHN FREEMAN and Mercy Prence married the 13th February, 1649.
       John Freeman, son of John Freeman, was borne the 2cond of February, 1650. This deceased.

Alsoe, another son, named John, borne in December, 1651.

Thomas Freeman, the son of John Freeman, was borne in Septem̃, 1653.

Edmond Freeman, the son of John Freeman, was borne in June, 1657.

Marcye Freeman, the daughter of John Freeman, was borne in July, 1659.

Nathaniel Mayo and Hannah Prence were marryed the 13th of February, 1649.

Thomas Mayo, the son of Nathaniell Mayo, was borne the 7th December, 1650.

Nathaniell Mayo, the son of Nathaniell Mayo, was borne the 16th of Nouember, 1652.

Samuell Mayo, the son of Nathaniel Mayo, was borne the 12th of October, 1655.

Hannah Mayo, the son [daughter] of Nathaniel Mayo, was borne the 17th of October, 1657.

Theophilus Mayo, the son of Nathaniel Mayo, was borne the 17th of December, 1659.

John Mayo was married to Hannah Reycraft the first of January, 1650.

John, the son of John Mayo, was borne the fifteenth of December, 1652.

Wiłłam, the son of John Mayo, was borne the 7th of October, 1654.

James, the son of John Mayo, was borne the third of October, 1656.

Samuell, the son of John Mayo, was borne the 2cond of March, 1658.

Wilłam, the son of Wilłam Walker, was borne the 2ᶜᵒⁿᵈ of August, 1659.   EASTHAM.

Stephen, the son of Wilłam Twining, was borne the sixt of February, 1659.

Eliazer, the son of Thomas Paine, was borne the 10th of March, 1658.

Hannah, the daughter of John Smalley, borne att Plymouth the 14th of June, 1641.

John, the son of John Smalley, borne att Plymouth, the 8th of Septem: 1644.

Isacke and Mary, the son and daughter of John Smalley, were borne the 11th of December, 1647.

*Jemineth, the daughter of Robert Vixon, was borne the 30th of   [*32.]
August, 1655.

Titus, the son of Robert Vixon, was borne the 2ᶜᵒⁿᵈ of December, 1657.

Elizabeth, the daughter of Roberˀ Vixon, was borne the 29th of May, 1660.

Jonathan, the son of Richard Higgens, was borne att Plymouth in July, 1637.

Benjamine, the son of Richard Higgens, was borne att Plymouth in July, 1640.

John Yeates, the son of John Yeates, deceased, which said John Yeates, Juniʳ, is son in law to the said Richard Higgens, was borne att Duxburrow the 15th of August, 1650.

Mary, the daughter of Richard Higgens, was borne the 27th of Septem: 1652.

Eliakim, the son of Richard Higgens, was borne the 20th of October, 1654.

Wilłam, the son of Richard Higgens, was borne the 15th of December, 1654.

Jadiah, the son of Richard Higgens, borne the fift of March, 1656.

Rebeckah, the daughter of Jonathan Sparrow, was borne the 30th of October, 1655.

John, the son of Jonathan Sparrow, was borne the 2ᶜᵒⁿᵈ of Nouember, 1656.

Presilla, the daughter of Jonathan Sparrow, was borne the 13th of February, 1658.

Apthia, the daughter of Samuell Freeman, was borne the 11th of December, 1660.

Apthia, the daughter of Samuell Freeman, deceased the 19th of February, 1660.

Mary, the daughter of Daniel Cole, was borne the 10th of March, 1658.

Josepth Harding was married to Bethya Cooke the 4th of Aprill, 1660.

Josepth Rogers was married to Susanna Deane the 4th of Aprill, 1660.

EASTHAM.   Marke Snow was married to Jane Prence the 9th of January, 1660.

John Banges was married to Hannah Smalley the 23 of January, 1660.

Jonathan Higgens was married to Elizabeth Rogers the 9th of January, 1660.

Wilłam, the son of Gyles Hopkins, was borne the 9th of January, 1660.

Isacke, the son of Wilłam Merricke, was borne the 6th of January, 1660.

Wilłam Twining, Senir, died the 15th of Aprill, 1659.

Josepth Rogers, Junir, deceased the 27th of January, 1660.

SCITUATE.   *The Record of the Marriages, Beirthes, and Burials of Scittuate,
[*33.]   as followeth.

WILŁAM HATCH married to Susanna Annible, the 13th of May, 1652.

Lydia, the daughter of Wilłam Hatch, was borne Aprill the 28th, 1653.

Lydia, the daughter of Wilłam Hatch, died May the 2cond, 1653.

Abia, the daughter of Henery Ewill, was borne the 27th of September, 1653.

P me, JAMES TORREY, Towne Clark.

Isacke Chettenden was married to Mary Vinall in Aprill, 1646.

Sarah and Rebecka Chettenden, twines, the daughters of Isacke Chettenden, were borne the 25 of February, 1646.

Mary, the daughter of Isacke Chettenden, was borne August the 17th, 1648.

Israell, the son of Isacke Chettenden, was borne October the 10th, 1651.

Stephen, the son of Isacke Chettenden, was borne Nouember the fift, 1654.

Elizabeth, the daughter of Isacke Chettenden, was borne Septem: 9th, 1658.

Sarah, the daughter of Rodulphus Elmes, was borne the 29th of Septem: 1645.

Mary, the daughter of Rodulphus Elmes, was borne June the 9th, 1648.

Joanna, the daughter of Rodulphus Elmes, was borne the 28th of March, 1651.

Hannah, the daughter of Rodulphus Elmes, was borne December 25, 1653.

John, the son of Rodulphus Elmes, was borne the sixt of July, 1655.

Josepth, the son of Rodulphus Elmes, was borne the sixteenth of March, 1658.

Waitestill, the daughter of Rodulphus Elmes, was borne February the , 1660.

Bethya, the daughter of Walter Hatch, was borne March the 31, 1661.

Myles, the son of William Parker, was borne June the 25, 1655.

Josepth, the son of William Parker, was borne the 4th of October, 1658.

Nathaniel, the son of William Parker, was borne the eight of March, 61.

John, the son of John Cushen, was borne the 28th of Aprill, 1662.

*Scittuate Register. [*34.]

Gorge Younge was married to Hannah Pinson the 15th of January, 1661.

Stephen Tilden was married to Hannah Little January the 15th, 1661.

Stephen Vinall was married to Mary Baker the 26 of February, 1661.

Thomas Pinsen, Junir, was married to Elizabeth White the 18th of ptember, 1662.

Edward Wright was married to Lydia Rawlins, widow, May the , 1664.

Hannah, the daughter of Stephen Tildin, was borne the 14th of Octo- ·, 1662.

Mary, the daughter of Stephen Vinall, was borne Nouember the 29th, 1662.

Joanna, the daughter of James Torrey, was borne May the fourth, 1663.

Deborah, the daughter of Henery Ewell, was borne June the 4th, 1663.

Isacke, the son of Isacke Chettenden, was borne the 30th of Septem: 1663.

Thomas, the son of John Cushen, was borne the 26th of September, 1663.

Charles, the son of Charles Stockbridge, was borne the 4th of Feb- ary, 1663.

Nathaniell, the son of Nathaniell Rawlins, was borne the 7th of ptem: 1662.

Nathaniell Rawlins, Senir, deceased the 23 of December, 1662.

Lydia, the daughter of Samuell Vtley, was borne December the 28th, 1659.

Margarett, the daughter of Humphery Johnson, was borne in Decem- ·, 1659.

Samuell, the son of Josepth ∧ was borne the 12th of Septem- ·, 1660. This to be enquired.

Thomas, the son of Thomas Oldum, was borne the 30th of October, 1660.

Sarah, the daughter of James Torrey, was borne the 9th of February, 1660.

Samuell Utley was married to Hannah Hatch December the sixt, 1648.

The Regester of Eastham.

WILLIAM, the son of William Merecke, was borne the 15th of Se tember, 1643.

Stephen, the son of William Mericke, was borne the 12th of May, 164

Rebeckah, the daughter of William Merricke, was borne the 28 July, 1648.

Mary, the daughter of William Merricke, was born the 4th of N uember, 1650.

Ruth, the daughter of William Merricke, was borne the 15th May, 1652.

Sarah, the daughter of William Merricke, was borne the first August, 1654.

John, the son of William Merricke, was borne the fifteenth of Januar 1656.

Isacke, the on of Henery Atkins, was borne the 14th of June, 1657.

Annah, the daughter of Marke Snow, was borne the 7th of July, 1656

Mehetabell, the daughter of Richard Knowles, was borne the 20th May, 1653.

Barbery, the daughter of Richard Knowles, was borne the 28th Septem: 1656.

Anna, the daughter of Josias Cooke, and wife of Marke Snow, died t 24th of July, 1656.

Taunton Regester.

THOMAS AUGER married to Elizabeth Packer the 14th of Nouer ber, 1665.

Thomas Linkoln, Seni^r, married to Elizabeth Street, widdow, the 10 December, 1665.

Patience, the daughter of John Bundey, died the 27th of March, 166

Johanna, the daughter of Nathaniel Thayer, was borne the 13th Decem: 1665.

Taunton, the 28th of February, 1665.

SHADRACH WILBORE, Towne Clarke.

JOHN BRYANT married to Abigaill Bryant the 23 of Nouember, 1665.

John Waterman married to Ann Sturtivant the 7ᵗʰ of December, 1665.

Edward Gray married vnto Dorithy Lettice the 12ᵗʰ of December, 1665.

John Robins married to Jehosabath Jourdaine the 14ᵗʰ of December, 1665.

Isacke Barker married to Mistris Judith Prence the 28ᵗʰ of December, 1665.

Jonathan Barnes married to Elizabeth Hedge the 4ᵗʰ of January, 1665.

Ephraim Tilson married to Elizabeth Hoskins the 7ᵗʰ of July, 1666.

Isacke, the son of Ephraim Tinkham, was borne the 11ᵗʰ of Aprill, 1666.

Samuell, the son of John Waterman, was borne the 16ᵗʰ of October, 1666.

John, the son of Sachariah Eedey, was borne the 10ᵗʰ of October, 1666.

Hannah, the daughter of William Harlow, was borne the 28ᵗʰ of Octo-
r, 1666.

Jacob Michell married to Sussanna Pope the 7ᵗʰ of Nouember, 1666.

Benjamine Bosworth married to Hannah Morton the 27ᵗʰ of Nouem-
r, 1666.

Robert Barrow married to Ruth Bonum the 28ᵗʰ of Nouember, 1666.

Nathaniel, the son of Nathaniel Morton, died the 17ᵗʰ of February, 1666.

Marcye, the wife of Joseph Dunham, died the 19ᵗʰ of February, 1666

John Phillips married to Faith Dotey the 14ᵗʰ of March, 1666.

John Cole married to Elizabeth Ryder the 21 of Nouember, 1667.

John Nelson married to Sarah Wood, the daughter of Henery Wood,
e 28ᵗʰ of Nouember, 1667.

John Doged, of Martins Vineyard, married to Bathshebath Prat, widdow,
e 29ᵗʰ of August, 1667.

Joseph Williams married to Elizabeth Watson the 28ᵗʰ of Nouember, 1667.

Nathaniel Holmes married to Marcye Faunce the 29ᵗʰ of December, 1667.

Edward, the son of Edward Gray, born the 31 of January, 1666.

Rowland, the son of Mʳ John Cotton, was borne the 27ᵗʰ of Decem-
r, 1667.

Joseph, the son of Samuell Sturtivant, was born the 16ᵗʰ of July, 1666.

Gabriel Fallowell, aged fourscore and three yeares, died the twenty
ght of December, 1667, and was buryed the 31 of the same month with
eat respect and honor, and much lamented in respect of the loss of him
hoe was a good old man and a faithfull servant of the Lord.

John Fallowell married to Sarah, the daughter of John Wood, the 13ᵗʰ
February, 1667.

Bathshua, the daughter of William Harlow, was borne the one and twentyeth of Aprill, 1667.

*Abigaill, the daughter of Jonathan Pratt, was born the sixteenth of June, 1665.

Bathshebah, the daughter of Jonathan Pratt, was borne the 20th of February, 1666.

Ruth, the daughter of Jacob Cooke, was borne the seauenteenth of January, 1665.

John Ivey, of Boston, was married to Marcye Bartlett, the 25th of December, 1668.

Susanna, the daughter of Edward Gray, was borne the 15th of October, 1668.

Jonathan, the son of Jonathan Pratt, was borne the 20th of March, 1668.

John Doten, the son of John Doten, was borne the 24th day of August, 1668.

Edward, the son of John Doten, was borne the 28th of June, 1671.

Jacob, the son of John Dotey, was born the 24th of May, 1673.

Elizabeth, the daughter of John Waterman, was born the fifteenth of January, 1668.

John Dunham, Senir, of Plymouth, aged about fourscore yeares, died the 2cond of March, 1668. Hee was an approued seruant of God, and a vsefull man in his place, being a deacon of the church of Christ att Plymouth.

Gyles Rickard, Senir, was married to Hannah Churchill, Senir, the 25th of June, anno Dom 1669.

Joseph Dunham was marryed to Hester Wormall the 20th of August, 1669.

Jacob Cooke, Senir, was marryed to Elizabeth Shirtliffe, widdow, the 18th of Nouember, 1669.

On the eight day of December, anno Dom 1669, the honored Capt Thomas Southworth changed this life for a better, being then about the age of fifty three yeares, who was a majestrate of this jurisdiction, and otherwise a good benifactor to both church and comonwealth, and that which is more than all hath bine named, hee was a very godly man, and soe liued and died full of faith and comfort, being much lamented by all of all sorts, sects, and conditions of people within our jurisdiction of New Plymouth.

Eliezer, the son of Robert Barrow, was borne on the fifteenth day of September, 1669, and died on the thirteenth day of December, 1669.

Eliezer Jackson, the son of Abraham Jackson, was borne   ^   ^   of October, 1669.

Hannah, the daughter of Benjamine Bosworth, was borne the one and wenty day of December, 1669.

Joannah, the daughter of Wilłam Harlow, was born the 24ᵗʰ of Iarch, 1669.

*On the 26 day of March, 1670, Mistris Allice Bradford, Seniʳ, changed [*37.] iis life for a better, haueing attained to fourscore yeares of age, or therabouts. hee was a godly matron, and much loued while shee liued, and lamented, iõ aged, when shee died, and was honorabley enterred on the 29 day of the ιonth aforsaid, att New Plymouth.

On the 12ᵗʰ day of December, 1671, Mistris Allice Bradford, Juniʳ, ιanged this life for a better, about the age of 44 yeares. Shee was a racious woman, liued much desired, died much lamented, and was buried on ιe 14ᵗʰ day of the month aforesaid, att Plymouth abouesaid.

Sarah, the daughter of Mʳ John Cotton, was borne on the fift day of prill, 1670.

Maria, the daughter of Mʳ John Cotton, was borne on the 14ᵗʰ of ιnuary, 1671.

Hannah, the daughter of Jonathan Prate, was borne on the 28ᵗʰ of ιne, 1671.

Elizabeth, the daughter of Zacariah Eedey, was borne the third day ʼ August, 1670.

Nathaniel Bosworth, Juniʳ, of Nantaskett, allies Hull, was married to lizabeth Morton, of Plymouth, on the seauenth day of December, 1670.

Joseph Prince, of Nantaskett, alies Hull, was married vnto Joanna Morton, ʼ Plymouth, on the 7ᵗʰ of December, one thousand six hundred and seauenty.

Richard Willis was married to Patience Bonum on the 28ᵗʰ of De- mber, 1670.

Lydia Bumpas, the daughter of Joseph Bumpas, was borne the 2ᶜᵒⁿᵈ August, 1669.

Francis Curtice was married to Hannah Smith on the 28ᵗʰ of De- mber, 1671.

John Laythorpe was marryed to Mary Cole, Juniʳ, on the third of ιnuary, 1671.

Nathaniel Southworth marryed to Desire Gray the tenth of January, ▸71.

Joseph Churchill married to Sarah Hickes the third of June, 1672.

Thomas Faunce married to Jane Nelson the 13ᵗʰ of December, 1672.

*Mercye, the daughter of Joseph Warren, was borne the 23 of Sep- [*38.] ιmber, 1653.

5

34 PLYMOUTH COLONY RECORDS.

PLYMOUTH.

Abigaill, the daughter of Joseph Warren, was borne the 15th of March, 165

Joseph, the son of Joseph Warren, was borne the 8th of January, 165

Patience, the daughter of Joseph Warren, was borne the 15th March, 1660.

Elizabeth, the daughter of Joseph Warren, was borne the 15th August, 1662.

Benjamine, the son of Joseph Warren, was borne the 8th of January, 167

Lydia, the daughter of Joseph Bumpas, was borne the 2cond day August, 1669.

Wybra, the daughter of Joseph Bumpas, was borne the fifteenth May, 1672.

[*39.]   *Mehittabell, the daughter of Willam Harlow, was borne the 4th October, 1672.

The 23th of February, 1672, Mr John Howland, Senir, of the towne Plymouth, deceased. Hee was a godly man and an ancient professor in t wayes of Christ; hee liued vntill hee attained aboue eighty yeares in the worl Hee was one of the first comers into this land, and proued a vsefull instrume of good in his place, & was the last man that was left of those that came ou in the shipp called the May Flower, that liued in Plymouth; hee was wi honor intered att the towne of Plymouth on the 25 of February, 1672.

Thomas Prence, Esquire, Gour of the jurisdiction of New Plymou died the 29th of March, 1673, and was interred the 8th of Aprill followin After hee had serued God in the office of Gour sixteen yeares, or nea thervnto, hee finished his course in the 73 yeare of his life. Hee was a wort gentleman, very pious, and very able for his office, and faithfull in t discharge therof, studious of peace, a welwiller to all that feared God, and terrour to the wicked. His death was much lamented, and his body honora buryed att Plymouth the day and yeare aboue mensioned.

Nathaniel Bosworth, the son of Nathaniel Bosworth, Junir, of Na taskett, was borne the 22cond of March, 1672, at Plymouth.

Elizabeth Bosworth, the wife of Nathaniel Bosworth, Junir, of Na taskett, died the sixt day of Aprill, 1673, being the Lords day. Shee wa vertuous young woman; her death was much bewaild by her husband a relations and other frinds. Shee was honorably buried att Plymouth t 8th day of Aprill, 1673, which was the same day that Gour Prence v interred, about two houres before him.

Samuell, the son of Zachariah Eedey, was born the 4th day of June, 16

John Eedey, the son of Obadiah Eedey, was borne the 22cond of March,16

Hasadiah Eedey, the daughter of Obadiah Eedey, was borne the 10th Aprill, 1672.

Jabez Howland, the son of Jabez Howland, was borne on the 15th day
Nouember, anno 1669.

Bethya Howland, the daughter of Jabez Howland, was borne on the
ird day of June, 1674.

John Howland, the son of Jabez Howland, was borne about the 15th
y of January, 1672, and soone after deceased within the same month.

Mistris Lydia Morton, the wife of Nathaniel Morton, Seni[r], deceased on
e 23 of September, 1673, after shee had liued with her said husband neare
e space of 38 yeares. After much dollorous paine and sicknes, shee ended
r life with much peace and comfort. Shee was a good woman, and liued
uch desired, and died much lamented, especially by her poor sorrowfull hus-
nd ; shee was honorably buried on the 25th of the said monthe att Plymouth.

Mistris Elizabeth Warren, an aged widdow, aged aboue 90 yeares, deceased
. the second of October, 1673, whoe, haueing liued a godly life, came to
r graue as a shoke of corn fully ripe. Shee was honorably buried on the
th of October aforsaid.

John Morton, Seni[r], of Middleberry, died on the third of October, 1673 ;
e was a godly man, and was much lamented by sundry of the inhabitants
that place. It pleased God, notwithstanding, to put a period to his life,
er a longe sicknes and somtimes som   ×   ×   hopes of recouery.

*Jabez Pratt, the son of Jonathan Pratt, was borne on the first of
ouember, 1673.

Melletiah, the daughter of Jonathan Pratt, was born the eleuenth of
ecember, 1676.

Nathaniel Morton, of Plymouth, was married to Anne Templar, of
artstowne, the 29[th] day of Aprill, 1674.

Judith, the daughter of Serj: Willam Harlow, was born the 2[cond] of
gust, 1676.

Mary, the daughter of John Rickard, the son of Gyles Rickard, was borne
e 27[th] of October, 1677.

---

aunton Regester of Beirthes, Marriages, and Burialls, p[r]sented to
the Court, Anno 1668.

ARAH, the daughter of John Bundy, borne the 4[th] of March, 1668.

Samuell, the son of Thomas Caswell, borne the 26 of January, 1662.

Elizabeth, the daughter of Thomas Casewell, borne the 10[th] of January,
34.

TAUNTON.
Abigaill, the daughter of Thomas Caswell, borne the 27th of October, 166

Richard, the son of Richard Briggs, borne the 7th of Aprill, 1668.

Sarah, the daughter of John Dean, born the 9th of Nouember, 1668.

John, the son of John Lincon, borne the 11th of Octob: 1665.

Thomas, the son of John Lincon, borne the 15th of September, 1667.

Hannah, the daughter of Daniell Fisher, borne Febru: ye first, 1666.

John, the son of Daniell Fisher, born the last of Nouemb: 1667.

John, the son of Jabez Hackett, born the 26th of December, 1654.

Jabez, the son of Jabez Hackett, born the 12th of Septem: 1656.

Mary, the daughter of Jabez Hackett, borne the 9th of January, 1659.

Sarah, the daughter of Jabez Hackett, borne the 13th of July, 1661.

Samuell, the son of Jabez Hatckett, borne the 29th of July, 1664.

Hannah, the daughter of Jabez Hackett, borne the 25 of January, 1666.

Mary, the daughter of John Richmond, borne att Bridḡwater, Ju 2cond, 1654.

John, the son of John Richmond, born at Bridḡwater, the 6th of June, 165

Thomas, the son of John Richmond, born att Newport, on Rhode Ilan the 2cond of February, 1658.

Sussanna, the daughter of John Richmond, borne att Bridḡwater, t 4th of Nŏember, 1661.

Josiah Richmond, the son of John Richmond, borne att Taunton t 8th of December, 1663.

Edward, the son of John Richmond, borne the eight of February, 166

Samuell, the son of John Richmond, borne the 23 of September, 1668

This was taken out of Taunton Towne Record.

Attested by SHADRACH WILBORE, Towne Clarke.

March 1, 1668–69.

Taunton Register of Mariages, Beirth, and Burialls, 1667.

JAMES, the son of John Bundy, borne the 29th of December, 1664.

Patience, daughter of John Bundy, died the 27th of March, 1665.

Hannah, the daughter of Samuell Smith, was borne the 17 of Se tem: 1662.

Sarah, the daughter of Samuell Smith, was borne the 25 of January, 166

Sarah, daughter of Samuell Smith, died the 18th July, 1665.

Samuell, the son of Samuell Smith, borne the 15 of October, 1666.

Steuen, the son of Thomas Casewell, borne the 15 of February, 1648.

Thomas, the son of Thomas Casewell, was born 22 of February, 1650.

Peter, the son of Thomas Caswell, was borne the last of October, 1652.

Mary, the daughter of Thomas Caswell, was borne the last of August, 1654.

John, the son of Thomas Casewell, was borne the last of July, 1656.

Sarah, the daughter of Tho: Caswell, borne the last of Nouember, 1658.

Wilłam, the son of Thomas Casewell, borne the 15 of September, 1660.

Mary, the daughter of Shadrach Wilbore, borne the 18th of March, 1661.

Sañiell, the son of Shadrach Wilbore, was borne the first of Aprill, 1663.

Rebeckah, the daughter of Shadrach Wilbore, was borne the 13 of January, 1664.

Hannah, the daughter of Shadrach Wilbore, born the 24th of February, 1667.

Sañiell, the son of Sañiell Hall, was borne the 11th of December, 1664.

John, the son of Samuell Hall, was borne the 19th of October, 1666.

Johanna Thayer, the daughter of Nathaniell Thayer, borne 13 of December, 1665.

*Edward Shoue, son of Mr Gorge Shoue, was borne the 28th of Aprill, 1665.   [*42.]

Edward Shoue, the son of Mr Gorge Shoue, died, buried the 7th of August, 1665.

Elizabeth, the daughter of Mr Gorge Shoue, was borne the 10th of August, 1666.

Seeth, the son of Mr Gorge Shoue, was borne the 10th of December, 1667.

Elizabeth, the daughter of John Smith, was borne the 7th of September, 1663.

Henery, the son of John Smith, was borne the 27th of May, 1666.

Hannah, the daughter of Samuell Hallowey, was borne the first of March, 1667.

Wilłam, the son of Wilłam Briggs, was borne the 25 of January, 1667.

Gared, the son of Garett Talbutt, was borne the 20th of March, 1667.

Mary Eedy, the daughter of John Eedey, was borne the 14th of March, 1666.

Wilłam, the son of Richard Briggs, was borne the 21 of Nouember, 1663.

Rebecka, the daughter of Richard Briggs, borne the 15th of August, 1665.

Samuell, the son of John Dean, born the 24th of January, 1666.

Samuell, the son of Samuell Lincon, borne the first of June, 1664.

Hanna, the daughter of Samuell Lincon, borne the 24th of March, 1666.

Tamisen, the daughter of Samuell Lincon, born the 27th of October, 1667.

John, the son of Robert Crosman, borne the 16th of March, 1654.

TAUNTON.   Mary, the daughter of Robert Crosman, borne the 16 of July, 1655.

Robert, the son of Robert Crosman, borne the third of August, 1657.

Joseph, the son of Robert Crosman, borne the 25 of Aprill, 1659.

Nathaniell, the son of Robert Crosman, borne the 7th of August, 1660.

Eliezer, the son of Robert Crosman, borne the 16 of March, 1663.

Elizabeth, the daughter of Robert Crosman, born the 2d of May, 1665.

Samuell, the son of Robert Crosman, borne the 25 of July, 1667.

Eliezer, the son of Robert Crosman, died the 26 of October, 1667.

Ester Allin, the daughter of Jonah Allin, Junir, was borne the 3 of January, 1662.

Mary, the daughter of Jonah Allin, was borne the 12 of May, 1663.

Sarah, the daughter of Jonah Allin, was borne the 4th of Nouember, 1665

Jonah Allin, the son of Jonah Allin, borne the 17th of August, 1667.

[*43.]   *Thomas Auger married to Elizabeth Packer, of Bridgwater, the 14th of Nouember, 1665.

Thomas Lincone, Senir, married to Elizabeth Street, widdow, the 10th of December, 1665.

Agnis Smith, wife of Francis Smith, died the sixt of January, 1665.

William Briggs married to Sarah Macomber, of Marshfeild, the sixt of Nouember, 1666.

Samuell Hallowey married to Jane Brayman the 26th of March, 1666.

Garett Talbutt married to Sarah Andrewes, the first of Aprill, 1664.

John Eedey married to Sussannah Padducke, of Dartmouth, the last of Nouember, 1665.

Richard Briggs married to Rebecah Hoskins, of Lakenham, the 15th of August, 1662.

John Dean married to Sarah Edson, of Bridgwater, the 7th of Nouember, 1663.

Joseph Gray married to Rebecka Hill the 25th of February, 1667.

Constant Allin, the wife of Jonah Allin, Senir, died the 22cond of Aprill, 1667

Jonah Allin, Senir, married Francis Hill, of Vnketey, the 14th of December, 1667.

Timothy Poole, the son of Mr William Poole, died the 15 of December, 1667. Hee was drowned in a little pond att Wesquabenansett where it was thought hee did swime after a fowle which hee had shott.

John Parker died the 14th of February, 1667.

This is a true coppy drawne out of Taunton regester the first of March 1667 or 68, and attested by

SHADRACH WILBORE, Clarke.

Tauntō Regester of Beirthes, Marriages, and Burialls, March, 1670.

A NNA BURT, the wife of James Burt, died the 17th of August, 1665. Elizabeth Wilbore, the wife of Joseph Wilbore, died the 9th of Nouember, 1670.

John Dean, the son of John Deane, died the sixt of August, 1670.

Sussanna, the daughter of Samuell Smith, was borne the 20th of July, 1669.

Samuell, the son of Samuell Bundy, was borne the 4th of October, 1670.

Easter, the daughter of Thomas Casewell, was borne the 4th of June, 1669.

Joseph, the son of Shadrach Wilbore, was borne the 27th of July, 1670.

Nicholas Hall, the son of Samuell Hall, was borne the 28th of October, 1670.

Thomas, the son of Wilłam Brigges, was borne the 9th of September, 1669.

Sarah, the daughter of Wilłam Briggs, was borne the 10th of September, 1669.

John, the son of John Deane, was borne the 28th of July, 1670.

Elizabeth, the daughter of Thomas Lincolne, was borne the 24th of Aprill, 1669.

Mercye, the daughter of Robert Crosman, was borne the 20th of March, 1669.

Mercy Hoare, the daughter of Hezekiah Hoar, was borne the last of January, 1654.

*Nathaniell, the son of Hezekiah Hoare, was borne the last of March, 1656.   [*44.]

Sarah, the daughter of Hezekiah Hoare, was borne the first of Aprill, 1658.

Elizabeth Hoare, the daughter of Hezekiah Hoar, was borne the 26 of May, 1660.

Edward, the son of Hezekiah Hoar, was borne the 25 of September, 1663.

Lydia, the daughter of Hezekiah Hoar, was borne the 24th of March, 1665.

Mary, the daughter of Hezeka Hoare, was borne the 22[cond] of September, 1669.

Mehittabell, the daughter of Joseph Gray, was borne the 21 of February, 1668.

Jonathan, the son of Jonathan Briggs, was borne the 15th of March, 1668.

Dauid, the son of Jonathan Briggs, was borne the sixt of December, 1669.

Mary Lincon, the daughter of Thomas Lincon, was borne the 12 of May, 1652.

Sarah, the daughter of Tho: Lincon, was borne the 25 of September, 1654.

Thomas, the son of Thomas Lincon, was borne the 21 of Aprill, 1656.

TAUNTON.   Samuell, the son of Thomas Lincon, was borne the 16th of March, 1658.

Jonah, the son of Thomas Lincon, was borne the 7th of July, 1660.

Hannah, the daughter of Thomas Lincon, was borne the 15th of March,1663.

Constant, the daughter of Thomas Lincon, was borne the 16th of May, 1665.

Marcye, the daughter of Thomas Lincon, was borne the 3 of Aprill, 1670.

Vnis, the daughter of James Leonard, Junir, was borne att Braintree, the 25 of Nouember, 1668.

Prudence, the daughter of James Leonard, Junir, was borne the 24th of January, 1669.

Edward, the son of Edward Bobbit, was borne the 15 of July, 1655.

Sarah, the daughter of Edward Bobbitt, was borne the 20th of March, 1657.

Hannah, the daughter of Edward Bobbitt, was borne the 9th of March, 1660.

Damaris, the daughter of Edward Bobbitt, was borne the 15th of September, 1663.

Elkana, the daughter of Edward Bobbitt, was borne the 15th of December, 1665.

Dorcas, the daughter of Edward Bobbitt, was borne the 20th of January, 1666.

Ester, the daughter of Edward Bobbitt, was borne the 15th of Aprill, 1669.

James, the son of James Phillips, was borne the first of January, 1661.

Nathaniell, the son of James Phillipps, was borne the 25 of March, 1664.

Sarah, the daughter of James Phillipps, was borne the 17th of March, 1667.

Wiłłam, the son of James Phillipps, was borne the 21 of August, 1669.

Elizabeth, the daughter of Joseph Williams, was borne the 30th of July, 1669.

Jane, the daughter of James Bell, was borne the 4th of Aprill, 1658.

John, the son of James Bell, was borne the 15th of August, 1660.

[*46.]   *James Bell, the son of James Bell, borne the 10th July, 1663.

Nathaniel, the son of James Bell, was borne the seauenth of January, 1664.

Sarah, the daughter of James Bell, was borne the 15th of September, 1666.

Elizabeth, the daughter of James Bell, was borne the 15th of Nouember, 1668.

Mary, the daughter of James Bell, was borne the seauenth of July, 1669.

John, the son of Joseph Staples, was borne the 28th of January, 1670.

This is a true coppy of what was brought to mee.

Taken out of Taunton regester this sixt of March, $\frac{1670}{71}$.

Attested by SHADRACH WILBORE,

The Towne Clarke of Taunton.

1677. Heer followeth diuers other registers which might haue bin
more methodically, as I could desire, because the order of Court hath
not bin attended in bringing in the regesters of the townes as might haue
bine; and p̄tely alsoe in that I haue bine interͬupted therͬin by the
troubles of the late warr.

A Coppy of the Marriages, Beirthes, and Burialls of sundry Pʳsons, BARNSTABLE.
p̄sented from the Record att Barnstable.

JANE, the wife of Anthony Annible, buried about December, 1643.
The said Anthony married with Anne Alcocke 1 of March, 1645.
His son Samuell borne about the 2ᶜᵒⁿᵈ of January, 1646.
His son Ezek ^ ^ ^ ^ ^ ^
His daughter Desire about the begiñing of October, 1653.
Abraham Blush his daughter Sarah borne 2ᶜᵒⁿᵈ of Decemb: 1641.
His son Joseph the 5ᵗʰ of Aprill, 1648.
He buried his wife Anne 16 May, 1651.
And married with Hannah Barker, viḋ.
His son Abraham, borne about 16 October, 54.
He buried his wife Hannah about the 16ᵗʰ of March, 1658.
And marrẏed with Allice Derbey, viḋ, 4 January, 1658.
Joseph Benjamine and Jeremiah Lumbert, 10 June, 1671.
Nicholas Bonham and Hannah Fuller married January the 1, 1658.
His daughter Hannah borne the 8ᵗʰ of October, 1659. Mary the
4ᵗʰ of October, 1661.
Thomas Burman and Hannah Annible marryed March first, 1645.
His daughter Hannah borne about the end of May, 1646.
His son Thomas about the middest, 1648.
Sam̃ell about the end of July, 1651.
Desire about the end of May, 1654.
Mary the middest of March, 1656.
Mehittabell the begiñing of September, 1658.
Trustrum the begiñing of August, 1661.
Sam̃ell Bacon and Martha Foxwell maryed the 9ᵗʰ of May, 1659.
His son Sam̃ell borne the 9ᵗʰ of March, 1659–60.
His daughter Martha the sixt of January, 1661.
Austine Beirse his daughter Mary borne 1640.
Martha, 1642.
Presilla, 10ᵗʰ of March, 1643.

6

BARNSTABLE.   Sarah the 28th of March, 1646.

Abigaill the 18th of December, 1647.

Hannah the 16th of Nouember, 1649.

Joseph, the 25th of January, 1651.

Hester, the 2^{cond} of October, 1653.

Lydia the latter end of September, 1655.

Rebecka, September 26, 1657.

His son James the latter end of July, 1660.

[*47.]   *Nathaniel Bacon and Hannah Mayo marryed the 4th of Decem ber, 1642

His daughter Hannah borne the 4 of Septem: 1643.

His son Nathanieli the 5th of February, 1645.

Mary, the 12th of August, 1648.

Samuell, the 25th of February, 1650.

Elizabeth, the 28th of January, 1653.

Jeremiah, the 8th of May, 1657.

Mercye, the 8th of February, 1659.

James Cleaguehorne and Abigaill Lumbert marryed the sixt of January, 1654.

His son James borne the 29th of January, 1654.

Mary borne the 28th of October, 1655.

Elizabeth borne Aprill the ^ 1658.

Sarah, the third of January, 1659.

Robert, the 27th of October, 1661.

Mr Henery Cobb his son John borne att Plymouth the 7th of June, 163?

His son James borne att Plymouth, the 14th of January, 1634.

His daughter Mary borne att Scittuate, March the 24, 1637.

His daughter Patience att Barnstable, about the 19th of March, 1641

Gershom, the 10th of January, 1644.

Eliezer, the 30th of March, 1648.

His wife Patience buried the 4th of May, 1648.

Hee married with Sarah Hinckley, the 12th of December, 1649.

His daughter Mehittable borne in Septem: 1651.

And buried the 8th of March, 1652.

Samell borne the 12 of October, 1654.

Sarah, the 15 January, 58; and buried the 25th of January, 1658.

Jonathan, the 10th of Aprill, 1660.

Mr John Chipman his daughter Hope borne August the 13th, 1652.

His daughter Lydia, the 25th of December, 1654.

His son John, the 2^{cond} of March, 56–57, and died the 29th of BARNSTABLE.
May following.

Hannah, the 14 January, 1658.

Samuell, the 15th of Aprill, 1662.

Wilłam Crocker his son, John Crocker, borne the last of May, 1637.

His daughter Elizabeth, the 22^{cond} of Septemb: 1639.

Samell, the 3 of July, 1642.

Job, the 9th of March, 1644.

Josiah, the 19th of Sept: 1647.

Eliezer, the 21 of July, 1650.

Joseph, 1654.

Hee buried his daughter Elizabeth, May, 1658.

His son John Crocker married with Mary Botffish, Nouember, 1659.

Elizabeth, daughter of the said John, borne October, 1660.

John Dauis and Hannah Lynnitt married the 15 of March, 1648.

His son John, borne about the middest of January, 1649.

Samell, the middest of December, 1651.

His daughter Hannah and Mary, the 3 of January, 1653.

His son Joseph and Benjamine, June, 1656.

Symon, the middest of July, 1658.

Dolar, the begiñing of October, 1660.

*Edward Fitsrandalls daughter Hannah, borne Aprill, 1649.   [*48.]

Mary, the last of May, 1651.

His son John, the 7th of October, 1653.

Joseph, the first of March, 1656.

Thomas, the 16th of August, 1659.

Hope, the 2^{cond} of Aprill, 1661.

Richard Foxwell his daughter Mary, borne the 17th of August, 1635.

Martha, the 24 of March, 1638.

Ruth, the 25 of March, 1641.

Samell Fuller, Seni^r, his son Thomas, borne the 18th of May, 1650.

His daughter Sarah, the 14th of Decem: 1654.

Item, a child borne 8th February, 1658, and buryed 15 dayes after.

Roger Goodspeed and Allis Layton married December, 1641.

His son Nathaniell, borne October 6, 1642.

John, the middest of June, 1645.

His daughter Mary, the latter end of July, 1647.

BARNSTABLE.　　　　Benjamine, the sixt of May, 1649.

Ruth, the 10th of Aprill, 1652.

Ebenezer, latter end of December, 1655.

Elizabeth, in May, 1658.

John Gorum his daughter Desire, borne att Plymouth, the 2^{cond} o
　　　Aprill, 1644.

These borne ⎧ Temperance, the 5th of May, 1648.
att ⎨ James, the 28th of Aprill, 1650.
Marshfeild. ⎩ John, 20th of February, 1651.

　　　⎧ Joseph, borne the 16th of February, 1653.
Att ⎨ Jabez, the third of August, 1656.
Yarmouth. ⎪ Mary, the 20th of January, 1658.
　　　⎩ Lydia, the 11th of Nouember, 1661.

His daughter Desire marryed att Barnstable, the 7th of October, 1661

Saṁell Hinckley his son Saṁell, borne the 4th of July, 1642.

His son John, the 24th of May, 1644.

Hee buried Sarah, his wife, August 19, 1656, and married with
　　　Bridged Botfish, Decemb: 15, 1657.

Mr Thomas Hinckley married with Mary Richards the 4th of De
cember, 1641.

His daughter Mary, borne the 3 of August, 1644.

Sarah, the 4th of Nouember, 1646.

Melletiah, 25 of December, 1648.

Hannah, the 15th of Aprill, 1651.

His son Samuell, the 14th of February, 1652.

Thomas, the 5th of December, 1654.

Bethshuah, the 15th of May, 1657.

Mehittable, the 24th of March, 16$\frac{58}{59}$.

Hee buried Mary, his wife, the 25th June, 1659, and married Mary
　　　Glouer, viz:, the 16 March, 59–60.

His daughter Admire, borne 28 January, 1661, and buried the 16^t
　　　of February, 1661.

His son Ebenezer, borne the 22^{cond} February, 1662.

Thomas Huckens marryed with Mary Wells, 1642.

His daughter, borne about the 4th of July, 1644, and buryed th
　　　28th of the same month, July, 1644.

His daughter Mary, borne the 29th of March, 1646.

Elizabeth, the 2^{cond} of February, 1647, and buryed the 28th of
　　　December, 1648.

His wife Mary, buried the 28 July, 1648, and hee married with Rose BARNSTABLE. Hollier, viz$\int$, the 3 of Nouemb^r, 1648.

His son John, borne about the 2^{cond} of August, 1649.

*Thomas, the 25 of Aprill, 1651.   [*49.]

Hannah, the 14th of October, 1653.

Joseph, the 21 of February, 1655.

Deborah Hillies, daughter of the said Rose, by her husband, Hugh Hillies, borne att Yarmouth, October the 30th, 1643.

Saṁell Hillies, att Yarmouth, about the 30th of July, 1616.

James Hamblen his son Bartholomew, born Aprill, 1642.

John, the 26th of June, 1644.

Sarah, the 7th of Nouember, 1647.

Eliezer, the 17th of March, 1649.

Israell, the 25th of June, 1655.

John Haddawey and Hannah Hollett married the first of July, 1656.

His first borne son, about October, 57, and buried ten dayes after.

His son John, borne about the 16th of Augst, 1658.

Trustrum Hull his daughter Mary, borne the latter end of September, 1645.

Sarah, the latter end of March, 1650.

Joseph, in June, 1652.

John, the latter end of March, 1654.

Hannah, February, 1656.

John Jenkens and Mary Ewer were marryed the 2^{cond} of February, 1652.

His daughter Sarah, borne the 15th of Nouember, 1653.

Mehitable, the 2^{cond} of March, 1654, 55.

Samuell, the 12th of September, 1657.

John, the 13th of Nouember, 1659.

Ralph Jones his son Shuball, borne the 27th of August, 1654.

Jedadiah, the 4th of January, 1656.

John, the 14th of August, 1659.

Gorge Lewis, Juni^r, marryed with Mary Lumbert, December, 1654.

His son Gorge, borne the latter end of September, 1655.

Mary, the 9th of May, 1657.

Sarah, the 12th of January, 1659.

Thomas Lewis and Mary Dauis marryed the 15th of June, 1653.

His son James, borne the last of March, 1654.

His son Thomas, the 15th of July, 1656.

Mary, the 2^{cond} of Nouemb^r, 1659.

BARNSTABLE.　　　James Lewis and Sarah Lane marryed October, 1655.

His son John, borne att the latter end of October, 1656.

Samuell, the 10th of Aprill, 1659.

Thomas Lumbert, Seni^r, his son Jededia, borne the 20th of September, 16x.

Benjamine, the 26th of August, 1642.

[*50.]　　　*Dauid Linnitt and Hannah Shilley marryed the 15th of March, 1652.

His son Samuell, borne the 15th of December, 1655.

Elisha, the 1 of June, 1658.

Hannah, the 15th of December, 1660.

Barnard Lumbert his daughter Martha, borne the 19th of September, 1640.

Jabez, the 1 of July, 1642.

Jabez Lumbert married to Sarah Darbey, the first of December, 1660.

His first borne son, borne the 18th of February, 1661, and died the same day.

Joseph Laythorp, married with Mary Ansell, the 11th of December, 1650.

His son Joseph, borne the 3th of December, 1652.

Mary, the 22^{cond} of March, 1654.

Benjamine, the 25th of July, 1657.

Elizabeth, the 18th of December, 1659.

John, the 28th of Nouember, 1661.

Joshuah Lumbert and Abigaill Linnett marryed the latter end of May, 1650.

His daughter Abigaill, borne the 6th of Aprill, 1652.

Mercye, the 15th of January, 1655.

Jonathan, the 28th of Aprill, 1657.

Joshua, the 16th of January, 1660.

Thomas Laythorp his daughter Mary, borne 4th of October, 1640.

Hannah, the 18th of October, 1642.

Thomas, the 7th of July, 1644.

Melletie, the 2^{cond} of Nouember, 1646.

Bethya, the 23 of July, 1649.

His daughter Mary marryed the 20 Nouemb: 1656.

Gorge Lewis, Seni^r, his son John, borne att Scittuate, the 2^{cond} of March, 1637.

Ephraim, the 23 of July, 1641.

Sarah, the second of February, 1643.

John Martin married to Martha Lumbert the 1 of July, 1657.

His son John, borne about the middle of June, 1658.

Gorge, borne in the first weeke in October, 1660.

Elisha Parker and Elizabeth Hinckley married the 15 July, 1657.

His son Thomas, borne the 15th of May, 1658.

Elisha, about the begiñing of Nouember, 1660.

Robert Parker marryed with Sarah James the 28th of January, 1656.

His daughter Mary, borne the 1 of Aprill, 1658.

The son Samuell, the latter end of June, 1660.

*John Phinney and Abigaill Coggen married the 10th of June, 1650.   [*51.]

And his wife Abigaill buried the 6th of May, 16x.

And his wifes son, Thomas Coggen, buried the 26 of January, 1658.

The said John Phinney marryed to Elizabeth Bayley, the 26 of June, 1654.

His son Jonathan, born August 14, 1655.

Robert, the 13th of August, 1656.

Hannah, the 2cond of September, 1657.

Elizabeth, the 15th of March, 1658–59.

Josiah, the 11th of January, 1660.

Moses Rowley and Elizabeth Fuller marryed the 22cond of Aprill, 1652.

His daughter Mary, borne the 20th of March, 1653.

His son Moses, the 10th of Nouember, 1654.

A child, that died the 15th of August, 1656.

Shuball and Mehittable, January 11, 1660.

Henery Tayler and Lydia Hatch marryed the 19th of December, 1650.

His daughter Lydia, borne the 21 of June, 1655.

His son Jonathan, the 20th of Aprill, 1658.

Robert Dauis his daughter Deborah, borne in January, 1645.

Mary, in May, 1648.

Andrew, in May, 1650.

John, first of March, 1652.

Robert, in August, 1654.

Josias, in September, 1656.

Hannah, in September, 1658.

Sarah, in October, 1660.

Presented to the Court this sixt of March, 1661–62.

P me,   THOMAS HINCKLEY.

SWANSEY. *A List of such Marriages, Beirthes, and Burialls, as were brough[into the Towne Clarke of Swansey, to be recorded, from the 27 of February, 1672, to this p'sent February the 27, 1673.*

Marriages.

JOHN PADDUCKE and Anna Jones were married on the one an[twentyeth day of December, 1673.

Saṁell Bullucke and Mary Thirber were married on the 12th day o[Nouember, 1673.

Beirthes.

Anne, the daughter of Leiftenant John Browne, and of Anne, his wif[was borne the 19th of September, 1673, att 4 a clocke in the morning.

Benjamine, the son of John Crabtree, and of Mary, his wife, was born[on the 12 day of October, 1673.

Elizabeth, the daughter of Thomas Easterbrooke, and of Sarah, his wif[was borne on the 19th of December, 1673.

Elizabeth, the daughter of Daniell Allin, and of Mary, his wife, wa[borne on the 28th day of September, 1673.

Hannah, the daughter of Jonathan Bosworth, was borne Nouembe[the 5th, 1673.

[*52.]   *Hannah, the daughter of Jarrett Ingraham, was borne the 29th of De[cember, 1673.

John, the son of Gedian Allin, and of Sarah, his wife, was borne Octo[ber the 20th, 1673.

Mellatia, the son of John Martin, and of Jone, his wife, borne the 3[of August, 1673.

Margery, the daughter of Wilłam Haward, and of Sarah, his wife, wa[borne Sept: 10th, 1673.

Nathaniell, the son of Nathaniell Lewis, and of Mary, his wife, wa[borne July the 17th, 1673.

Saṁell, the son of Thomas Lewis, and Hannah, his wife, was born[Aprill the 23, 1673.

Burialls.

Mistris Dorrithy Browne, the wife of M[r] John Browne, Seni[r], decease[January the 27, being the 90th yeer of her life, or therabouts, and was burie[on the 29th of January, 1673.

Taken out of the Booke of Records, att Swansey, by mee,

JOHN MYLES, Juni[r], Towne Clarke.

*A Coppy of the Beirthes and Buriall of Swansey, from March the SWANSEY.
first, 1671, to this instant March, 1672.*

CALEB, the son of Caleb Eedey, and of Elizabeth, his wife, were borne on the 29th of May, 1672.

Jonathan, the son of William Haward, and Sarah, his wife, was borne the 8th of Aprill, 1672.

Joseph, the son of Joseph Lewis, and of Mary, his wife, was borne ne the sixt, 1672.

John, the son of John Cobleich, and of Mary, his wife, was borne the t of January, 1672.

Thomas, the son of Nathaniell Chaffey, and of Experience, his wife, s borne October the 19th, 1672.

℞ me,   JOHN MYLES, Junir, Towne Clarke.

Scittuates Register.   SCITUATE.

THOMAS OLDHAM, marryed to Mary Witherell, Nouember the 20th, 1656.

Jonas Pickles was married to Allice Hattee, December the 23, 1657.

John Louell, of Boston, married to Elizabeth Siluester, the daughter of hard Siluester, the 24th of January, 1658, ℞ Mr Hatherley.

Daniell Hickes was married to Elizabeth Hanmore, Sept: 19th, 1657.

*John Bryant was marryed to Elizabeth Witherell, December the 1651.   [*53.]

Mary, the daughter of Thomas Oldham, was borne August the 20th, 1658.

Jonas, the son of Jonas Pickles, was bore the fift of February, 1658.

Steuen, the son of Joseph Tilden, was borne May the 14th, 1659.

Ichabod, the son of Henery Ewell, was borne in June, 1659.

Abigaill, the daughter of Thomas Clapp, was borne January 29, 1659.

Mary, the wife of John Bryant, deceased July the 2cond, 1655.

Elizabeth, the daughter of Nathaniel Rawlins, deceased February 17, 1659.

Ephraim Kempton, deceased ⌃ 24, 1655.

Hannah, the wife of Ephraim Kempton, deceased March 31, 1656.

℞ me, JAMES TORREY, Towne Clarke.

SCITUATE. *A true Lists of all Beirthes that haue bine brought in to mee, Isacke Bucke, Towne Clarke of Scittuate, in the Yeer 1674. As for marriages and burialls, there hath not one bine brought in to mee this yeer to record.*

MARCYE TILDEN, the daughter of Steuen Tilden, was borne the first of May, 1674.

John Cushen, the son of John Cushen, was borne the 14ᵗʰ September, 1674.

Samuell Chandeler, the son of Benjamine Chandeler, was borne the 30ᵗʰ of Nouember, 1674.

James Hatch, the son of Jeremiah Hatch, was borne the 4ᵗʰ of May, 1674.

James Perrey, the son of Thomas Perrey, was borne the 12ᵗʰ of March, 1673.

Sarah Leichfeild, the daughter of Josiah Leichfeild, was borne the 2? of December, 1674.

Rodulphus Hatch, the son of Thomas Hatch, was borne the 26ᵗʰ of December, 1674.

Hannah Cudworth, the daughter of Jonathan Cudworth, was borne the eight of May, 1674.

Transcribed out of the Records of Scittuate, p̃ me,

ISACKE BUCKE, Towne Clarke of Scittuate.

[*54.] *Scittuate, the 3 of March, 167⁵⁄₆. A true Lists of the Marriage Beirthes, and Burialls, that haue bine brought in to mee, Isack Bucke, in the Yeer 1676.*

JOSEPH GARRETT married to Ruth Bucke, the 17ᵗʰ day of January, 1676.

Ichabod Turner, the son of John Turner, Junⁱʳ, was borne the 9ᵗʰ of Aprill, 1676.

Wiłłam Blackmore, deceased the 21 of Aprill, 1676.

Transcribed out of the Records of Scittuate,

P̃ ISACKE BUCKE, Towne Clarke of Scittuate.

Swansey Regester of Marriages, Beirthes, and Burialls, 1674.　　

BENJAMINE, the son of Robert Jones, was borne the 8th day of May, in the yeer 1674.

Edward, the son of Hezekiah Luther, was borne the 27th of Aprill, 1674.

Hephzibath, the daughter of Thomas Lewis, was borne the 15th of Nouember, 1674.

James, the son of John Myles the younger, was borne the 26th of December, 1674.

John, the son of Joseph Chafey, was borne the 16th day of Septem, 1673.

Israell, the son of Israell Pecke, was borne the 18th day of December, 1674.

Rachell, the daughter of Nathaniel Chafey, was borne the 7th of Septem, in the yeer 1673.

Thomas Manning and Rachell Blisse were married the 28 of October, 1674.

Mr John Faireweather and Elizabeth Dicksey were married, and not recorded.

Burialls.

Mary, the daughter of Joseph Chafey, deceased the 7th of May, 1674.

Mary, the wife of Samuell Bullocke, deceased the 4th of October, 1674.

Sollomon, the son of Joseph Carpenter, deceased the 25 of October, 1674.

Capt Thomas Willett, the 3 day of August, 1674.

This is a true accompt of all the beirthes, marriages, and burialls, that haue bine to my knowlidge within the towne of Swansey, for to be returned this yeer.

Dated Swansey, the 26 of the 12th month, 1674.

NICHOLAS TANNER, Towne Clarke.

1673. Beirthes, Marriages, and Burialls of the Towne of Rehoboth, in the Yeer of our Lord 1673.　　

Birthes.

ANTIPAS NEWMAN, son of Samuell Newman, borne the 29 of March.

Rachell, the daughter of Rice Leonard, the 26 of January.

Mehittable, the daughter of William Sabin, the 10th of May.

Israell, the son of Samuell Sabin, the 16 of June.

Nathaniell, the son of Gorge Robinson, the 1 of Nouember.

Judith, the daughter of Thomas Cooper, the 11th of September.

Henry, the son of Ensigne Henery Smith, the 4th of December.

Robert, the son of Jonathan Fuller, the 2cond of March.

Benjamine, the son of Benjamine Sabin, the 2cond of December.

Sarah, the daughter of Jeremiah Wheaten, 29th of Septeṁ.

Mary, the daughter of John Perren, Junir, the 16th of Aprill.

Ruth, the daughter of John Wilmoth, the 5th of October.

Hannah, the daughter of John Albey, the 10th of October.

Elizabeth, the daughter of Wilłam Hamon, the 24th of Septeṁ, 1661.

Elizabeth, the daughter of John Johnson, 19 of May.

1673.   Marriages.

Mr James Willett married to Elizabeth Hunt, the 17th of Aprill.

John Fuller to Abigaill Titus, 25th of Aprill.

John Titus to Lydia Redwẹy, the 17th of July.

Isack Allin to Mary Bowin, the 30th of May.

Robert Beere to Elizabeth Bulluck, the 25 of June.

Joseph Allin to Hannah Sabin, the 10th of Nouember.

Peter Hunt, Junir to Rebeckah Paine, the 24th of December.

Saṁell Fuller to Mary Iyde, the 12th of December.

John Woodcocke, Junir, to Sarah Smith, the 26th of February.

1673.   Burialls.

Elizabeth, the daughter of John Savage, was buried the 3th of March.

Mary, the daughter of Jarett Ingram, the 25 of May.

Antipas, the son of Saṁell Newman, the 17 of July.

Sarah, the daughter of John Reed, Jur, 19 July.

Sarah, the wife of Saṁell Pecke, the 27 of October.

Daniell, the son of Leift Peter Hunt, the 15th of Septeṁ.

Roger Annadowne, the 13th of Nouember.

Nathaniell, the son of Gorge Robinson, the 9 of Nouember.

Sarah, the wife of Mr Wilłam Blackston, the middle of June.

Allice, the wife of John Kinsley, the 14 of January.

Transcribed out of the Towne Records, by mee,

WILŁAM CARPENTER, Clarke.

he Marriages, Beirthes, and Burialls in the Towne of Rehoboth, REHOBOTH.
in the Yeer 1674. [*56.]

̄OHN KINSLEY married to Mary Maury, the 16th of March.
Thomas Wilmouth married to Mary Robinson, the 7th of June.
Wiltam Blanding married to Bethya ̬ , the 4th of September.
John Butterworth married to Hannah Wheaten, the 4th of September.
Thomas Manning married to Rachell Blisse, the 28th of October.
Steuen Burph married to Elizabeth Perry, the 29th of May.
Thomas Jordaine married to Easter Hall, the 24th of December.

1674. Beirthes.

Mathew Buckland, son of Joseph Buckland, borne the 16 of September.
Meriam Carpenter, daughter of William Carpenter, borne the 16th of ober.
Sollomon Miller, son of Robert Miller, borne the sixt of March.
Mehittable Whittaker, daughter of Richard Whittakar, borne the 27th of ember.
Elizabeth Ormsbey, daughter of John Ormsbey, borne the 27th of No-ber.
Rebeckah Pecke, daughter of John Pecke, borne the 5th of Aprill.
Isacke Bowine, son of Obadiah Bowine, borne the 30th of September.
Nathaniel Smith, son of Daniell Smith, borne the 7th of August.
Thomas Cooper, son of Nathaniel Cooper, borne the 12th of July.
Jacob Ormsbey, son of Jacob Ormsbey, borne the 23 of August.
Sarah Sauage, daughter of John Sauage, borne the 10th of March.
Mary Bullocke, daughter of Samuell Bullocke, borne the 5th of October.
John Fuller, son of John Fuller, borne the 8th of Septem̄.
Isacke Allin, son of Isacke Allin, borne the 3th of January.
Lydia Titus, daughter of John Titus, borne the sixt of December.
Nathaniell Gylson, son of James Gylson, borne the 24 of January.
Jonathan Sabin, son of Joseph Sabin, borne the 12th of July.
Dauid Sabin, son of Nehemiah Sabin, borne the 10th of November.
*Benjamine Beer, son of Robe ̃ Beer, borne the sixt of June.   [*57.]
John Woodcocke, son of John Woodcocke, Junir, borne the 18th of mber.
Gilbert Steuens, son of Francis Steuens, borne the 26th of February.

REHOBOTH.   1674. Burialls.

John Perren, Seni^r, buried the 13th of September.

Samuell Holmes, son of Samuell Holmes, buried the 13th of Sept.

Richard Bowine, Seni^r, buried 4th of February.

Dauid Sabin, son of Nehemiah Sabin, buried the 4th of February.

Experience Walker, daughter of Phillip Walker, buried the 10th Nouember.

Elizabeth Reed, the wife of Thomas Reed, buried the 23 of February.

Transcribed out of the Records, by mee,

WILLIAM CARPENTER, Clarke.

TAUNTON.   *To the honored Court holden att Plymouth, March, 1671 or 72*

HEER followeth the beirthes, marriages, and burialls that were brou to mee the yeer past, according to order of Court, by the inha ants of Taunton.

Imp^r, Mehittable Dean, daughter of John Dean, borne the 9th of tober, 1671.

John Austine, the son of Jonah Austine, was borne the first of July, 1(

Hannah Leanard, the daughter of James Leanard, was borne att Br trey, the 2^{cond} of October, 1671.

Ruth Bobbitt, the daughter of Edward Bobbitt, was borne the 7th August, 1671.

Richard Williams, the son of Joseph Williams, was borne the 26th Nouem̃, 1671.

Thomas Armsbee, the son of Thomas Armsbee, was borne the 2$^{?}$ February, 1668.

Mary Armsbee, the daughter of Thomas Armsbee, was borne the 3^{t} October, 1671.

Abigaill Tisdall, the daughter of John Tisdall, was borne the 15$^{?}$ July, 1667.

John Tisdall, the son of John Tisdall, borne the 10th of August, 16

William Hacke, the son of William Hacke, was borne the 15th of uember, 1663.

Richard Steuens, the son of Richard Steuens, was borne the 23 of Feb- TAUNTON.
ry, 1669.

John Dean, the son of John Dean, died the sixt of August, 1670.

John Tisdall, Junir, marryed to Hannah Rogers, of Duxburrow, the 23 Nouember, 1664.

Taunton, the 3th of March, 71 : 72.

Ᵽ me, SHADRACH WILBORE, Clarke.

The first of March, 1674. To the honored Court. [*58.]

EER followeth the marriages, beirthes, and burialls of all those that 'were brought to mee ; but many neglect to bringe in theire names nee.

John Pollard married to Mary Leanard, of Bridḡwater, the 24th of ember, 1673.

Mary Wilbore, the daughter of Shadrach Wilbore, died the 19th of 1ary, 1674.

Nicholas Stoughton married to Elizabeth Knapp, the 17 of Feb- y, 1673.

Martha Bundey, the wife of John Bundey, died the first of May, 1674.

Sarah Hall, the daughter of Samuell Hall, borne the 14th of October, 1674.

Hopestill Shoue, the wife of Mr Gorge Shoue, died the 7th of March, 3 or 74.

Dorcas Bobbitt, the daughter of Edward Bobbitt, died the 9th of ll, 1674.

Joseph Bell, the son of James Bell, was borne the 27th of June, 1670.

Easter Bell, the daughter of James Bell, borne the 15th of August, 1672.

Amey Staples, the daughter of Joseph Staples, borne the 13th of ll, 1674.

Thomas Steuens, the son of Richard Steuens, borne the 3th of Feb- r, 1674.

Abigaill Paule, the daughter of Wilłam Paule, borne the 15th of May, 1673.

James Walker, Junir, married to Barsheba   ^   , the 23 of De- er, 1647.

Hannah Lenard, the *son* [daughter] of James Leanard, died the 25th of 1ary, 1674.

Taunton, the first of March, 1674.

Attest, by mee, SHADRACH WILBORE, Clarke.

EASTHAM. *To the honered Court holden att Plymouth, the first Tusday in Marc*
1670, allies 71.

WHERAS it is ordered by the Court, that the clarkes or register kee
ers of euery towne shall exhibite a true and ꝑfect coppy, faire
written, yeerly, att March Court, vnto the Court, of all the marriage
beirthes, and burialls of the yeer past, according to that trust put vp
mee, and may bee expected from mee, doe ꝑsent to the honored Court
true coppy of all the marriages, beirthes, and burialls recorded in t
yeer 1670.

Prence Freeman, the son of Mr John Freeman, was borne the 3d day
February, in the ⌃ 1665.

Nathaniell Freeman, the son of Mr John Freeman, was borne the 2
day of March, in the yeer 1669.

Symon Crosbey, the son of Mr Thomas Crosbey, was borne the fift d
of July, in the yeer 1665.

Sarah Crosbey, the daughter of Mr Thomas Crosbey, was borne the 2
day of March, in the yeer 1667.

Joseph Crosbey, the son of Mr Thomas Crosbey, was borne the 27th
of January, 1668.

Mr Thomas Crosbey had 2 children, which were borne att a beirth
4th day of December, in the yeer 1665.

The said children, vizʃ, the two last intimated of Mr Crosbeyes childr
the one of them deceased the 10th day of February, 1670, and the othe
named John.

[*59.]   *Jonathan Banges and Mary Mayo were marryed the 16th day
July, 1664.

Edward Banges, the son of Jonathan Banges, was borne the last day
September, 1665.

Rebeckah Banges, the daughter of Jonathan Banges, was borne the
day of February, 1667.

Jonathan Banges, the son of Jonathan Banges, was borne the eleue
of May, 1670.

Jonath Banges, the son of Jonathan Banges, deceased the 11th of May, 1

William Merricke and Abigaill Hopkins were married the 23 da
May, 1667.

Rebeckah Merricke, the daughter of William Merricke, was borne
28th day of Nouember, 1668.

William Merricke, the son of William Merricke, was borne the first day August, 1670. EASTHAM.

John Cole and Ruth Snow were married the 10th of December, 1666.

Ruth Cole, the daughter of John Cole, was borne the eleuenth day of arch, 16$\frac{67}{68}$.

John Cole, the son of John Cole, was borne the sixt day of March, 16$\frac{69}{70}$.

Constant Done, the son of Daniell Done, was borne the 7th day of arch, 16$\frac{69}{70}$.

Ephraim Done and Mercye Knowles were married the 5th of Feb- ıry, 1667.

Patience Done, the daughter of Ephraim Done, was borne the 28th of ıuary, 1668.

Apphiah Done, the daughter of Ephraim Done, was borne the 28th of ly, 1670.

John Smith and Hannah Williams were married the 24th of May, 70.

Elizabeth Smith, the daughter of John Smith, was borne the 24th of ɔruary, 1668.

John Knowles and Apphiah Banges were married the 28th of Decem- , 1670.

Steuen Merricke and Mercy Banges were married the 28th of Decem- , 1670.

From Eastham, the 4th day of March, 1670.

℘ me, MARKE SNOW, Towne Clark.

Jonathan Sparrow, the son of Jonathan Sparrow, was borne the 9th of y, 1665.

Richard Sparrow, the son of Jonathan Sparrow, was borne the 17th of rch, 16$\frac{69}{70}$.

Apphiah Freeman, the daughter of Samuell Freeman, was borne the of January, 1666.

Constant Freeman, the son of Samuell Freeman, was borne the last day March, 1669.

*Joseph Higgens, the son of Jonathan Higgens, was borne the 14th day February, in the yeer 1666. [*60.]

Nathaniell Mayo, the son of John Mayo, was borne the second day of ill, 1667.

Thomas Mayo, the son of John Mayo, was borne the 24th of June, 1670.

Isacke Done, the son of John Done, was borne the second of June, 1670.

EASTHAM.   Mary Smith, the daughter of Samuell Smith, was borne the 3th day c
January, 1669.

Joshuah Higgens, the son of Benjamine Higgens, was borne the first da
of October, 1668.

Lydia Higgens, the daughter of Benjamine Higgens, was borne the latte
end of May, 1670.

Josiah Cooke, the son of Josiah Cooke, was borne the 12th of N_c
uember, 1670.

Thomas Snow, the son of Marke Snow, was borne the 6th of Au
gust, 1668.

Steuen Hopkins and Mary Merricke were marryed the 23 day o
May, 1667.

Elizabeth Hopkins, the daughter of Steuen Hopkins, was borne the la
week of June, 1668.

Steuen Hopkins, the son of Steuen Hopkins, was borne the 15th day o
July, 1670.

James Rogers and Mary Paine were married the 11th of January, 167

Joshuah Banges and Hannah Scudder were married the first day of De
cember, 1669.

℞ MARKE SNOW, Towne Clarke of Eastham.

TAUNTON.   *Beirthes, Marriages, and Burialls, from the Towne of ‡Swansey,‡*
‖ Taunton ‖

ANDREW SMITH married to Mary Bundey, the 5th of January, 167
Elizabeth Briggs, the daughter of Wilłam Briggs, borne the 4th c
Nouember, 1672.

Thomas Crosman, the son of Robert Crosman, borne the 6th of O
tober, 1671.

Sussanna Crosman, the daughter of Robert Crosman, was borne the 14
of February, 1672.

Eliezer Fisher, the son of Daniell Fisher, was borne the 12th c
May, 1673.

John Richmond, the son of John Richmond, was borne the 5th of D
cember, 1673.

Joseph Gray, the son of Joseph Gray, was borne the 31st of December, 167

Hannah Leanard, the *son* [daughter] of James Leanard, Juni^r, borne at TAUNTON.
raintrey, the 2^{cond} of October, 1671.

*James Leanard, the son of James Leanard, Juni^r, borne att Taunton, the [*61.]
st of February, 1672.

Ephraim Gray, the son of Joseph Gray, bŏne the 20th of June, 1673.

Deliuerance Bobbitt, the daughter of Edward Bobbitt, was borne the
5 of Decemb, 1673.

Judith Armbey, the daughter of Thomas Armesbey, borne the 8th of
anuary, 1673.

Anna Tisdall, the daughter of John Tisdall, Juni^r, borne the 27th of
anuary, 1672.

Steuen Casewell, the son of Steuen Casewell, was borne the 11th of
ecember, 1673.

Elizabeth Cobb, the daughter of Agustine Cobb, was borne the 10th of
ebruary, 1670.

Morgan Cobb, the son of Agustine Cobb, was borne the 29th of De-
mber, 1673.

Taunton, the 2^{cond} of March, 1673.

By mee,   SHADRACH WILBORE.

Heer followeth the beirthes, marriages, and burialls of such as are
ought in to mee, Shadrach Wilbore, Clarke.

Mr Gorge Shoue married to Hopestill Newman, of Rehoboth, the 12th
July, 1664.

Lydia Smith, the wife of John Smith, Seni^r, died the 21 of Ju-
, 1672.

Mr John Poole married to Mistris Elizabeth Brenton, the 28th of
arch, 1672.

Thomas Deane married to Katheren Steuens, the 5th of January, 1669.

Stephen Casewell married to Hannah Thrasher, the 29th of De-
mber, 1672.

John Smith, Seni^r, married to Jaell Packer, of Bridgwater, the 15th of
ouember, 1672.

Ester Smith, the daughter of Samuell Smith, borne the sixt of Jan-
ry, 1671.

Shadrah Wilbore, the son of Shadrach Wilbore, borne the 5th of De-
mber, 1672.

Mary Hall, the daughter of Samuell Hall, borne the 3th of Octo-
r, 1672.

TAUNTON.   Nathaniell Shoue, the son of Mr Gorge Shoue, borne the 29th of January, 1668.

Samuell Shoue, the son of Mr Gorge Shoue, was borne the 16th of June,1670

Sarah Shoue, the daughter of Mr Gorge Shoue, was borne the 30 o July, 1671.

Mary Talbutt, the daughter of Jarudd Talbutt, was borne the 14th o December, 1671.

Samuell Fisher, the son of Daniell Fisher, was borne the 3^d of December, 1669.

Sarah Richmond, the daughter of John Richmond, was borne the 26 o February, 1670.

James Leanard, the son of James Leanard, was borne the first of February, 1672.

[*63.]   *Rebeckah Armesbey, the daughter of Thomas Armsbey, was borne th 26 of May, 1672.

Mary Steuens, the daughter of Richard Steuens, was borne the 8th o June, 1672.

Anna Wilbore, the daughter of Joseph Wilbore, was borne the 7th o May, 1672.

Hannah Jones, the daughter of Thomas Jones, was borne the third c October, 1675.

Lydia Jones, the daughter of Thomas Jones, was borne the 26th c July, 1659.

Thomas Jones, the son of Thomas Jones, was borne the 4th of May, 166

Joseph Jones, the son of Thomas Jones, was borne the 5th of May, 166

James Paule, the son of William Paule, borne the 7th of Aprill, 1657.

John Paule, the son of William Paule, borne the 10th of July, 1660.

Edward Paule, the son of William Paule, borne the 7th of February, 166

Mary Paule, the daughter of William Paule, was borne the 8th of February, 1667.

Sarah Paule, the daughter of William Paule, borne the 5th of July, 166

Thomas Dean, the son of Thomas Deane, was borne the first of February, 1670.

Thomas Dean, the son of Thomas Dean, died the 26th of February, 167

Hannah Dean, the daughter of Thomas Dean, was borne the 14th February, 1671.

Taunton, the first of March, 72 or 73.

Attested p^r me,   SHADRACH WILBORE, Clarke.

Swansey, the 4th of March, 1675. In obedience to an order of Court,
haue sent an accompt of beirthes, and marriages, and burialls which were
s last yeer : first, beirthes.

Christian, the daughter of Daniell Allin, was borne the 26 of Jan-
ry, 1674.

Elizabeth, the daughter of Thomas Barnes, was borne the 14 of Feb-
ry, 1674.

Experience, the daughter of Samuell Luther, was borne the 3^d of
rch, 1674–75.

Elisha, the son of Nathaniel Pecke, was borne the 19th of Aprill, 1675.
John, the son of John Martine, was borne the 15 of March, 1674–75.
John, the son of Capt John Browne, was borne the 28th day of Aprill, 1675.
Margeritt, the daughter of Joseph Carpenter, was borne the 4th of
y, 1675.

*Nathaniel, the son of William Lohun, was borne the 2^{cond} of Feb-   [*64.]
ry, 1674.

Sibill, the daughter of Joseph Lewis, was borne the 18th of March, 1674.
Samuell, the son of Caleb Eedy, was borne the 15th of July, 1675.
Hezekiah Willett and Andia Browne were married the 7th day of Jan-
y, 1675.

Burialls.

Deliuerance, the wife of Nathaniell Pecke, died the 30th of Aprill, 1675.
Gershom Cobb buried the 24th of June, 1675.
Joseph Carpenter was buried the 6th of May, 1675.
Joseph Lewis was buried the 24th of June, 1675.
John Salsbury was buried the 24th of June, 1675.
John Jones was buried the 24th of June, 1675.
John Fall buried the 24th of June, 1675.
John Druce was buried the 2^{cond} of July, 1675.
Capt John Gorum was buried the 5th of February, 1675.
Nehemiah Allin was buried the 24 of June, 1675.
Robert Jones was buried the 24th of June, 1675.
William Lohun was buried the 24 of June, 1675.
Willam Salsbury was buried the 24th of June, 1675.
Willam Hamon was buried the 29th of June, 1675.

By mee, NICHOLAS TANNER,
Towne Clarke of Swansey.

Rehoboth. *Marriages, Beirthes, and Burialls, att Rehoboth, in the Yeers 16⁚*
and 1676.

SAMELL BULLOCKE married to Thankfull Rouse, the 26 of M⁚
1675.

Thomas Read marryed to Anna Perren, the 16ᵗʰ of June, 1675.

John Woodward married to Sarah Crosman, the 11ᵗʰ of Nouemb⁺, 16⁚

Beirthes.

Dauid Carpenter, the son of Samuell Carpenter, borne the 17ᵗʰ
Aprill, 1675.

Mary Sabin, the daughter of Wiltam Sabin, borne the 18ᵗʰ of S⁚
tem: 1675.

Dauid Buckland, the son of Benjamine Buckland, borne the 22ᶜᵒⁿᵈ
March, 1675.

Thomas Wilmouth, the son of Thomas Wilmouth, was borne the 7ᵗʰ
July, 1665.

Mary Kinsley, the daughter of Eldad Kinsley, was borne the 7ᵗʰ
October, 1675.

Sibell Newman, the daughter of Mʳ Noah Newman, × the 31
March, 1675.

Ellice Sauage, the daughter of John Sauage, the eleuenth of January, 16⁚

Mehittabell Wilmoth, the daughter of John Wilmoth, the 19ᵗʰ
June, 1675.

Jeremiah Woodcocke, the son of John Woodcock, the sixt of June, 16⁚

Nathaniell Chaffey, the son of Nathaniell Chaffey, the 8ᵗʰ of F⁚
ruary, 1675.

[*65.]   *Experience Sabin, the daughter of Samuell Sabin, was borne the 5ᵗʰ
October, 1676.

Ellice Wilmoth, the daughter of Thomas Willmoth, the first of ⁚
tem: 1676.

Ebinezer Walker, the son of Phillip Walker, the 15ᵗʰ of Nouember, 1⁚

Ebinezer Smith, the son of Mʳ Daniell Smith, the 29ᵗʰ of July, 167⁚

Abiell Fuller, the son of John Fuller, the 30ᵗʰ of December, 1676.

Abiell Smith, the son of Ensigne Henery Smith, the 24ᵗʰ of Dec⁚
ber, 1676.

Elizabeth, the wife of Francis Steuens, was buried the fourth
March, 1675.

Deliuerance, the wife of Nathaniell Pecke, buried the first of May, 1675. REHOBOTH.

Widdow Bowine buried in ˄ , 1675.

Sibill New: the daughter of Mr Noah Newman, the 24th of September, 1675.

Isacke Kenricke, the son of Gorge Kenricke, the 13th of January, 1675.

Martha, the wife of Noah Mason, the sixt of February, 1675.

Sarah, the daughter of John Read, in January, 1675.

Nathaniell, the son of John Perren, the third of September, 1675.

John Read, Juni^r, buried in Aprill, 1676.

John Fitch, Juni^r, buried in Aprill, 1676.

Robert Beares, the 29th of March, 1676.

Sarah Woodcocke, the wife of John Woodcocke, the 10th of May, 1676.

Nathaniel Woodcocke, the 28th of Aprill, 1676.

John Iyde, the middle of December, 1676.

Experience Sahon, the daughter of Samuell Sahon, the 28th of No-mber, 1676.

John Read, the son of Thomas Read, the 4th of December, 1676.

James Redway was buried the 28 of October, 1676.

The wife of Nicholas Iyde buried the third of Nouember, 1676.

Nathaniel Wilmoth, the 12th of Nouember, 1676.

Ensigne Henery Smith, the 24th of Nouember, 1676.

Lydia Titus, the wife of John Titus, the 25th of Nouember, 1676.

Rachell Man, the wife of Thomas Man, in June, 1676.

Ellice Willett, the wife of James Willett, in July, 1676.

Nathaniell Sahen, in the latter end of May, 1676.

Nathaniell Pecke, the 25th of August, 1676.

Elizabeth Skaffe, the 25 of June, 1676.

*Samuell Fuller, the 15th of August, 1676.   [*67.]

John Fuller, the 23 of August, 1676.

Mary Hunt, the 23 of August, 1676.

Peter Hunt, Juni^r, the 25th of August, 1676.

Tabithay Hunt, the 14 of October, 1676.

Jasiell Perry, in September, 1676.

Mehittable Perry, in September, 1676.

Sampson Mason, in September, 1676.

Sarah Fuller, the wife of Robert Fuller, the 14th of October, 1676.

Jeremiah Fitch, the 15th of October, 1676.

A younge child of Nicholas Pecke, in August, 1676.

The wife of Thomas Wilmouth, Seni^r, in February, 1676.

Elizabeth Smith, the daughter of Mr Henery Smith, the first of rch, 1676.

REHOBOTH. Sarah Leanard, the daughter of Krie Leanard, the 16th of March, 1676

Nehemiah Buckland, the son of Joseph Buckland, buried in May, 1677

Thomas Graunts child buried in September, 1676.

Thomas Mans child buried in June, 1676.

Jacob Ormsbey, ‡Senir,‡ son, buried the 2cond of March, 1676.

Jacob Ormsbey, Junir, buried the 16th of February, 1676.

By mee, WILŁAM CARPENTER, Clarke.

SANDWICH. *[Sandwich: Births, Marriages, and Deaths.]*

JOHN REDDING and Mary Bassett were marryed the 22 of the eigh month, 1676.

Job Gibbs, the son of John Gibbs, was borne the 27th of Aprill, ann Dom̃ one thousand six hundred seauenty and six.

Michaell Blackwell, the son of John Blackwell, was borne the 16th c the 9th, 1676.

Thomas Tupper, Senir, deceased the 28th of March, anno Dom̃ on thousand six hundred seauenty and six; hee died in the 98th yeer of his ag and 2cond month.

Anne Tupper deceased the 4th of June, anno Dom̃ one thousand si hundred seauenty and six, whoe deceased in the 90th yeer of her age.

Transcribed out of the Regester of Sandwich, this fift of the first, 167

ꝑ THOMAS TUPPER, Clarke for the Towne of Sandwich.

PLYMOUTH. *[Plymouth: Deaths.]*

[*68.] *MARTHA NELSON, the daughter of John Nelson, died the 19th February, 1675.

Sarah, the wife of John Nelson, died the 4th of March, 1675.

John, the son of John Nelson, died the fift of June, 1676.

[Taunton : Births, Marriages, and Deaths.]

[*69.]

TO the honored Court to be holden att Plymouth the first Tusday in March, 1676 or 77 : but there be many that doe neglect to attend the Court order.

Imprimis.   Elias Irish married to Dorrethy Witherill, the twenty-sixt of ugust, 1674.

Hannah Wilbore died the 3th of December, 1675.

Mistris Hopstill Shoue, the wife of Mr Gorge Shoue, died the 7th of arch, 1673 or 74.

Mr Gorge Shoue married to Mistris Walley, the 18th of February, i74, or 75.

Mary Shoue, the daughter of Mr Gorge Shoue, borne the 11th of Au- ıst, 1676.

John Bundey married to Ruth Surney, of Mendum, this 9th of Jan- ry, 1676.

Jonah Austine died the 10th of May, 1676.

John Wilbore, the son of Shadrach Wilbore, borne the second of arch, 1674–75.

Saṁell Hallowwey, the son of Saṁell Hallowey, born the 14th of Sep- ıber, 1668.

Nathaniel Halloway, the son of Saṁell Hallowey, was borne the 2cond July, 1670.

Easter Hallowey, the daughter of Samuell Hallowey, was borne the 14th May, 1673.

John Hallowey, the son of Samuell Hallowey, was borne the 24th of bruary, 1674.

Mary Briggs, the daughter of William Briggs, was borne the 14th of gust, 1674.

Mathew Briggs, the son of William Briggs, was borne the 5th of Feb- ıry, 1676.

Ebenezer Richmond, the son of John Richmond, borne att Newport, on ode Iland, the 12th of May, 1676.

James Leanard, the son of James Leanard, died the 30th of December, 1674.

James Leanard, Junir, married to Lydia Calipher, of Milton, the 29th October, 1675.

Mehittable Williams, the daughter of Joseph Williams, borne the 7th of ıe, 1676.

9

TAUNTON.   Sañiell Cobb, the son of Augustine Cobb, was borne the 9th of Nouex
ber, 1675.

John Hall married to Hannah Peniman, the 4th of February, 1667.

John Hall, the son of John Hall, borne the 27th of June, 1672.

Joseph Hall, the son of John Hall, borne the 7th of Aprill, 1674.

James Hall, the son of John Hall, borne the 8th of December, 1675.

John Pollard, the son of John Pollard, was borne the 20th of March, 167

Mary Smith, the daughter of Andrew Smith, borne the third of C
tober, 1675.

John Williams, the son of Nathaniell Williams, was borne the 27th
August, 1675.

Taken out of the Regester Booke of the Towne of Taunton, the 5th
March, 167⅞. . By mee,

SHADRACH WILBORE, Towne Clarke.

REHOBOTH.   *The Marriages, Beirthes, and Burialls of Rehoboth, in the Ye
[*71.]   1677.

DANIELL REED married to Hannah Pecke, August 20th.

Isacke Williams married to Judith Cooper, the 13 of Nouem.

Samuel Pecke married to Rebeckah Hunt, the 21 of Nouember.

Moses Read married to Rebeckah Fitch, December the sixt.

Noah Mason married to Sarah Fitch, December the sixt.

Abrah Perren married to Sarah Walker, the 27th of December.

Nicholas Iyde, Junir, married to Mary Ormsbey, the 27th of December

John Titus married to Sarah Miller, the 3 of July.

Beirthes.

Sollomon Carpenter, the son of Samuell Carpenter, borne the 23
December.

Mary, the daughter of John Ormsbey, borne the 4th of Aprill.

Dorethy, the daughter of Preserued Abell, was borne the 16 of N
uember.

Ebenezer, the son of Jeremiah Wheaton, was borne the 7th of March.

Mary, the daughter of John Butterworth, was borne the 20th of Octob

Mehittable, the daughter of John Perren, was borne the 19th of April

Amose, the son of John Carpenter, was borne the 19th of Nouember.

Nathaniel, the son of John Wilmoth, was borne the 29th of September.

Joseph, the son of John Johnson, was borne the third of October.

John, the son of Thomas Gaunt, was borne the 21 of January.

Anne Pecke, the *son* [daughter] of John Pecke, borne the 17th of July.

Abijah Cooper, the *daughter* [son] of Nathaniel Cooper, was borne the st of May.

Burialls.

Samuell, the son of Mr Noah Newman, was buried the second of tober.

Steuen Paine buried the 24th of January.

Michell Walker buried the 16th of February.

Peter Cooper buried the 28th of February.

Abijah Cooper buried the 22^{cond} of May.

John Buckline buried the 20th of June.

Nehemiah Buckline buried the 19th of May.

Transcribed out of the Towne Records, p me,

WILLAM CARPENTER, Towne Clarke of Rehoboth.

[*Plymouth : Births, &c.*]

ᔈLIZABETH, the daughter of John Drew, of Plymouth, borne the fift day of February, 1673.

Bethyah, the daughter of Jonathan Pratt, was born the eight of Au- st, 1679.

Mary, the daughter of Samuell Sauory, was born the third of y, 1678.

*John, the son of Joseph Churchill, was borne on the 22^{cond} of   [*72.] y, 1678.

Hannah Churchill, the daughter of Eliezer Churchill, was borne the 23 August, 1676.

Joannah Churchill, the daughter of Eliezer Churchill, was borne the 25 Nouember, 1678.

Thomas, the son of Thomas Doten, was borne the 22^{cond} of July, 1679.

Jabez Howland, the son of Jabez Howland, was borne the 15 of Sep- ber, 1669.

PLYMOUTH.   Josia Howland, the son of Jabez Howland, was borne the sixt of A
gust, 1676.

John Howland, the son of Jabez Howland, was borne the 26 of J
ly, 1679.

Mary, the daughter of John Rickard, Seni^r, was borne the 27th of C
tober, 1677.

Lydia, the daughter of John Rickard, Seni^r, was borne the 12th of D
cember, 1679.

Joseph Faunce marryed to Judith Rickard, the third January, 1677.

Hannah, the daughter of Joseph Faunce, was borne the 12th
June, 1679.

Elisha Cobb, son of John Cobb, was borne the third of Apr
anno 1678.

TAUNTON.   *Tauntons Register of Beirthes of theire Children.
[*73.]

IMP^R NATHANIELL SMITH, son of Samuell S., borne the 26th
July, 1675.

Sarah Hall, the daughter of Samuell Hall, died the 26 of May, 1677.

Samell Talbott, the son of Jarerd Talbott, was borne the 29th of F
ruary, 1675.

Josiah Talbot, the son of Jared Talbot, was borne the 21 of C
tober, 1678.

John Briggs, the son of Richard Briggs, borne the 13th of February, 16

Joseph Briggs, the son of Richard Briggs, was borne the 15th
June, 1674.

Benjamine Briggs, the son of Richard Briggs, was borne the 15th
September, 1677.

John Dean, the son of John Deane, was borne the 18th of S
tem: 1674.

Elizabeth Dean, the daughter of John Dean, was borne the 15th
March, 1676.

Ebinezer Lincolne, the son of Samuell Lincolne, was borne the 15
October, 1673.

Rachell Lincolne, the daughter of Samuell Lincolne, was borne the
teenth of Septem: 1677.

Mary Fisher, the daughter of Daniell, borne the 30th of May, 1675.

Mercye Fisher, the daughter of Daniell Fisher, was borne the 12th of TAUNTON. December, 1677.

Tamsen Steuens, the daughter of Richard Steuens, was borne the 3 of July, 1677.

Samuell Smith, the son of Andrew Smith, was borne the 15 of May, 1678

John Cobb, the son of John Cobb, was borne the 31 of March, 1678.

John Woodward, the son of John Woodward, was borne the second of March, 1678.

Wiłłam Hoskins marryed to Sarah Casewell, the 3 of July, 1677.

Anne Hoskins, the daughter of Wiłłam Hoskins, borne the 14 February, 1678.

Edward Rew died the 16th of July, 1678.

Elizabeth Walker, the wife of James Walker, Seni[r], died the 30th of July, 1678.

James Walker, Seni[r], marryed to Sarah Rew, the 4th of Nouem: 1678.

Attest, by SHADRACH WILBORE, Clarke.

Eliezer Wilbore, the son of Shadrach Wilbore, was borne the first of July, 1677.

Ebenezer Hall, the son of Samuell Hall, was borne the 19th of March, 1677.

James Leanard, the son of James Leanard, was borne the 11th of May, 1677.

Mary Staple, the daughter of Joseph Staple, borne the 26th of January, 1677.

Remember Tisdall, the daughter of John Tisdall, borne the 8th of July, 1675.

Benjamine Hall, the son of John Hall, borne the sixt of December, 1677.

Israell Woodward married to Jane Godfrey, the 4th of Auğst, 1670.

Elizabeth Woodward, the daughter of Israell Woodward, borne the teenth of June, 1670.

Israell Woodward died the 15th of June, 1674.

Israell Woodward, the son of Israell Woodward, was borne the 4th of ctober, 1674.

John Tisdall, Seni[r], killed by the Indians, the 27th of June, 1675.

Sarah Tisdall, the wife of John Tisdall, Seni[r], died in December, 1676.

*Richard Marshall marryed to Easter Bell, the 11th of February, 1676. [*74.]

John Cobb marryed to Jane Woodward, the 13th of June, 1676.

Hannah Paule borne the 4th of October, 1657.

TAUNTON.   John Bundey, the son of John Bundey, borne the sixt of October, 1677

Ephram Gray, the son of Joseph Gray, died the 21 of June, 1675.

Rebeckah Gray, the wife of Joseph Gray, died the 13th of May, 1676.

Nathaniel French marryed to Mary Tisdall, the 9th of January, 1676.

Nicholas White, Juni[r], marryed to Vrsilla Maycomber, of Marshfeild the 9th of December, 1673.

Nicholas White, the son of Nicholas White, borne the 25th of October, 1676

Samuell Phillipps marryed to the widdow Cobb, the 15th of May, 1676

Mehittable Phillipps, the daughter of Samuell Phillips, borne the 9th of January, 1676.

John Gould marryed to Mary Crossman the 24 August, 1673.

Mary Gould, the daughter of John Gould, borne the 19th of June, 1674

Hannah · Gould, the daughter of John Gould, borne the 9th of Nouember, 1677.

Isack Dean married to Hannā Leanard, the 24th of January, 1677.

Thomas Gilbert married, att Boston, to Anna Blacke, of Milton, the 1 of December, 1676.

Hannah Gilbert, the daughter of Thomas Gilbert, was borne the 28th of Septem: 1677.

Taunton, the 4th of March, 1677.

Attested by SHADRACH WILBORE, Clarke.

REHOBOTH.   *Beirthes, Marriages, and Burialls of the Towne of Rehoboth, in the Yeer 1678.*

NEHEMIAH BUCKLAND, son of Joseph Buckland, born the 31 of March, 1678.

Obadiah Carpenter, son of Wiltam Carpenter, borne the 12th of March, 1678.

Noah Pecke, the son of Samuell Pecke, borne the 21 of August, 1678.

Jonathan Ormsbey, son of John Ormsbey, borne the 26th of August, 1678

Noah Mason, son of Noah Mason, was borne the 17th of December, 1678

Nathaniel Kingsley, the son of Eldad Kingsley, was borne the 5th of February, 1678.

James Reddaway, son of John Reddaway, was borne the 10th of January, 1678.

John Titus, son of John Titus, Juni^r, was borne the 12th of March, 1678.

Abigaill Sabin, daughter *the daughter* of Joseph Sabin, was borne the 16th August, 1678.

Jonathan Chaffey, son of Nathaniell Chaffey, was borne the 7th of Aprill, 1678.

Hannah Read, daughter of Daniell Read, was borne the 30th of June, 1678.

*Thomas Read, son of Thomas Read, was borne the 25th of March, 1678.   [*75.]

Mary Sauage, the daughter of John Sauage, was borne the 5th of June, 1678.

Mary Wilmoth, daughter of Thomas Wilmoth, Juni^r, was borne the 29 of Decemb: 1678.

Judith Smith, the daughter of Daniell Smith, was borne the 7th February, 1678.

Elizabeth Fuller, the daughter of Jonathan Fuller, was borne the 12 of May, 1678.

Nathaniell Ide, the son of Nicholas Ide, Juni^r, was borne the 14th of Nouember, 1678.

Nathaniell Ide, the son of Nicholas Ide, Juni^r, was borne the 14th of Nouember, 1678.

Hannah Ormsbey, daughter of Thõ Ormsbey, was borne the 23 of Sepem: 1678.

Ephraim Whittacar, the *daughter* [son] of Richard Whittacar, was borne the 27 of January, 1678.

Zacheriah Read, the son of Moses Read, was borne the 25th of October, 1678.

Marriages.

Enacke Hunt marryed to Mary Paine, the 29th of October, 1678.

Samell Perry married to Mary Miller, the 12th of December, 1678.

John French married to Mary Palmer, the 27th of Nouember, 1678.

Tho: Wilmoth, Seni^r, married to Rachell Read, the 27th of June, 1678.

Thomas Man married to Mary Wheaton, the 9th of Aprill, 1678.

Burialls.

The Reuerend Mr Noah Newman was buried the 18th of Aprill, 1678.

Julian Sutton buried the 4th of June, 1678.

John Kingsley buried the sixt of January, 1678.

Mary Kingsley buried the 29th of January, 1678.

John Sauage buried the 22^{cond} of August, 1678.

Zacheriah Read, son of Moses Read, buried in January, 1678.

Transcribed out of the Records of Rehoboth,

℞ me, WILŁAM CARPENTER, Clarke.

*New Plymouth Register.

JOSIAH COTTON, the son of Mr John Cotton, was borne the eight o
January, 1679.

James Warren, the son of Richard Warren, was borne the 13th of Ja▮
uary, anno 1679.

Hugh Cole was marryed January the 8th, 1654.

The Beirthes of the Children of Hugh Cole, now of Swansey, whoe w▮
soñitimes inhabitant of the towne of Plymouth, in this jurisdiction ▮
New Plymouth.

James Cole, the son of Hugh Cole, was borne in the yeer 1655, N
uember the 8th.

Hugh Cole, the son of Hugh Cole, was borne the 15th of March, 1658
John Cole, the son of Hugh Cole, Seni^r, was borne the 16th of May, 166▮
Martha Cole, daughter of Hugh Cole, was borne the 14th of Aprill, 166
Anna Cole, the daughter of Hugh Cole, was borne on October the 14th, 166▮
Ruth Cole, the daughter of Hugh Cole, borne on the 17th of January, 166▮
Joseph Cole, the son of Hugh Cole, was born the 15th of May, 1668.

Patience Faunce, daughter of Thomas Faunce, was borne the seauen▮
of Nouember, 1673.

John, the son of Thomas Faunce, was borne the 16th day of Septe▮
ber, 1678.

Martha, the daughter of Thomas Faunce, was borne the 17th day
December, 1680.

---

*1680. Marriages, Beirthes, and Burialls in the Towne of Rehobo▮
as followeth.

Marriages.

SAMUELL PALMER married to Elizabeth Kingsley, 12th of Januar▮
Gorge Robinson married to Elizabeth Gaille, 12 of Nouember.
Jonathan Wilmouth married to Ester Pecke, the 29th of December.
Joseph Browne married to Hannah Fitch, the 10th of Nouember.
Joseph Rockett married to Mary Wilmouth, the 5 of January.

Beirthes, 1680.

Zacheriah Carpenter, son of Samuell Carpenter, born the first of July.

Margarett Sabin, daughter of William Sabin, was born the 10th of Aprill.

Jaell Pecke, the daughter of Samuell Pecke, was born the 14th of June.

Sarah Fuller, the daughter of Jonathan Fuller, was born the 23th of Aprill.

John Mason, son of Noah Mason, was born the 28th of Nouember.

Nathaniel Shepherdson, son of Daniell Shepherdson, was born the 28 of October.

Nathaniell Read, son of Thomas Read, born the 30th of March.

Nathaniel Pecke, the son of John Pecke, born the sixt of July.

Rebeckah Smith, the daughter of Mr Daniell Smith, born the 20th of Aprill.

Jacob Ormsbey, the son of Thomas Ormsbey, was born the 13th of September.

Presillah Carpenter, the daughter of John Carpenter, was born the 20th of January.

Dorithy Wilmouth, the dāghter of John Wilmouth, borne the 26th of August.

Samuel Titus, son of John Titus, Junir, born the 29 of July.

Dauid Chaffey, the son of Nathaniell Chaffey, was born the 22cond of August.

Daniell Read, the son of Daniel Read, was born the 20th of January.

Samuell Blandinge, the son of William Blanding, was boře the 11th of Aprill.

Mehittable Perry, daughter of Samuell Perry, was born the 30th of Aprill.

Mary Man, daughter of Thomas Man, was born the 11th of January.

Mary Miller, the daughter of Robert Miller, was borne the 14th of June.

Martha Ormsbey, the daughter of John Ormsbey, was born the 7th of May.

Presilla Shaue, daughter of John Shaue, was boře the 22 of June.

Lydia Buckland, the daughter of Joseph Buckland, was borne the 5th September.

Sarah Penfeild, the daughter of Thomas Penfeild, was born the 20th of ʒbruary.

*Burialls att Rehoboth, 1680. [*79.]

Jaell Pecke, the daughter of Samuell Pecke, buried July the 6th.

Elizabeth Cooper, the wife of Deacon Cooper, was buried the first of ʒbruary.

REHOBOTH.   Elizabeth Miller, the wife of John Miller, Seni^r, was buried the 18th of Aprill.

[*80.]   *Lott none marnell att the promiscuous and disorderly setting downe o the names of such as are or may be married, or doe or may be born, or ma dye ; for they are sett as they were brought to mee, as disorderly as they a sett downe.   If the Courts order had bin minded respecting this matter, the had bine otherwise placed then they are.

PLYMOUTH.   *Plymouth Register.*

JOHN RICKARD, the son of John Rickard, Juni^r, was born on the day of February, 1679.

Hugh Cole, Seni^r, was married in January the 8th, 1654.

James Cole was born in the yeer 1655, Nouember the third.

Hugh Cole, Juni^r, was born in the yeer 1658, the 8th of March.

John Cole was borne in the yeer 1660, the 15 of May.

Martha Cole was borne in the yeer 1662, the 16 of Aprill.

Annah Cole was borne in the yeer 1664, the 14 of October.

Ruth Cole was borne in the yeer 1666, the 8th of January.

Patience Faunce, the daughter of Thomas Faunce, was borne the of Nouember, 1673.

John Faunce, the son of Thomas Faunce, was borne the 16th of Se tember, 1678.

Martha Faunce, the daughter of Thomas Faunce, was borne the 17th December, 1680.

Hannah, the daughter of Gorge Morton, was borne the 27th of Nouer ber, 1668.

Mannasses, the son of Gorge Morton, was borne the third of F ruary, 1668.

Ephraim Morton, son of Gorge Morton, was borne the 12th Aprill, 1670.

Joannah, the daughter of Gorge Morton, was borne the 27th June, 1673.

Ruth Morton, the daughter of Gorge Morton, was borne the 20th December, 1676.

Gorge Morton, son of Gorḡ Morton, was borne the 8th of July, 1678.

Timothy Morton, the son of Gorge Morton, was born the 12th of Iarch, 16⅜⅟.

James Cobb, the son of John Cobb, was born the 20th of July, 1682.   ✳

Mary, the daughter of John Rickard, son of Gyles Rickard, was borne ıe 27th of October, 1677.

Lydia, the daughter of John Rickard, son of Gyles Rickard, was born ıe 12 of December, 1679.

John, the son of John Rickard, the son of Gyles Rickard, was born the 9 of December, 1681.

John, the son of Francis Curtice, was born the 26 of July, 1673.

Benjamine, the son of Francis Curtice, was born the 11th of August, 1675.

Francis, the son of Francis Curtice, was borne about the middle of prill, 1679.

*‡William Hoskins, the son of Wilłam Hoskins, was borne the 30th of   [*81.] ıne, 1681.‡

Elizabeth, the daughter of Francis Curtice, was borne the fifteenth day June, 1681.

Elisha Curtice, son of Francis Curtice, was borne in March, 1683.

James, the son of Richard Warren, was born in January, 1682.

Samuell Warren, the son of Richard Warren, was borne the seauenth March, 16⅜⅔.

Samuell Gaurdiner was married to Susannah Shelley, the 20th of De-mber, 1682.

Samuell Gardiner, the son of Samuell Gardiner, was born the 27 of ptember, 1683.

Mercye, the daughter of John Rickard, the son of John Rickard, de-ased, was borne the 12th of February, 1682.

John Rickard, the son of John Rickard, deceased, was born the 12th of ʒbruaıy, 1684.

[The following entries are in an unknown chirography.]

Zechariah Eedey, ye son of Zachariah Eedy, born Aprill ye 10th, 1664.

John, the son of Zachariah Eedey, was borne the 10th of October, 1666.

Samuel Eedy, the sone of Zachariah Eedey, Senr, late of Plimouth, was ·rne the 3^d day of June, anno 1673.

Ebenezer, the son of said Zachariah, was borne the 8th of Febr^y, 1675.

Caleb, the son of s^d Zachariah, was borne the 21 of Septemb^r, 1678.

Joshua, the son of s^d Zachariah, was borne the 21th of February, 1680.

Obadiah, the son of s^d Zachariah, was borne the 2^d day of Septemb^r, 1683.

PLYMOUTH.   Alice, the daughter of Zachariah Eedey, Jun[r], was borne y[e] 28th of N
vemb[r], 1684.

Elinor, the daughter of s[d] Zachariah Eedy, Jun[r], was borne y[e] 16th da
of May, anno 1686.

[The records follow in the handwriting of Secretary Morton.]

REHOBOTH.   *The Marriages, Beirthes, and Burialls in the Towne of Rehobot.
[*83.]   in the Yeare 1681.

Marriages.

THOMAS KENRICKE married to Marye Perrey, the 17th of June, 168
Samuell Walker married to Martha Iyde, the 11th of Nouember, 168
Daniell Thurston married to Hannah Miller, the 16th of December, 168
Joseph Brooman married to Sarah Sauage, the 29 of Septeᵐ, 1681.
John Martin married to Marcye Billington, the 27 of June, 1681.

Beirthes.

Ames Angeir, son of the Reuerend M[r] Samuell Anger, was borne t
29 of June, 1681.

Elizabeth Paine, the daughter of M[r] Nathaniel Paine, was born the si
of Noueᵐ, 1681.

Ephraim Carpenter, the son of Wilłam Carpenter, was borne the 25
Aprill, 1681.

Rebecka Pecke, the daughter of Samuell Pecke, was borne the 22[cond]
October, 1681.

Mary Fuller, the daūhter of Jonathan Fuller, was borne the first
October, 1681.

Joannah Abell, the daughter of Preserued Abell, was born the 11th
January, 1681.

Peter Hunt, the son of Enocke Hunt, was borne the 22 of Septem
1681.

Mehittabell Wilmouth, the daughter of Thomas Wilmouth, was bor
the 4th of March, 1681.

Mehittabell Wheaton, the daughter of Jeremiah Wheaton, was bor
the 2[cond] of Aprill, 1681.

Hannā Graunt, the daughter of Thomas Graunt, was borne the 4th
Aprill, 1681.

Thankfull Bullocke, the daughter of Samuell Bullocke, was borne 1681. REHOBOTH.

John French, the son of John French, was borne the 13 of Aprill, 1681.

Rachell Johnson, the daughter of John Johnson, was born the 23 of December, 1681.

Experience Sabine, the daugher of Joseph Sabine, was borne the 14 of March, 1681.

Elizabeth Perren, the daughter of Abraham Perren, was born the 3ᵈ of December, 1681.

Zacheriah Read, the son of Moses Read, was borne the 20th of Octo-er, 1681.

Jacob Iyde, the son of Nicholas Iyde, was borne the 4th of July, 1681.

*Ester Wilmouth, the daughter of Jonathan Wilmoth, was borne the 8th of Nouember, 1681. [*84.]

John Robinson, the son of Gorge Robinson, was born the fift of Sep-em̄, 1681.

Joseph Browne, the son of Joseph Browne, was borne the 21 of No-ember, 1681.

Hannah Browne, the daughter of Joseph Browne, was borne the 21 of Nouember, 1682. . . . . 1681.

Richard Euens, the son of Richard Euens, was born the 10th of Au-ust, 1681.

Elizabeth Bosworth, daughter of Joseph Bosworth, was born the 17th of Nouember, 1681.

Mary Titus, the daughter of Sylas Titus, was born the 30 of March, 1681.

Jane Woodcocke, the daughter of Deborah Woodcocke, was borne the 1th of March, 1681.

Burialls att Rehoboth.

Experience Sabin, the daughter of Joseph Sabine, buried the 13th of ꞏay, 1681.

Peter Hunt, the son of Enocke Hunt, buried the 12th of October, 1681.

Amos Carpenter, the son of John Carpenter, was buried the sixt of ꞏly, 1681.

Judith Pecke, the daughter of Samuell Pecke, buried the 20th of Feb-ary, 1681.

Transcribed out of the Towne Records,

P WILꞭAM CARPENTER, Clarke.

The Beirthes, Marriages, and Burialls in the Towne of Rehoboth, Anno 1682.

Beirthes.

HANNAH ANGIER, the daughter of Mr Samuell Angier, was borne the 10th of August, 1682.

Abraham Carpenter, the son of Samuell Carpenter, was borne the 20th of September, 1682.

Noah Whittacar, the son of Richard Whittacar, was borne the 31 of January, 1682.

Jacob Ormsbey, the son of John Ormsbey, the 16th of March, 1682.

Elizabeth Hunt, the daughter of Enoch Hunt, was borne the 2^{cond} of October, 1682.

Hannah Read, the daũgter of Thomas Read, was borne the 12th of Aprill, 1682.

Daniell Perren, the son of John Perren, was borne the 18th of March, 1682.

Bethya Ormsbey, the daughter of Thomas Ormsbey, was borne the 15th of Aprill, 1682.

[*85.] *Sarah Willmoth, the daughter of John Willmouth, was borne the 21 of December, 1682.

John Redway, the son of John Redway, was borne the 10th September, 1682.

Hannah Titus, the daũgter of John Titus, Juni^r, was borne the 10th of Nouember, 1682.

Joseph Saben, the son of Joseph Saben, was borne the 18th of Nouember, 1682.

Jaciell Perrey, the son of Samuell Perrey, was borne the sixt of May, 1682.

Anne Shaw, the daughter of John Shaw, was borne the fifteenth of March, 1682.

Elizabeth Butterworth, the daughter of John Butterworth, was borne the 15th of January, 1682.

John Palmer, the son of Samuell Palmer, borne the 25 of March, 1682

Jasiell Kennericke, the son of Thomas Kennericke, borne the 23 of March, 1682.

John Martin, the son of John Martin, was borne the 10th of June, 1682

Elizabeth Paine, the daughter of John Paine, was borne the 12th of July, 1682.

Samuell Walker, the son of Samuell Walker, was borne the 11ᵗʰ of REHOBOTH. Nouember, 1682.

Experience Brayman, the daughter of Joseph Brayman, was born the 0ᵗʰ of Nouember, 1682.

Jonath Johnson, son of John Johnson, was borne the 20ᵗʰ of February, 1682.

Mary Mason, the daughter of Noah Mason, was borne the 12ᵗʰ of Deember, 1682.

John Read, the son of Daniell Read, was borne the 25ᵗʰ of February, 1682.

Dauid Graunt, the son of Thomas Graunt, was born the 2ᶜᵒⁿᵈ of February, 1682.

Marriages.

Samuell Mason married to Elizabeth Miller, the second of March, 1682.

Samuell Miller married to Ester Bowin, the 20ᵗʰ of July, 1682.

John Thompson marryed to Sarah Smith, the 19ᵗʰ of Septeṁ, 1682.

[Burials.]

*Samuell Carpenter, Seniʳ, buried the 20ᵗʰ of February, 1682.   [*86.]

Rebeckah Pecke, the daughter of Samuell Pecke, buried the 2ᶜᵒⁿᵈ of ouember, 1682.

Anthony Perrey, buried the first day of March, 1682–83.

John Read, the son of Daniel Read, buried the first of March, 16⅚.

Rachell Johnson, the daughter of John Johnson, buried in Aprill, 1682.

Transcribed out of Towne of Rehoboth theire Records,

Ᵽ me, WILƗAM CARPENTER, Clarke.

---

aunton Register followeth, vid: of all such as were brought to the TAUNTON. *Clarke.*

DEBORAH SMITH, the daughter of John Smith, was borne the 7ᵗʰ of March, 1676.

Hannah Smith, the daughter of John Smith, was borne the 22 of arch, 1678.

John Smith, the son of John Smith, was borne the sixt of December, 1680.

TAUNTON.　　　John Lincon, the son of Samuell Lincon, was born the 15 of Se
tember, 1679.

Lydia Leanard, the daughter of James Leanard, was borne the 10th (
March, 1679.

Stephen Leanard, the son of James Leanard, borne the 14th of Decer
ber, 1680.

Joseph Caswell, the son of Stephen Caswell, borne the 18 of May, 167

Ephraim White, the son of Nicholas White, was borne the 8th of Fe
ruary, 1678.

Dorcas White, the daughter of Nicholas White, borne the 24th of Se
tem, 1680.

Thomas Gilbert, the son of Thomas Gilbert, was borne the 11th
July, 1681.

Israell Woodward, the son of John Woodward, was borne the 30th
July, 1681.

Sarah Hoskins, the daughter of William Hoskins, was borne the 31
August, 1679.

[*87.]　　　*Wiłtam Hoskins, the son of Williams Hoskins, was borne the 30th
June, 1681.

John White, the son of John White, was borne the 16 of August, 168

Mary Leanard, the daughter of Joseph Leanard, was borne the seco
of October, 1680.

Thomas Maycomber, the son of John Maycomber, was borne the 3(
of Aprill, 1679.

William Witherell, Junir, married to Elizabeth Newland, the 14th
March, 1681.

Nathaniel Hoare married to Sarah Wilbore, the 2cond of February, 168

SWANSEY.　　　　　　　*Swansey Regester.*

MARGARETT, the daughter of James Browne, Junir, was borne t
28 of June, 1682.

Ruth, the daughter of Thomas Thurbur, was borne the 16th of July, 168

Jotham, son of Benjamine Carpenter, was borne the first of June, 168

Dorithy, the daughter of Joseph Chaffey, was born Septem the 4th, 168

Hezekiah Bowin, son of Obadiah Bowin, Junir, was borne Nouem
the 19, 1682.

Zacheryah Eedey, son of Caleb Eedey, was borne January the 28, 1682.   SWANSEY.

Mʳ John Myles, pastour of the church of Swansey, deceased February e third, 1682.

Zacheryah Eedey, son of Caleb Eedey, died February the 26, 1682.

This is a true coppy or accompt as aboue expressed and written by

WILŁAM INGRAHAM,

Towne Clarke of Swansey.

A List of the Names of all the Children that haue bin brought in to   SANDWICH.
the Register that haue bine born in the Yeare 1675.   [*88.]

ELDAD TUPPER, the son of Thomas Tupper, was borne the last day of May, anno Doɱ 1675.

Elizabeth Psuall, the daughter of James Pursuall, was born the 10ᵗʰ of pteɱ, anno Doɱ 1675.

Mercy Harper, the daughter of Robert Harper, was born the 12ᵗʰ of ɪe, anno Dominie 1675.

Bethiah Nye, the dauḡter of Ebenezer Nye, was borne the 5ᵗʰ of Octo-, anno Doɱ 1675.

Bethyah Gibbs, the dauḡter of Thomas Gibbs, Junier, was borne the ʰ of December, anno Doɱ 1675.

Sandwich Register of Marriages in Sandwich in the Yeer 1675.

Elisha Bourne and Patience Skiffe were married the 26 of October, 1675.

Taunton Marriages and Burialls that were brought in as followeth.   TAUNTON.

GORḠE HALL, the son of Samuell Hall, born the 25 of January, 1680. Joann Shoue, the daughter of Mʳ Gorge, was born the 28 of Sep-, 1678.

John Briggs, the son, born the 19 of March, 1680.

Sarah Briggs, the wife of William Briggs, died the 20 of March, 1680.

Nathaniell Talbut, the son ˄ Jared Talbutt, born the 21 of Febuary, 1679.

TAUNTON.

Benjamine Briggs, the son of Richard Briggs, born the 15ᵗʰ Septeṁ, 167

Joseph Staple, the son of Joseph Staple, born the 12ᵗʰ March, 1680.

Nathaniel Steuens, the son of Richard Steuens, born the 30 July, 168

Mercy Cobb, the dãghter of Augustine Cobb, bõne the 12ᵗʰ of August, 168

Sussannah Smith, the daughter of Andrew Smith, borne the 2 of N uember, 1680.

Sarah and Mary Gilbert, the dãghters of Thomas Gilbert, born the 11 of August, 1679.

Sarah Leonard, the daughter of Benjamine Leonard, borne the 21 May, 1680.

Israell Thrasher, the son of Christopher Thrasher, born the 15ᵗʰ Septeṁ, 1648.

Israell Thrasher marryed to Mary Caswell, the 15ᵗʰ Augᵗ, 1676.

Mary Thrasher, the daughter of Israell Thrasher, born the 7 August, 1677.

Henery Hodgis maryed to Hester Gallop, the 17 of December, 1674.

Mary Hodgis, the daughter of Henery Hodgis, born the 3ᵈ of Fe ruary, 1675.

Ester Hodgis, the daughter of Henery Hodgis, born the 17 of Fe ruary, 1677.

William Hodgis, the son of Henery Hodgis, born the 18 of March, 168

Samuell Pitts married to Sarah Bobitt, the 25 of March, 1680.

Samuell Ryder marryed to Lydia Tilden, of Plymouth, the 14 of Jur in Taunton, by James Walker, Seniʳ, 1680.

Benjamine Deane maried to Sarah Williams, the sixt of January, 168

Thomas French, the son of Joseph French, born the 12 of Deceṁ, 1680.

Thomas French, the son of Joseph French, buried the 29 of Dece ber, 1680.

Mary Leanard, the daughter of Joseph Leonard, born the 2 of Oc ber, 1680.

Taunton, the 28ᵗʰ of February, 1680.

Attest by SHADRACH WILBORE, Towne Clarke.

[*89.]

*Joseph Bundy, the son of John Bundy, born the 1 of January, 1679

Sarah Hall, the *son* [daughter] of Samuell Hall, Seniʳ, the 2ᶜᵒⁿᵈ March, 1679.

John Eedey married to Sussanah Padducke, of Dartmouth, the 12ᵗʰ Nouember, 1665.

Mary Eedy born the 14ᵗʰ of March, 1666 or 67.

John Eedy was born the 19th of January, 1670.

Susannah Eedy, the wife of John Eedy, died the 14 of March, 1670.

John Eedy marryed to Deliuerance Owin, of Braintrey, the first of May, 1672.

Marcye, the daughter of John Eedy, borne the fift of July, 1673.

Hañah Eedy, borne the 5 of July, 1676.

Ebenezer Eedy, the son of John Eedy, born the 16 of May, 1679.

Abigaill Richmond, the daughter of John Richmond, born the 26 of February, 1678.

Hezekiah Hoare, the son of Hezekiah Hoare, was borne the 10 of November, 1678.

Joseph Williams, the son of Joseph Williams, born the 13 February, 1678.

Bethya Cobb, the daughter of Augustine Cobb, born the 5th of Aprill, 1678.

Nathaniel Woodworth, the son of John Woodworth, was born the 31 of July, 1679.

Isacke Negus married to Hannah Andrewes, the 7th of Aprill, 1679.

Robert Crosman, Junir, married to Hannah Brooks, the 21 of July, 1679.

Benjamine Leanard married to Sarah Thrasher, 15 January, 1678.

Hañah Stoton, the daugter of Nicolas Stoton, born the 4 of July, 1679.

Joseph Wood married to Hester Walker, January the first, 1679.

Richard Godfrey, Junir, married to Mary Richmond, 1 January, 1679.

Esra Dean married to Bethyah Edson, of Bridgwater, 17 Decem, 1678.

Bethya Dean, the daughter of Esra Dean, born the 14 of October, 1679.

Bethya Dean, daghter of Esra Deane, died 27 of Nouember, 1679.

John White married to Hañah Smith, 24 of February, 1679.

Attested by SHADRACH WILBORE, Town Clarke.

---

o the honored Court att Plymouth, the first Tusay in March. Heer followeth the Names of the Beirth, Marriages, & Deathes that haue bin in Taunton in the Year past; all that are brought in to mee, but many doe neglect to bring them to mee to be recorded.

JONAH AUSTIN, Senir, died the 30 day of July, 1683.

Benjamine Wilbore, the son of Shadrach Wilbore, born the 23 of July, 1683.

Henery Hoskins, the son of William Hoskins, born the 13 of March, 1683.

TAUNTON.   Benjamine Leanard, the son of Benjamine Leanard, born 25 January, 1683

Seth Dean, the son of Esra Dean, born the third day of June, 1683.

Wiłłam Maycomber, the son of John Maycomber, born the 31 of January, 1683.

Hugh Brigg, of Taunton, married to Martha Euerson, of Plymouth, the first day of March, 1683.

Taunton, the third of March, 1683.

Attest by SHADRACH WILBORE, Towne Clarke.

SWANSEY.   *Swanseys Register of Marriages, Beirthes, and Burials.
[*90.]

JOHN CRABTREE was maried to Mary, his wife, the 1st of Novem ber, 1683.

Thomas Birch was married to Bathshebah Sanford, the 24 of January, 1683

Zacheriah Eedey, Junir, was married to Mercye Baker, the 13th of February, 1683.

An Accoumpt of Beirthes.

Marcye, the daughter of William Haward, and Sarah, his wife, was born January 30, 1680.

Joanna, the daŭgter of John Martin, and Joan, his wife, was born th 15 of February, 1682–83.

John, the son of Nathaniel Togood, and Elizabeth, his wife, was born the 20th of Aprill, 1679.

Elizabeth, daughter of Nathaniel Togood, and Elizabeth, his wife, was born the 25 of July, 1682.

Elizabeth, the daŭgter of John Thurber, and Mary, his wife, was bor the 24th of August, 1678.

Rachell, the daughter of John Thurber, and Mary, his wife, was bor the 5th of March, 1682–83.

Jeremiah, the son Jarrt Ingraham, and Rebecka, his wife, was born th 12th of July, 1683.

Benjamin, the son of John Medbery, and Sarah, his wife, was born th 5th of March, 1682.

Sarah, the daŭgter of Humphery Tiffeny, and Elizabeth, his wife, wa born the sixt of July, 1683.

William, the son of John West, and Mehitabel, his wife, was born the SWANSEY.
ᵗʰ of September, 1683.

Mary, the dauḡter of John Thurbery, and Mary, his wife, was born
y the 10ᵗʰ, 1674.

Thomas, the son of John Thurbery, and Mary, his wife, was borne the
ᵗʰ of Nouember, 1676.

Abigaill, the daughter of Thomas Thurbē, & of Ruth, his wife, was born
last day of October, 1683.

Bethyah, the daughter of Israell Pecke, and Bethyah, his wife, was born
second of January, 1683.

Mary, the daughter of John Crabtre, and Mary, his deceased wife, was
n the 25ᵗʰ day of May, 1683.

Richard, son of Richard Johnson, and Elizabeth, his wife, was born the
ɔf January, 1683.

Samuell, the son of Samuell Wheaton, and Elizabeth, his wife, was born
21 day of July, 1683.

Jeremiah, the son of Jeremiah Child, and Martha, his wife, was born the
nd of Septem̃, 1683.

An Account of Burialls.

Mary Crabtre, wife of John Crabtree, deceased the 31 of May, 1683.
Nathaniel Lewis, deceased the 13ᵗʰ of October, 1683.
Samuell Wheaton, Seniʳ, deceased the 2ᶜᵒⁿᵈ of February, 1683.

WILLIAM INGRAHAM,
Clarke of the Towne of Swansey.

---

unton Register of the Marriages, Beirthes, and Burieles that   TAUNTON.
were brought in to mee att Taunton.   [*91.]

ISTRIS ALLICE PAINE died the 5ᵗʰ of December, 1682.
Edward Bundy, the son of John Bundy, born the 13ᵗʰ of August, 1681.
Mistris Margery Peacocke, the mother of Mʳ Gorge Shoue, buried the 17
ɔf Aprill, in the yeare 1680.

Edward Shoue, the son of   ˄   Shoue, born in October, 1680.
Eliezer Eedy, the son of John Eedy, born the 16 of October, 1671.
Yett Mercye Shoue, the dauḡter of Gorge, born the 7 of Nouember, 1682.

TAUNTON.   Eliezer Eedy, the son of John Eedy, born the 16th of October, 1671.

Israel Fisher, the son of Daniell Fisher, born the 27 of March, 1680.

Nathaniel Fisher, the son of Daniell Fisher, was born the 9th of Fe
rnary, 1681.

Hannah Staples, the daughter of Joseph Staples, born the 17th of May, 168

Jeremiah Ormsbey, the son of Thomas Ormsbey, born the 25 Noũm̃, 167

Andrew Smith, the son of Andrew Smith, born the 2^{cond} of Aprill, 168

Esra Dean, the son of Esra Dean, born the 14 of October, 1680.

Samuell Dean, the son of Esra Dean, born the 11th of Aprill, 1681.

Samuell Dean, the son of Esra ͜ , died the 16 of February, 1682.

Hannah White, the daughter of John White, born the 19th of Aprill, 168

Charity Hodges, the daughter of Henery Hodgis, born the 5 of Aprill, 168

Ebinezer French, the son of Joseph French, born the 27 of June, 168!

Edward Cetill married to Susanna Godfree, the 10th of July, 1682.

Mary Cettle, the daughter of Edward Cettle, born the fift of Aprill, 168

Anthony Newland, son of Jeremiah New̃, born the first of August, 16£

Anthony Newland married to Easter Austin, the 16 of December, 168

Abigaill Hoar, the daughter of Nathaniel Hore, born the 2 of Nouem̃, 168

Walther Mery married to Martha Cotterell, the 17th of February, 168

James Reed married to Susaña Richmon, the 18th of Aprill, 1683.

Attest by SHADRACH WILBORE, Town Clarke.

Taunton, the 5th of June, 1683.

REHOBOTH.   *The Beirthes, Marriages, and Burialls, in the Towne of Rehobo
[*92.]   Anno 1679.

Beirthes, Anno 1679.

MARY SABIN, daughter of Samuell Sabin, born the 4 of March.
          Mary Hunt, daughter of Enoch Hunt, born the 7th of Septem̃.

John Butterworth, son of John Butterworth, bor̃ the 7th of May.

Noah Perram, son of John Perram, born the 24 of December.

Eliphilett Carpenter, son of John Carpenter, born the 17th of April.

Hannah French, the son [daughter] of John French, born the 19 of Octo

Rebeckah Johnson, daughter to John Johnson, born the 17th of Novem

Sarah & Rebeckah, daughters of Abraham Perram, born the 11th of Octo

Rachell Man, daughter of Thomas Man, born the 15th of Aprill.   R<small>EHOBOTH</small>.

Bethya Reed, daughter of Moses Reed, born the 2^{cond} of Nouember.

Anno 1679.   Marriages.

Mr Thomas Medselfe married to Mistris Ann Paine, 2 of December.

Thomas Cushman married to Abigaill Fuller, the 16th of October.

Anno 1679.   Burialls.

Mr Steṗen Paine, Seni^r, buried the 21 of August.

Decon Philip Walker, the 21 of August.

Rebeckah, the dauġter of Abraham Perram, buried the 14 of October.

Eldad Kingsley buried the 30 of August.

Transcribed out of the Towne Records, by mee,

WILLIAM CARPENTER, Towne Clarke of Rehoboth.

The Records of the Beirth, Marriages, and Burialls.

Beirthes.

ȚATHANIEL WEATON, son of Jeremiah Wheaton, born the sixt of March.

Abigaill Pecke, daughter of John Pecke, born the 12 of March.

Experience Chaffey, the daughter of Nathaniel Chaffey, born the 24 ᴹarch.

Martha Iyde, daughter of Nicholas Iyde, Junier, borne the 18 of March.

Bethya Man, daughter of Thomas Man, born the 12th of March.

Elisha Pecke, son of Leifť Nicholas Pecke, born the 4th of Aprill.

Noah Fuller, son of Jonathan Fuller, born the 12th of February.

Nathaniell Peren, the son of John Peren, born the 9th of February.

Obadia Blanding, son of William Blanding, born the 14th of Aprill.

Samuell Robinson, son of Gorge Robinson, Junī, born the 16 of Nouember.

Jabez Browne, son of Joseph Browne, born the 30th of December.

John Penfeild, son of Samuell Penfeild, born the 30th of May.

Sillas Titus, the son of Silas Titus, bourn the 12 of August.

*Samuell and John Palmer, sonnes of Samuell Palmer, borne the 4th of ᴸary.   [*93.]

Joseph Bosworth, son of Joseph Bosworth, borne the 27 of September.

REHOBOTH.   Robert Marten, son of John Marten, born the 9th of September.

Samuell Mason, son of Samuel Mason, born the 9 of June.

Enos Hunt, son of Enoch Hunt, born the 28 of January.

Peter Hunt, son of John Hunt, borne the 7th of February.

Anne Willmouth, daughter of Thomas Willmouth, Junr, born the 22 o
August.

Mary Rockett, the daughter of Joseph Rockett, deceased, borne the 14
of December.

Dorethy Carpenter, daugher of John Carpenter, born the 9 of February

Katheren Allin, the daughter of Isacke Allin, born the 18 of January.

Sarah Thurston, daugter of Daniell Turston, deceased, born the 2^{ec}
of January.

Rebeckah Reed, daughter of Moses Reed, born the 14th of Stember.

Mary Kendrick, daugter of Thomas Kenericke, born the 2^{cond} of Januar

Ester Miller, daugter of Samuell Miller, born the 4th of Aprill.

Rebeckah Wilmoth, daugter of Jonathan Wilmouth, borne the 30
August.

Marriages.

Nathaniel Pery married to Sarah Carpenter, the 17th of May.

Samuell Tharsher, of Taunton, married to Bethya Brookes, of Reh
both, the 4th of December.

Benjamin Onion, of Deadham, married to Deborah Woodcocke, of R
hoboth, the 24th of May.

Samuel Carpenter married to Patience Iyde, the 8th of January.

Richard Bowine marryed to Mary Titus, the 9th of January.

Dauid Freeman, of Rehoboth, married to Margarett Ingraham, of Swa
sye, the 4th of Aprill.

James Welch, of Swansey, married to Mercye Sabin, of Rehoboth, t
9 of Nouember.

Burialls.

Elizabeth Hunt, the daughter of Enocke Hunt, buried the 29 of Marc

Joseph Sabine, son of Joseph Sabin, buried the 8th of May.

John Palmer, the son of Samuell Palmer, buried the 15th of July.

Josepth Rocked buried the 21 of July.

William Buckland buried the first of Septeṁ.

John Palmer, son of Samuel Palmer, buried the 5th of January.

Nathaniell Peren, the son of John Peren, buried the 24th of February.

Ephraim Hawner buried the 27 of August.

By mee, WILLIAM CARPENTER, Seni^r, Towne Clarke.

[In an unknown handwriting.]

*Marshfeild, An° 1687.

OHN BESBEY and Joanna Brookes were marreyed September the 13th, 1687.

Martha, the daughter of John Besbey, was borne October yᵉ 13th, 1688.

John, yᵉ son of John Besbey, was borne September 15, 1690.

Elijah, the son of John Besbey, was borne the 29th of January, 169½.

Mary, yᵉ daughter of John Besbey, was borne March yᵉ 28ᵗʰ, 1693.

Moses, the son of John Besbey, was borne October 20th, 1695.

Elisha, the son of John Besbey, was borne the third of May, 1698.

[The following entries are in a handwriting of a more modern date, and are crossed out in the ginal volume. The persons mentioned were of the town of Plymouth.]

Josiah Cotton & Hannah Sturtevant were married at Plymᵗʰ, by Mʳ
ₒhᵐ Little, January 8ᵗʰ, 170⁷⁄₈.

The Birth of yʳ Children.

Hannah Cotton, yʳ daughter, born Apˡ 3, 1709.

Mary Cotton, yʳ daughter, born August 14, 1710.

John Cotton, yʳ son, born April 5, 1712.

Bethiah Cotton, yʳ daughter, born June 8, 1714.

Theophilus Cotton, yʳ son, born March 31, 1716.

Lucy Cotton, yʳ daughter, born February 19ᵗʰ, 17¹⁷⁄₁₈.

Josiah Cotton, yʳ son, was born January 19ᵗʰ, 17¹⁸⁄₂₈.

12

TREASURY ACCOUNTS.

PLYMOUTH RECORDS.

TREASURY ACCOUNTS OF THE COLONY OF NEW PLYMOUTH IN NEW ENGLAND.

[The following pages include that portion of the Plymouth Colony Records generally known as the Treasurer's Accounts. The original manuscript volume contains about one hundred and twelve pages, a large portion of the writing being on one side of the paper only. Originally it comprised the third part of the volume in which were recorded a portion of the Laws, the Indian Deeds, the Treasurer's Accounts, and the fourth volume of Court Orders. The first record is that of the tenth of June, 1658, and the last, that of the fifth of June, 1686, the whole covering a period of twenty-eight years. The writing is by various hands.]

*CAPT: JOSIAS WINSLOW, Leiftenant Thomas Southworth, M^r Ed- **1658.** mond Hawes, and Josias Cooke, being ordered to take an account of the Tresurer this 10th of June, 1658.

10 June.

[*1.]

It, the Tresurer is debter by money of the countrey, alreddy receiued, ... } 79 : 16 : 00

It, by fines not yett levied, ... 30 : 06 : 00

It, p^r more, four barrells of oyle, ... 08 : 00 : 00

It, by money due on Kenebecke, it the yeare 1656, . . . 04 : 07 : 03

It, more, for one yeare and an halfe rent now dew, . . . 052 : 10 : 00

In totall due, . . . 174 : 19 : 06

We haue not heerin meddled with fines about the oath of fidelitie, nor any fines condemned by this p̃sent Court, held June the fift, 1658. Att which Court, Roᵇ Harper, Ralph Allin, Seni^r, John Allin, Thomas Green- feild, Edward Perrey, Richard Kerbey, Juni^r, Wiłłam Allin, Thomas Vre, Wiłłam Gifford, Mathew Allin, Daniell Wing, Francis Allin, and John Jen- kens, all of Sandwich, for refusing to take the oath of fidelitie, fined euery of them the som̄e of £10, in all, ... 130 : 00 : 00

1658.

10 June.

George Webb, for refusing to take the oath of fidelitie within the time prefixed, fined, ... } 05 : 00 : 0

The said Gorge Webb engageing to depart the goûment, in case hee sc
doe, the other fine pound is remitted.

Gorḡ Allin, takeing the matter about the oath into consideratͭ, is likͤ
wise for p̄sent ·not required to pay the one halfe of his fine, which is fiͥ
pound ; neverthelese, for his refusing to take the said ŏth within the tiͫ
p̄fixed in the order, is fined, ... 05 : 00 : C

Anthony Loe, of Warwick, for selling a pistoll to an Indian, was fined the sumē of . . . . } 03 : 00 : 0

Moses Rowley and Robert Parker, for striking each other,
fined each, ... } 00 : 03 : ͫ

[*2.] *The Tresurer is pͬ contra credit by seuerall disburŝments, 69 : 10 : ͫ

By debts now owing.

Impͬ, to the Gouͬ, by the appointment of the countrey, . 10 : 00 : ͫ
To Mͬ John Howland, ... 01 : 00 : ͫ
To the marshall, ... 02 : 00 : ͫ
To Mistris Bradford, ... 15 : 01 : ͫ
To Captͭ Winslow, ... 04 : 10 : ͫ
To Mͬ Constant Southworth, ... 04 : 00 : ͫ
To Mͬ John Barnes, ... 04 : 07 : ͫ

40 : 18 :

Itͭ, more to bee alowed to him for his two yeares seruice, . 12 : 00 :

52 : 18 :
69 : 10 :

The totall of the Tresurers creditt, ... 122 : 09 :

Rest to the countrey on ballence due from the
Tresurer, ... 52 : 09 : 06
Itͭ, by mistake in one barrell of oyle, lesse . . 02 : 00 : 00

This is a trew account, errors excepted.

The countrey haue alowed more to the Tresurer, ... 04 : 00 :
Soe that now remaines due to the countrey, ... 46 : 09 :

Att the Court held att Plymouth the 29ᵗʰ of September, 1658.

THE Court of Majestrates and Deputies ordered a smale gratuity of ten
pounds vnto Major Josias Winslow, in some p̃te of consideration of
me emergent charges that hee should bee att in journeyes and otherwise, for
e discharge of his said cheife milletary office in this jurisdiction.

---

*Att the Court holden att Plymouth the 3ᵈ of December, 1658.

THO: GREENFEILD, for striking of Gorg̃ Barlow, the marshall of
Sandwich, &c̃, in the execution of his office, fined three pounds.

Thomas Greenfeild, Daniell Wing, and Richard Kerbey, Juniʳ, for re-
ing to aid the said marshall in the execution of his office, fined each twenty
llings.

Wiłłam Newland, for being att the meeting of those called Quakers
hteen times, fined nine pounds ; and for his wife being att the said meet-
s twenty times, fined ten pounds ; and for entertaining of John Copeland,
d another of those called Quakers, fined fiue pounds.

---

t the Generall Court holden att Plymouth, for the Jurisdiction of
New Plymouth, the first of March, 1658.

OHN SMITH, JUNIᴿ, of Plymouth, Goodwife Howland, the wife of
Henery Howland, Zoeth Howland and his wife, John Soule and Good-
e Soule, the wife of Gorge Soule, of Duxburrow, Arther Howland and
wife, of Marshfeild, Mⁱˢ Cudworth, Goodwife Coleman, Wiłłam Parker,
his wife, of Scituate, haueing bine p̃rsented for frequently absenting them-
es from the publicke worship of God, were sentanced by the Court to pay,
ording to order of Court, each ten shillings, to the collonies vse.

Richard Beare, for laciuiouse and filthy practices, was adjudgeᵈ by the
rt worthy of corporall punishment answarable to his demerritts ; notwith-

1 6 5 8-9. standing, vpon some speciall considerations, hee was sentanced by the Cou
1 March. to pay a fine of fiue pounds to the vse of the collonie.

    Wiłłam Newland, for his contempt of the Courts order, in neglecting bring his two daughters to the Court, to answare for theire miscarriage toward the marshall Barlow in the execution of his office, the said Wiłła Newland is fined the sume of forty shillings, twenty shillings wherof hee to pay to the said Barlow, the other twenty to the Treasurer.

    And the said Wiłłam Newland, for telling of a lye in the Court, fined te shillings.

1659.
June.
[*4.]

The Fines of Jūe Court, 1659.

For the refusing to take the oath of fidelitie.

		ll	s	
EDWARD PERREY,	. . . .	05 : 00 : 0
John Newland,	. . . .	05 : 00 : C
Ralph Allin, Seni^r,	. . . .	05 : 00 : C
Wiłłam Gifford,	. . . .	05 :
Wiłłam Allin,	. . . .	05 : 00 : C
Mathew Allin,	. . . .	05 : 00 : 0
John Allin,	. . . .	05 : 00 : 0
Thõ Ewer,	. . . .	05 : 00 : C
Rich Kerbey, Juni^r,	. . . .	05 : 00 : C
Roŧ Harper,	. . . .	05 : 00 : C
John Jenkens,	. . . .	05 : 00 : (
Gorᵹ Allin,	. . . .	05

For being drunke.

Daniell Mockenney, fined,	. . . .	00 : 05 : (
Jeremiah Newland, for being drunke,	. . . .	00 : 05 : (
Josepth Burgis, for takeing away a beast attached for the countrey, fined,	. . . .	01 : 00 : (
Henery Dillingham, fined,	. . . .	02 : 10 :
‡Experience Michell, fined,‡	. . . .	02 : 10 :

Remited by
the Court.

The Fines of October Court, 1659.

	ll	s	d
EDWARD PERREY, ...	05	00	00
John Newland, ...	05	00	00
Ralph Allin, ...	05	00	00
Wilłam Allin, ...	05	00	00
Mathew Allin, ...	05	00	00
Gorge Allin, ...	05	00	00
Joseph Allin, ...	05	00	00
Daniell Winge, ...	05	00	00
‡Thõ Ewer,‡	05	00	00
Rotͫ Harper, ...	05	00	00
John Jenkens, ...	05	00	00
Wilłam Gifford, ...	05		
Thõ Pope, ...	00	10	00
Thõ Butler, ...	02	10	00
Rich Kerbey, Junir, ...	05	00	00
Steuen Winge, ...	01	00	00
Edward Perrey, ...	01	00	00
Thõ Burgis, Junir, ...	00	10	00
Edmond Freeman, Junir, ...	00	10	00
Thõ Lucas, ...	00	10	00
Josepth Billington, ...	00	05	00

Thõ Butler was fined ten shillings att March, 1658, which I can not understand was taken into the former account.

---

*Att the Court held att Plymouth the seauenth of March, 1659.

	ll	s	d
THÕ LUCAS was fined, ...	01	10	00
Thõ Sauory, ...	00	05	00

Att this Court, Hailstones fine was remitted, and likewise Experience Michell his fine.

13

1660.   *Att the Court holden att Plymouth the first of May, 1660.*

1 May.   HENERY HOWLAND was fined, ... 07 : 00 :

John Smith, the younger, of Plymouth, ... 02 : 00 :

———

8 June.   *Att the Court held att Plymouth the 8ᵗʰ of June, 1660.*

THO: BURGIS, Juniʳ, fiined, ... 01 : 10 :

Henery Dillingham, ... 00 : 15 :

Thõ Butlér, and Dorithy, his wife, fined, ... 02 : 00 :

Joseph Allin, ... 02 : 10 :

About the oath of fidelitie were fined,

Edward Perrey, ... 05 : 00 :

John Newland, ... 05 : 00 :

Ralph Allin, ... 05 : 00 :

Wiłłam Gifford, ... 05 : 00 :

Wiłłam Allin, ... 05 : 00 :

Mathew Allin, ... 05 : 00 :

Gorge Allin, ... 05 : 00 :

Josepth Allin, ... 05 : 00 :

Daniell Winge, ... 05 : 00 :

Thõ Ewer, ... 05 : 00 :

Richard Kerbey, Juniʳ, ... 05 : 00 :

Robert Harper, ... 05 : 00 :

[*6.]   *Mʳ Constant Southworth debter to the countrey.*

ll   s

Pʳ Kennebecke, Aprill, 59, ... 07 : 07 :

Pʳ wampam, ... 00 : 08 :

Pʳ a bill of Jnᵒ Sprague, ... 04 : 10 :

Pʳ a bill of Thõ Turner, ... 02 : 05 :

Pʳ a bill of James Doughty, ... 01 : 15 :

Pʳ a debt from Edw̃ Jenkens, ... 05 : 10 :

Pʳ a debt from Wiłłᵃᵐ Shirtlife, ... 03 : 04

Pʳ a house bought of Capt̃ Willett, ... 20 : 00

Pʳ 2 heiffers of Mʳ Aldins, ... 04 : 10

Pʳ a horse receiued of Mʳ Aldin, ... 08 : 00

Pᵣ a mare and coult of Wilłam Newland, ...	14 : 00 : 00	**1660.**
Pᵣ a mare and a coult of Wilłam Allins, ...	14 : 00 : 00	8 June.
Pᵣ a horse coult, ...	05 : 15 : 00	
Pᵣ by money in Barlows handes, cash, ...	04 : 00 : 00	
Pᵣ a debt in the hands of Thõ Tupper, ...	04 : 00 : 06	
Pᵣ tarr of Gorge Barlows, ...	03 : 12 : 00	
Pᵣ a house and land of Thõ Johnsons, ...	10 : 00 : 00	
Pᵣ an house and land of Robbert Harppers, ...	10 : 00 : 00	
Pᵣ a paire of wheeles att Plymouth, ...	01 : 08 : 00	
Pᵣ oyle in Jnᵒ Ellices hand, ...	06 : 15 : 00	
More oyle in Jnᵒ Ellices hand, ...	09 : 07 : 06	
Pᵣ sheepe in Gorge Barlowes hand, 7 ewes & fiue lambes, .	11 : 10 : 00	
Pᵣ 4 cows att Wilłam Barstowes, ...	12 : 00 : 00	
Pᵣ a debt from Wilłam Barstow, wherof thirty shillings money, ... }	11 : 10 : 00	
Pᵣ 2 great oxen att Barstowes, ...	12 : 00 : 00	
Pᵣ 4 steers of 4 yeares old att Barstowes, ...	16 : 00 : 00	
Pᵣ a cow att Billingtons, ...	03 : 05 : 00	
Pᵣ a cow att Willᵃᵐ Shirtliffes, ...	03 : 10 : 00	
2 cow att Sam̃ Sturtivants, ...	07 : 00 : 00	
Pᵣ a cow and steer att Wilłam Clarkes, ...	06 : 10 : 00	
Pᵣ 7 cowes, 2 yearlings, one bull, and one steer, att Capt Thomas house, ... }	30 : 05 : 00	
Pᵣ a debt of Gorge Barlow, ...	01 : 02 : 00	
Pᵣ 15 cattle, still att Sandwich, vallued att	40 : 00 : 00	
Pᵣ 27 yards of trading cloth, att 8 shilling p yard, . . .	10 : 16 : 00	
Pᵣ a yard and halfe of broadclòth, att 18ˢ p yard, . . .	01 : 02 : 06	
Pᵣ 3 yards and an halfe of Red Rowle, att 6ˢ p yard, . .	01 : 01 : 00	
Pᵣ fines att Sandwich, alreddy judged, and warrants out with Gorge Barlow, ... }	116 : 04 : 09	
*Pᵣ a fine of Jnᵒ Smith, Junᵣ, of Plymouth, ...	00 : 10 : 00	[*7.]
Pᵣ a fine of Jnᵒ Soule, ...	00 : 10 : 00	
Pᵣ a fine of Zoeth Howland and his wife, ...	01 : 00 : 00	
Pᵣ a fine of Arther Howland and his wife, ...	01 : 10 : 00	
Pᵣ a fine of Wilłam Parker, ...	00 : 10 : 00	
Pᵣ a fine of Mistris Cudworth, ...	00 : 10 : 00	
Pᵣ a fine of Goodwife Coleman, ...	00 : 10 : 00	
Pᵣ a fine of Richard Beare, ...	05 : 00 : 00	

1660.

13 June.

Pᵣ a fine of Arther Howland, ... 04 : 00 :
Pᵣ a fine of Jnᵒ Barnes, ... 05 : 00 :
Pᵣ a fine of Wilłam Hailstones, ... 01 : 00 :
Pᵣ a fine of Edw̃ Holman, ... 00 : 12 :
Pᵣ Crosman, of Taunton, ... 00 : 05 :
Pᵣ Young Gilbert, of Taunton, ... 00 : 10 :
Pᵣ a fine of Nicholas Iyde, ... 02 : 10 :
Pᵣ a debt of Gorge Bonum, ... 00 : 04 :
Pᵣ a debt from Nicholas Hodgis, for a heiffer, ... 01 : 04 :

This is a true account, errors excepted.

JOSIAS WINSLOW, Juniᵣ,
THO: SOUTHWORTH,
JOSIAS WINSLOW.

[*8.]   *The countrey is debt̃.

                                                   ll   s

To the Gouᵣ, ... 11 : 00 :
To Mᵣ John Aldin, ... 16 : 00 :

More for moneyes disbursed of his own estate.

To Josias Winslow, Juniᵣ, to pay money, ... 03 : 00 :
To Josias Winslow, Juniᵣ, more, ... 10 : 00 :
To Nicholas Hodgis, Jnᵒ Smith, Jnᵒ Holmes, each 15ˢ, . 02 : 05 :
To Walter Brigges, for a woulfe, ... 00 : 15 :
To Jnᵒ Phillipes, for a woulfe, ... 00 : 15 :
To James Cole, Seniᵣ, ... 01 : 10 :
To the charge of Mᵣ Tildens jury, ... 03 : 04 :
To Duxburrow, for two men 2 daies seruice, ₵ ten pound ⎫
  of powder, ...⎭ 01 : 10 :
To Gyles Rickard, Seniᵣ, ... 00 : 14 :
To Capt̃ Willett, for trading cloth, ... 08 : 04 :
To Wilłam Harlow, ... 01 : 00 :
To Gorge Partrich, ... 00 : 03 :
To Constant Southworth, in (58) due by booke, ... 03 : 00 :
To Constant Southworth, in money disbursed, and horse ⎫
  hier to Secunke, ...⎭ 01 : 09 :
To him more, for the majestrates table, 9 daies ourplusse, . 10 : 04 :

To Mistris Bradford, for 9 daies ouerplusse, ... 04 : 18 : 00

To the Gou^r, for (58) . . . . 03 : 07 : 04

—————

80 : 10 : 05

This is a true account, as taken October 7, (59.)   Errors excepted.

JOSIAS WINSLOW, Juni^r,

THOMAS SOUTHWORTH,

JOSIAS WINSLOW.

———

THE Court haueing appointed Major Josias Winslow, Mr Josias Winslow, Seni^r, and Nathaneell Bacon, wee, by examination of the accoumpts, oe find —   [*9.] 13 June.

The Treasurer is debter.

Imprim̃, by moneys of the countreys, by him receiued, . 401 : 1 : 5

More by moneyes of the countreyes, that is, debts made by him, and by goods and cash in his hands, . . . } 114 : 2 : 1

More by fines not yett leuied, att Sandwich and elswhere, 227 : 4 : 5

More due to the countrey in oyle, att Sandwich and Yarmouth, ... } 03 : 4 : 0

More in debt of Goodman Tupper, ... 4 : 0 : 6

—————

In all amounting to . . . . 749 : 12 : 5

The Treasurer is p^r contra cred̃; by moneyes paid by him to the countreyes vse, and by theire order.   [*10.]

	ll	s	d
Imp^r, to the Gou^r, for what was due to him formerly, and for this last yeare, ...	22	7	4
To Mr Collyare, by the countreyes order, ...	10	00	0
To Mr Aldin, in reference to seruice as Treasurer, . . .	16	00	0
To Major Winslow, for what the countrey orders him for horses, and expenses on the com̃ission yoyag̃, ₵ moneyes due to him before, ...	29	00	00
To Leift̃ Southworth, by the countreyes order, and for expence on the com̃ission, ...	21	00	00
To Mistris Bradford, for the majestrates table, ...	16	18	00
To himselfe, on account of prouiding for the Court, . .	14	14	03
To James Cole, by the countreyes order, ₵ð, ...	11	12	00

To two barrells of powder bought for the countrey, . .	13 : 10 : 0
To moneyes to the comissioners, ...	10 : 00 : 0
To moneyes by order for woulues, ...	12 : 07 : 1
To Thomas Sauory, by the countreyes order, ...	14 : 10 : 0

More paied by him for charges of takeing up, driueing, grasing of the countreyes cattle, for horse hier att seuerall times, for money paied on account of trooping horses, and seuerall other charges p̃ticularly appeering in his accounts, ...   214 : 13 :

In all amounting to . . . .   406 : 12 :

Rest due to the countrey on ballence, ...   342 : 19 :

Out of which ballence there is in debts that the countrey doe owe as followet

Imp̃r, to the Gou̇r, yet vnpaied, ...	2 : 0 :
To Constant Southworth, cash, ...	5 : 0 :
More to him for 4 daies charge of this Court, ...	4 : 10 : 0
More to Mistris Bradford, for 4 daies of this Court, . .	1 : 18 : 0
To Gorḡ Bonum, ...	00 : 07 : 0
To Goodman Rickard, ...	00 : 16 : 0
To Gorḡ Barlow, allowed by this Court, ...	03 : 00 : 0
To trooping horses, not yett paied, ...	39 : 00 : 0
For woulues, more to pay, ...	09 : 00 : 0
More to Thomas Sauory, by the countres order, ...	20 : 00 : 0

85 : 12 :

[The following is out of place on page *9.]

Besides the ballence, the countrey haue an house bought of Captaine Wille
The house and land of Thõ Johnson, and the house and land of Rob
Harper.

And the oyle somĩtimes resting in the hand of John Ellis, being now
leased ; the fines for which it was taken are yett due, and not in the f
mencioned.

We haue taken notice that the Treasurer hath bine att much more cha
and trouble then any formerly, and therfore doe allow him twenty fiue poun
a great p̃te wherof is expended by him.

A true account, errors excepted. Taken this 13th of June, 1660, by

JOSIAS WINSLOW, Junir,
JOSIAS WINSLOW,
NATHANEEL BACON.

The Fines of the Court of Assistants held in August, 1660.   1660.

<table>
<tr><td></td><td>ll</td><td>s</td><td>d</td><td>August.</td></tr>
</table>

WILLIAM PARKER, of Scittuate, fined, ... 07 : 00 : 00   August.

Willam Newland, fined, ... 05 : 00 : 00   [*11.]

The Fines of October Court, 1660.   October.

SAQUATAM, an Indian, fined, ... 01 : 00 : 00

Quachevenett, fined, ... 00 : 10 : 00

Fined for being att Quakers meetings.

Robert Harper and his wife,

Josepth Allin,   Peter Gaunt,

Benjamine Allin,   Dorithy Butler,

John Newland and his wife,   Obadiah Butler,

Willam Allin,   John Jenkens,

Willam Gifford,   Rich Kerbey, Senir,

Mathew Allin,   Rich Kerbey, Junir,

The wife of Henery Dillingham,   Jone Swift,

Willam Newland and his wife,   John Smith, of Plymouth, ⅃

John Soule,   Deborah, his wife.

Rodulphus Elmes,   Lydia Hickes, of Plymouth.

Henery Howland, fined, ... 04 : 00 : 00

is following convicted for refusing to take the oath of fidelitie att this Court.

Robert Harper,   Joseph Allin,

John Newland,   Rich Kerbey, Junir,

Willam Gifford,   John Jenkens,

Mathew Allin,   Ralph Allin.

Teague Jones, fined, ... 6ll

Thomas Jones, of Taunton, fined, ... 10s

Thomas Lucas, ... 00 : 10

1 6 6 0-1.   *The Fines of the Court held the fift of March, 1660.*

5 March.

	ll : s : d
ROBERT WHETCOMB, fined, ...	10 : 00 : 00
Ezekiell Mayne, fined, ...	01 : 00 : 00
Thomas Lucas, fined, ...	02 : 00 : 00
James Cole, Seni[r], fined, ...	00 : 10 : 00
Gyles Rickard, Seni[r], fined, ...	00 : 10 : 00
[*12.] *Ephraim Done, ...	02 : 10 : 00
Thō Ridman, ...	02 : 10 : 00

1661.   **The Treasurers Account, giuen into the Court held att Plymouth
the 10th of June, 1661, for the Yeare 1660, is as followeth.*

10 June.

[*13.]

The Treasurer is debter.

IMP[R], p[r] the ballence of the last yeare, ...	342 : 19 : 0
P[r] the fines of June Court, (60)	81 : 05 : 0
P[r] the fines of August Court, ...	12 : 01 : 0
P[r] the fines of October Court, ...	67 : 10 : 0
P[r] the fines of March Court, ...	35 : 00 : 0
P[r] the fines of May Court, ...	18 : 00 : 0
P[r] debts { fines of Cap[t] Thomas, Henry Howland, { Willam Bassett, ...	08 : 02 : 0
P[r] oyle of the townes, ...	30 : 00 : 0
P[r] a horse in Trustrum Hulls hand, ...	10 : 00 : 0
P[r] a mare and coult sold to Taunton, ...	16 : 00 : 0
P[r] a horse taken from Joshua Copall, ...	12 : 00 : 0
P[r] nailes in the Treasurers hand, ...	00 : 08 : 0
P[r] oyle resting to the countrey att Eastham, ...	01 : 06 : 0
	634 : 12 : 0
P[r] a horse giuen to the troop, ...	07 : 00 : 0
P[r] goods and chattles in his hand, ...	28 : 01 : 0
In the totall, ...	669 : 13 : 0

*The Treasurer is per contra cred.

Pᵣ seuerall disbursments paied by the Treasurer for the countreyes vse, ... } 273 : 14 : 01

Pᵣ abatement of fines to Teage Jones, Wᵐ Parker, and a steer returned to Edw̃ Perrey, ... } 08 : 16 : 00

Pᵣ debt and fines that wee judge to bee current, ... 32 : 08 : 01

Pᵣ fines that wee thinke are desperate, ... 288 : 09 : 09

In the totall, ... 603 : 07 : 11

Rests due to ballence due to the countrey, ... 66 : 05 : 03

Out of which ballence the countrey doth yett owe —

To Major Winslow, ... 10 : 00 : 00
To Mᵣ Bradford, an old account, ... 02 : 10 : 09
To Ralph Smith, ... 00 : 15 : 00
To himselfe, for six dayes ouerplus of the Courts siting, . 06 : 14 : 06
To Mistris Bradford, for ouerplusse, ... 02 : 05 : 04
To Thomas Sauory, yett vnpayed, ... 05 : 18 : 01
To charge of the Kinges proclamation, ... 01 : 05 : 09

29 : 08 : 08

Besides which, the countrey haue a house bought of Captaine Willett, e house and land of Thomas Johnson, and the house and land of Thomas arper.

Wee haue allowed to the Treasurer for his care and paines this yeare, enty pound.

A true account, errors excepted, taken the tenth of June, 1661.

pᵣ JOSIAS WINSLOW,
JAMES TORREY,
JOSIAS COOKE,
NATHANIELL BACON,
NATHANIELL WARREN.

14

1662.   *June the 9th, 1662.*   June the 9th, 1662.

THE Treasurer is debtor to stocke publicke, as appeers by his accounte.

Debitor, ... 277 : 16 : 10

Pro contra credit, . . . 208 : 13 : 04

Remaines upon reduction, 69 : 03 : 06

The Treasurer is pro contra cred^r stocke publicke by disburšmen and debts appeering by his a count current att large.

Reduction upon reduction for the Treasurers sallary, concluded to bee twenty pound . . . } 49 : 03 : 06, remainder.

To which wee aded twenty pounds, or therabouts, in peage, now in t Treasurers hand, which makes the ballence due to the countrey, 69 : 03 :

It is agreed that Mr Aldin haue fiue pound allowed by the Treasurer f his last yeares more then ordinary trouble.

More to debts due.

Imp^r, to Major Winslow for comissioners horses, . . . 01 : 00 :

To one barrell of powder att the Treasurers, ... 0

To a barrell spent att the Kinges proclamation, ... 0

To 40^{ll} of Barnestb^e spent att the generall training, . . . 0

To Rehoboth, for woulues, ... 06 : 08 :

To Eastham, for woulues, ... 02 : 13 :

To Yarmouth, 2 woulues, & Taunton, 1 wolffe, ... 01 : 16 :

To James Walker, for transportation of letters, and other charges, ... } 00 : 09 :

To Bridgwater, one wolffe, ... 00 : 12 :

To Sauory, for whiping, ... 00 : 18 :

Signed by vs vnderwritten.

JAMES TORREY,
JOHN FREEMAN,
WILŁAM BRITT,
THOMAS HOWES,
PERIGRINE WHITE,
JOHN MORTON.

*June the fift, 1663.

THE Treasurer is debter to the countrey, as appeers by this account, . . $343 : 00 : 11$

The Treasurer per contra creditor to the countrey by disbursments and debts, as appeers vpon this account, $367 : 16 : 00\frac{1}{2}$

Soe there rests due to him, to ballence the account, . . . $24 : 15 : 01$

Debts due to the countrey in fines and otherwise.

	ll s d
Pr Samuell Howland, ...	$00 : 10 : 00$
Pr William Foard, Seni^r, ...	$00 : 05 : 00$
Pr Kanelme Winslow, Juni^r, ...	$00 : 10 : 00$
Pr Timothy Hallowey, ...	$00 : 10 : 00$
Pr John Palmer, Juni^r, ...	$05 : 00 : 00$
Pr Nathaniel Church & Elizabeth Soule, ...	$10 : 00 : 00$
Pr Josias Hallott, ...	$02 : 10 : 00$
Pr Thomas Starr, ...	$02 : 10 : 00$
Pr Elisha Hedge, ...	$01 : 10 : 00$
Pr Samuell Sturgis, ...	$01 : 10 : 00$
Pr Ephraim Done, ...	$01 : 05 : 00$
Pr Thomas Ridman, ...	$01 : 05 : 00$
Pr John Knowles, ...	$01 : 05 : 00$
Pr John Wilson, ...	$01 : 05 : 00$
Pr Ephraim Done, ...	$02 : 10 : 00$
Pr Thomas Ridman, ...	$02 : 10 : 00$
Pr Abraham Sampson, ...	$00 : 10 : 00$
	$35 : 05 : 00$

Due in rates not yett payed.

	ll s d
From Taunton, ...	$06 : 14 : 08$
From Cushenah, ...	$03 : 10 : 00$
From the farmes, ...	$01 : 10 : 00$
	$11 : 14 : 08$

More for a horse, ... $04 : 00 : 00$

The countrey is debter vpon the old account, and otherwise.
To a barrell of powder due to the countreyes stocke.

1663.

	ll	s
To 40 pound of powder to Barnstable.		
To the Goū, vpon the account of woulues, ...	00 : 09 : C
To Leiſt Freeman, ...	04 : C
To Rehoboth, for woulues, ...	08 : C
To the Goū, due to him of what the countrey allowed him the last yeare, ...	06 : 02 : 0

The Court doe allow vnto the Treasurer, for his charge and trouble th
last yeare, twenty fiue pounds sterlinge.

JAMES TORREY,
JOSIAS COOKE,
NATHANIELL WARREN,
JOHN CHIPMAN.

The Fines of June Court, 1663.

	s
ITEM, Josepth Rogers, of Namassakesett, ...	05 : 00 : (
Item, Christopher Winter, ...	00 : 10 :
Item, John Shilley, ...	01 : 00 :
Item, Nathaniel Fitsrandall, ...	10 : 00 : (
Item, Edward Sturgis, Senⁱ, ...	06 : 00 :
Item, Timothy Hallowey, ...	00 : 05 :
Item, Gorge Vaughan, ...	00 : 10 :
Item, Wiłłam Paule, of Taunton, ...	00 : 10 :
Item, more the said Wiłłam Paule, ...	00 : 03 :
Item, more the said Wiłłam Paule, ...	01 : 00 :
Item, John Hatheway, of Taunton, ...	00 : 03 :
John Doged, of Rehoboth, ...	01 : 00 :

The Fine of the Court of Assistants, August 4ᵗʰ, 1663.

JOSEPTH ANDREWS, ...	00 : 05 :

The Fines of the Court held att Plymouth, the fift of October, 1663. 1 6 6 3.

5 October.

JOSEPTH ROGERS, ...	02 : 10 : 00
Wilłam Tubbs, ...	02 : 10 : 00
Wilłam Norkett, ...	05 : 00 : 00
Nehemiah Bessey, ...	00 : 05 : 00
Thomas Ingham, ...	00 : 10 : 00
Ralph Earle, ...	01 : 00 : 00
Richard Berry, ...	2 : 00 : 00
Wilłam Griffin and his wife, ...	04 : 00 : 00
Richard Michell and his wife, ...	04 : 00 : 00

This fines of Berry and the rest were remitted att March Court, 1663. See booke of orders, and passages of the Court.

Att the Court of Assistants held the first of December, 1663. 1 December.

MYLES RICKARD, Seni^r, and Thomas Pope, each fined . 3^s : 4^d

---

*The Fines of March Court, 1663. 1 6 6 3-4.

	ll	s	d
JOHN BRIGGS, of Taunton, ...	00 : 10 : 00		
Timothy Hallowey, of Taunton, ...	01 : 00 : 00		
Ensigne Williams, ...	00 : 03 : 04		
John Bayley, of Scittuate, ...	00 : 03 : 04		
Richard Willis, ...	00 : 03 : 04		
Joseph Sauory, ...	00 : 03 : 04		
Ann, the wife of Wilłam Hoskins, ...	01 : 00 : 00		
Hester, the wife of John Rickard, ...	01 : 00 : 00		
Richard Willis, ...	00 : 10 : 00		
Francis Baddow, ...	00 : 10 : 00		
Robert Ransome, ...	00 : 10 : 00		
Abraham Hedge, ...	02 : 10 : 00		
Henery Green, of Taunton, ...	00 : 03 : 04		

March.

[*20.]

1664.   *Att the Court held the 3ᵗʰ of May, 1664.*

3 May.

FIUE Indians, att or neare Acushena, namely, Woomham, Poganatowam Weesunka, Sucquatamacke, and Chachapaquin, were fined, to the vse of the collonie, each twenty shillings.

---

16 June.   *June the 16ᵗʰ, 1664.*
[*23.]

THE account giuen in by the Treasurer vnto Mr Hawes, Cornett Studson Nathaniel Bacon, Richard Bourne, Mr Paine, Ensigne Eames, Leif Freeman, William Britt, Nathaniel Warren, James Walker, and Benjamin Bartlett, whoe were appointed by the Court, is as followeth.

The Treasurer is debter to the coun-   The Treasurer, pro contra creditt t
trey, as appeers by his account,   the countrey by disbursments an
                310 : 04 : 01   debts, as appeers vpon his account
                                                             339 : 9 :

Soe rests due to him, to ballence the account, ... 29 : 5 :

Debts due by fines and otherwise to the countrey.

Item, by Samuell Howland, ...	00 : 10 : 0
Item, William Foard, Senir, ...	00 : 05 : 0
Item, Kenelme Winslow, ...	00 : 10 : 0
Item, John Palmer, ...	03 : 10 : 0
Item, Nathaniel Church ₵ Eliz: Soule, ...	10 : 00 : 0
Item, Thomas Starr, ...	02 : 10 : 0
Item, Ephraim Done, ...	01 : 05 : 0
Item, John Knowles, ...	01 : 05 : 0
Item, Christopher Winter, ...	00 : 10 : 0
Item, Edward Sturgis, ...	04 : 00 : 0
Item, William Paule, ...	00 : 10 : 0
Item, more for William Paule, ...	01 : 00 :
Item, John Hathewey, ...	00 : 03 : 0
Item, Josepth Andrews, ...	00 : 05 : 0
William Tubbs, ...	02 : 10 : 0
Josepth Rogers, ...	02 : 10 : 0

Thomas Ingam, ...	00 : 10 : 00
Ralph Earle, ...	01 : 00 : 00
Thomas Pope, ...	00 : 03 : 04
Item, Gyles Rickard, ...	00 : 03 : 04
‡John Briggs,‡ this is remited, ...	00 : 10 : 00
Item, Timothy Hallowey, ...	01 : 00 : 00
Item, John Bayley, ...	00 : 03 : 04
Item, Richard Willis, ...	00 : 03 : 04
Item, Josepth Sauory, ...	00 : 03 : 04
Item, the wife of William Hoskins, ...	01 : 00 : 00
Item, Richard Willis, ...	00 : 10 : 00
Item, Abraham Hedge, ...	02 : 10 : 00
Item, Henery Green, ...	00 : 03 : 04
Item, Samuell Palmer, ...	03 : 00 : 00
Item, by fiue Indians, ...	05 : 00 : 00

1664.

16 June.

The country debter vpon old accounts and otherwise.

Item, one barrell of powder yett due to the countrey stocke.

Item, by Leift̃ Freeman, ... 4ˢ.

Wee doe alow to the Treasurer, for his charges and trouble this last ẽare, twenty fiue pounds.

Debts to the countrey.

	ll s d
From Taunton, ...	00 : 18 : 00
By the farmes, ...	01 : 10 : 00
By a cow in the Treasurers hands, ...	03 : 14 : 0
In peag now in the Treasurers hands, ...	08 : 00

The Fines of June Court, 1664. [*24.]

	ll s d	
TEM, ‡William Paybody,‡	05 : 00 : 00	This is remited.
Item, ‡Leiftenant Nash,‡	03 : 00 : 00	Remited, May, 1665.
Item, John Sprague, ...	03 : 00 : 00	
Item, Gyles Gilbert, ...	01 : 00 : 00	
Item, William Witherell, ...	01 : 00 : 00	
Item, Samuell Linkorne, ...	01 : 00 : 00	
Item, Josepth Gray, ...	01 : 00 : 00	
Item, Gorge Barlow, for Dorcas Presberry, ...	05 : 00 : 00	

1664.   *June 17, 1664.*

17 June.   WARRANTS were issued out for a rate of sixty pound, for the vse o
               the collonie, the one halfe money, the other halfe pease or wheate.

---

27 September.   *September 27ᵗʰ.*

WARRANTS were issued out for a rate of one hundred pounds, for th
intertainment of his maᵗⁱᵉˢ comissioners, to bee payed the one hal
therof in money, and the other halfe to bee payed in wheat, pease, barly, c
Indian corne, soe as the barley was not to exceed the one third of the sai
halfe; the wheat to bee payed att four shillings and six pence the bushell, th
barly att 4ˢ, the pease att three shillinges and six pence, and the Indian a
three shillinges the bushell.

The forfeiture of Elisha Hedge his bonds for the good behauior, the
being 4 pounds therof remited in May, 1665, there remaines . 06 : ^ : ^

October.   *The Fines of October Court, 1664.*

		li	s	
RUHAMAH TURNER, ...	05 : 00 : 0
James Bell, ...	00 : 03 : 0

1664-5.   *The Fines of March Court, 1664.*

March.   THOMAS CUSHMAN, ... 05 :
         Thomas Totman, of Scituate, ... 05 :
         William Randall, ... 00 : 03 : 0
         Thomas Somers, to bee payed by Edward Jenkens, . . . 00 : 05 : 0
         Thomas Linkorn, of Taunton, ... 00 : 03 :
         This is payed att the same Court hee was psented.

Fines of May Court, 1665.

RALPH SMITH, ... 00 : 10 : 00

  James Cole, Junir, ... 00 : 03 : 4

Ephraim Tilson, ... 00 : 03 : 4

June the 9th, 1665.

THE account giuen by the Treasurer vnto Mr Paine, Mr Hawes, Leiftenant Torrey, Mr Richard Bourne, and Nath Warren.

The Treasurers is debtor to the countrey, as appeers by his accounts, the sume of . . . . } 389 : 03 : 11

The Treasurer p contra credit to the countrey by disbursments and debts, as appeers by his accounts, the sume of } 393 : 02 : 07

Soe that there arresteth due to the Treasurer, to ballence the account, the sume of . . . . } 03 : 18 : 08

Debtes due by fines and otherwise to the countrey.

	ll	s	d
Item, Samuell Howland, ...	00	10	00
Item, Wilłam Foard, Senir, ...	00	05	00
Item, Kanelme Winslow, Junir, ...	00	10	00
Item, Thõ Starr, ...	02	10	10
Item, John Knowles, ...	01	05	00
Item, Christopher Winter, ...	00	10	00
Item, Wilłam Tubbs, ...	02	10	00
Item, Thomas Ingam, ...	00	10	00
Item, by Ralph Earle, ...	01	00	00
Item, Thomas Pope, ...	00	03	04
Item, by Gyles Rickard, ...	00	03	04
Item, Timothy Hallowey, ...	01	00	00
Item, John Hathewey, ...	00	03	04
Item, Josepth Sauory, ...	00	03	04
Item, by Abraham Hedge, ...	02	10	00
Item, by fiue Indians, ...	05	00	00
	19	10	02

Item, by Wilt Paybody, ... 05 : 00 : 0

Item, Ruhamah Turner, ... 05 : 00 : 0

Item, by James Bell, ... 00 : 03 : 0

Item, Thomas Cushman, Juni^r, ... 05 : 00 : 0

Item, by Thomas Totman, ... 05 : 00 : 0

Item, by James Cole, Juni^r, ... 00 : 03 : 0

Item, by Ephraim Tilson, ... 00 : 03 : 0

                                        23 : 10 : C

By iron in the Treasurers hand, ... 03 : 13 : C

The countrey is debter, vpon old account, a barrell of powder to th
countrey.

In reference of extreordinary paines and charge the Treasurer hath b
att in the countreyes busines this last yeare, the countrey alloweth vnto hi
the sume of thirty pounds.

The Fines of June Court, 1665.

                                             ll   s

THOMAS LITTLE, ... 01 : 10 : C

   Samuell Norman, ... 00 : 10 : C

   Fifty shillings of the fine of Ruhamah Turner was remitted vnto h
this Court.

   There is a fine of ten pound, vnpayed, due from Robert Whetcome.

---

*The Fines of October Court, 1665.

JOHN BARNES, ... 01 : 00 : C

   Gyles Rickard, Seni^r, ... 00 : 05 : C

   Thomas Lukas, ... 00 : 10 : C

   James Cole, Seni^r, ... 00 : 05 : C

   Thomas Phelpes, ... 00 : 10 : C

   John Shelley, ... 00 : 10 : C

December, 1665.

BRAHAM JACKSON, fined, ...   05 : 00 : 00

June 7ᵗʰ, 1665.

RATE of one hundred and fifty pounds being agreed on to bee leuied on the seuerall townshipps of this jurisdiction, warrants were
ıwith iſued forth for the ſume of forty pounds thereof to bee paied in
ey.

The 3ᵈ of October, 1665.

ARRANTS were issued forth to leuy the hundred and ten pounds
remaineing, which was to bee payed, one third p̃te therof in wheat,
the other two thirds in either wheat, pease, barly, or Indian corne.

The Fines of March Court, 1665.

	ll
HOMAS STARR, ...	05 : 00 : 00
Francis Baker, ...	00 : 03 : 04
John Casley, ...	00 : 03 : 04
John Barrow, ...	00 : 10 : 00
Benjamine Eaton, ...	02 : 00 : 00
Willłam Sabine, ...	02 : 10 : 00
Gorge Barlow,.	00 : 10 : 00
John Crow, ...	00 : 03 : 04

1666.

June the 8th, 1666.

THE account giuen in by the Treasurer vnto Mr Paine, Mr Nathaniel Bacon, and Josias Cooke.

The Treasurer is debter to the countrey, as appeers by his accounts, the sume of . . . . } 188 : 10 : 09

The Treasurer is p contra creditt to the countrey by disbursments and debts, as appeers by his accounts, the sume of . . . . } 205 : 16 : 09

Soe that there aresteth due to the Treasurer, to ballence the account, the sume of . . . . } 17 : 06 : 00

Debts due by rates to the countrey from these pticulars townes of the las yeare.

Item, Sandwich, . 00 : 17 : 08 }
Item, Scittuate, . . 00 : 02 : 00 } in all, ... 5 : 14 : 0
Item, Bridgwater, . 04 : 14 : 06 }

Debtes due by fines and otherwise to the countrey.

Kanelme Winslow, Junior, ... 00 : 10 : 0
Ralph Earle, ... 01 : 00 : 0
Thomas Pope, ... 00 : 03 : 0
Timothy Hallowey, ... 00 : 10 : 0
John Bayley, ... 00 : 03 : 0
Richard Willis, ... 00 : 13 : 0
Thomas Cushman, Juni^r, ... 03 : 00 : 0
Thomas Totman, for committing fornication, fined, . . . 05 : 00 : 0
Thomas Little, ... 01 : 10 : 0
Samuell Norman, ... 00 : 10 : 0
John Barnes, ... 01 : 00 : 0
Thomas Lucas, ... 00 : 10 : 0
Thomas Phelpes, ... 00 : 10 : 0
Abraham Jackson, ... 05 : 00 : 0
Francis Baker, ... 00 : 03 : 0
John Barrow, ... 00 : 10 :
Gorge Barlow, ... 00 : 10 :
James Cole, Seni^r, ... 00 : 05 :
Nathaniel Church, ... 05 : 00 :

Sarah Barstow, allies . . . . }
Sarah Church, ... } 05 : 00 : 00
John Carsley, ... 00 : 03 : 04

The countrey is debtor, vpon old account, a barrell of powder to the ntrey.

The countrey is debtor to Thomas Sauory, ... 7: 1: 1

In reference vnto the paines and charge the Treasurer hath bine att in countreyes busines this last yeare, hee is alowed the sume of twenty fiue nds.

June the 9ᵗʰ, 1666.

WARRANTS was issued forth from the Court to leuy by rate the sume of two hundred and thirty pounds, for the publicke charges of the trey for this yeare, besides the sume of seauen pounds to pay for cer- law bookes belonging to the countrey ; the said sumes to bee payed in ye, as followeth, vizſ : To bee payed one third therof in wheat, or e, or both ; one third in butter, or barly, or both ; and the other third in , Indian corne, peases, or rye, or any of these, or some tarr, prouided it ed not one third p̃te of the last third.

The wheat att four shillings and sixpence a bushell.

The porke att three pound and ten shillinges a barrell.

The barly att four shillings a bushell.

The butter att thirty shillings a firkin, if sizable.

The beife att forty fiue shilling a barrell.

The Indian corne att three shillinges a bushell.

The pease att three shillings and sixpence a bushell.

The rye att three shillinges and sixpence a bushell.

The tarr att nine shillinges a barrell.

To bee deliuered to the Treasurer, or att Boston or att Plymouth, as hee appoint, and the charge of transportation defrayed, by the first weeke in mber next.

e proportions of the seuerall townes to the said rate are as followeth : —

Plymouth, ... 19 : 08 : 06
Duxburrow with Bridgwater, ... 17 : 11 : 09

<u>1 6 6 6.</u>

9 June.

Scittuate, ...	31 : 15 :
Sandwich, ...	17 : 11 :
Taunton, ...	17 : 11 :
Yarmouth, ...	15 · 04 ·
Barnstable, ...	19 : 08 :
Marshfeild, ...	15 : 04 :
Rehoboth, ...	26 : 05 :
Eastham, ...	14 : 03 :
Sowams, ...	07 : 17 :
Dartmouth, ...	10 : 10

The p̃ticulares for which this rate is.

	ll
Item, to the Goũ, ...	50 : 00
Item, to the other majestrates, ...	50 : 00
Item, to the Treasurer in debt, &c̃, ...	42 : 06
Item, to the majestrates table, ...	40 : 00
Item, for law bookes, ...	7 : 00
Item, for Sauory, ...	6 : 13

Memorandum, that the ten pounds alowed to each of the Assistant
bee payed in specye, according to the two last thirds aboue expressed.

June.

The Fines of June Court, 1666.

	ll
ISACKE ROBINSON, Junⁱʳ, and his wife, for comĩiting carnall coppulation, before marryage, after contract, fined, . .	5 : 00
Wilłam Sutton, of Barnstable, for takeing away a Bible out of the meeting house att Barnstable, fined, . . .	1 : 0
And for telling a lye about the same, fined, ...	0 : 10
Job Judkin, for being drunke, ...	0 : 05
Wilłam Willis, for being drunke, ...	0 : 05
Richard Dwelly, for being drunke, ...	0 : 05
John Williams, Junⁱʳ, for his disturbance, and causing great expence to the countrey, in reference to the case about his wife, as is extant in the records of the Court, hee is fined, to the vse of the countrey, the sumĩe of . .	20 : 00

*July the fift, 1666.   **1 6 6 6.**

OHN SIMONS,   ⎫ for abusiue carriages on the Lords day ⎫   s
Edward Laud,   ⎬   att the meeting house att Duxburrow, ⎬ 00 : 10 : 00
and John Cooper, ⎭   fined, each of them, ... ⎭

---

*The Fines of October Court.   October.

[*32.]

		ll	s	d
OHN BATES, of Barnstable,	. . . .	00 : 03 : 04
William Burden, of Barnstable,	. . . .	00 : 03 : 04
More the said William Burden,	. . . .	00 : 05 : 00
John Siluester, of Marshfeild,	. . . .	00 : 10 : 00
John Palmer, Junir, of Scittuate,	. . . .	01 : 00 : 00
John Andrew, of Plymouth,	. . . .	00 : 10 : 00
More the said John Andrew,	. . . .	00 : 03 : 04
Joseph Bartlett, of Plymouth,	. . . .	00 : 03 : 04

The Fines of March Court, 1666.   **1 6 6 6-7.**

ILLAM NICARSON,	. . . .	20 : 00 : 00
Joseph Hallett, of Barnstable,	. . . .	10 : 00 : 00
William Lumpkin, of Yarmouth,	. . . .	00 : 10 : 00
Peter Worden, of Yarmouth,	. . . .	00 : 10 : 00
Jabez Howland,	. . . .	00 : 03 : 04
Joseph Billington,	. . . .	00 : 03 : 04
Arther Howland, Junir,	. . . .	05 : 00 : 00

---

*June sixt, 1667.   **1 6 6 7.**

HE account giuen in by the Treasurer vnto Cornett Robert Studson, Mr
Joseph Laythorp, Mr James Walker, Mr John Bourne, & Richard
.e.

1667.

6 June.

The Treasurer is debter to the country, as appeers by his accounts, the sūme of . . . . } 379 : 2 : ^{ll} ^s

The Treasurer p contra credditt to the countrey by disburŝments, as appeers by his accounts, ... } 378 : 16 :

Soe that there resteth due to the countrey, to ballence the account, the sūme of . . . . } 000 : 06 :

Debts due by rates and fines to the countrey, as followeth.

Kanelme Winslow, Juni^r, ...	00 : 10 :
Ralph Earle, ...	01 : 00 :
John Bayliffe, ...	00 : 03 :
Thomas Totman, ...	05 : 00 :
Samuell Norman, ...	00 : 10 :
Thomas Phelpes, ...	00 : 10 :
Abraham Jackson, ...	04 : 00 :
Francis Baker, ...	00 : 03 :
Wilłam Beerstow, ...	00 : 09 :
Rehoboth rate in part behind, ...	06 : 12 :
Wilłam Sutton, ...	00 : 10 :
John Bates, ...	00 : 03 :
Wilłam Burden, ...	00 : 08 :
John Andrew, ...	00 : 13 :
Joseph Bartlett, ...	00 : 03 :
Jabeze Howland, ...	00 : 03
Joseph Billington, ...	00 : 03
Wilłam Nicarson, ...	20 : 00
Joseph Hallott, ...	10 : 00
Wilłam Lumpken, ...	00 : 10
Arther Howland, Juni^r, ...	05 : 00
Mr Thomas Sumers, ...	00 : 17
Rest due for land att Rehoboth, ...	27 : 18

[*34.]   *The countrey is debtor vpon old account one barrell of powder for countreyes stocke.

Vpon new account as followeth.

To Mr Vsher, for bookes, in siluer, ...	07 : 00
To Mr John Winslow, of Boston, ...	31 : 09
To Mr Fuller, ...	04 : 09
To Widdow Abell, ...	11 : 04

To Mr James Walker,	01 : 00 : 00	
To William Harvey,	05 : 08 : 00	
To Abraham Sampson,	00 : 12 : 00	
To James Cole, Seni^r,	00 : 08 : 00	
Memorand, Arther Harris,	01 : 10 : 00	
To Joseph Laythorp,	02 : 00 : 0	
Wee judge meet to alow the major,	05 : 00 : 00	
To Capt Southworth,	02 : 00 : 00	
To the Treasurer, for his goeing to Rehoboth,	03 : 00 : 00	
To the cornett,	02 : 00 : 00	
For John Rogers, of Marshfeild,	00 : 10 : 00	
For John Dingleys horse,	00 : 10 : 06	
For Mr Aldens horse,	00 : 13 : 06	
For Robert Stanford,	00 : 10 : 00	
For Edward Southworth,	00 : 09 : 00	
For Francis Combe,	00 : 15 : 00	
For Joseph Howland,	00 : 15 : 00	
For William Clarke,	00 : 18 : 00	
For Joseph Bartlett,	00 : 15 : 00	
For Joseph Wadsworth,	00 : 10 : 00	
For John Tisdall, Juni^r,	00 : 03 : 00	
For John Richmond,	00 : 05 : 00	
Arther Harris,	00 : 10 : 00	
Roger Annadowne,	00 : 08 : 00	
Nicholas Iyde,	00 : 10 : 00	
Gorge Robinson,	00 : 06 : 00	
Goodman Fallowells mare,	00 : 07 : 06	
Dockt^r Fuller,	05 : 00 : 00	

1667. 6 June.

In reference vnto the paines and charge the Treasurer hath bin att in e countreyes busines, this last yeare, hee is allowed the sume of twenty ght pounds, being his paines hath bine extreordinary.

The Fines of June Court, 1667.

June. [*36.]

	ll	s	d
OSEPH BURGE, of Sandwich,	01	00	00
Samuell Jackson, of Scittuate,	00	03	04

16

The Fines of July Court, 1667.

MR MYLES, ...   05 :

Mr Browne, ...   05 :

Mr Tanner, ...   01 :

Samuell Fuller, the son of Samuell Fuller, of Barnstable, fined,   01 : 00 : 00

Richard Dwelley, ...   00 : 10 : 00

Sarah Smith, of Barnstable, ...   05 : 00 : 00

Danah Siluester, ...   10 : 00 : 00

The Fines of October Court, 1667.

SIX Indians, viz§, Lawrance, Quequequantest, James, Moses, Wamant and Monchassucke, for being p̄tenors in the imbezeling away of liquor taken out of the boate of Simon Steuens, att Cape Codd, were centanced b⸱ the Court to pay ten pound, to be deliuered to Leif͠t Freeman, att his hous⸱ att Eastham, in Indian corne, or porke, or feathers, for the collonies vse, be⸱ twixt this Court and the first day of May next insueing the date heerof.

James Doughty, for his eregulare carryage in indeauoring to releas⸱ Thomas Summers out of prison, is fined forty shillinges.

Abraham Sutliffe, for being drunke, fined, ...   00 : 05 : 0

And for expressing vngodly speeches in his drunkenes̃, fined,   04 : 00 : 0

William Nicarson, for sending scandalous writtinges to Generall Nicolls, is fined, ...   } 10 : 00 : 0

Robert Eldred, for consenting to one of the said writtings, fined, ...   } 05 : 00 : 0

Nathaniel Couell, for the same, fined, ...   05 : 00 : 0

Thomas Delanoy, and his now wife, for comīting carnall coppulation before mariage, fined, ...   } 10 : 00 : 0

The Fines of March Court, 1667.

JOSEPH TURNER, for breakeing the kingess peace, fined,   00 : 03 : 0

Joseph Turner, for publishing a pnisious writing, fined, .   05 : 00 : 0

Joseph Bartlett, for breakeing the kinges peace, fined, . .   00 : 03 : 0

Francis, the Indian sachem of Nausett, for his abusing of Captaine Allin, by vnhumaine and beastly carriages towards him, when hee was cast on shore att Cape Codd, ... } fined, 10 : 00 : 00

---

*Att the Court held att Plymouth the fift of June, 1667.

WARRANTS were issued out from the Court, to leuy, by rate, vpon the seuerall townships of this gou^rment, the sume of two hundred eighty x pound eighteen shillinges and eight pence, for the publicke charges of the ountrey, to be payed, one quarter p̄te therof in wheat or butter, the wheat att ᵃ 6ᵈ a bushell, and the butter att six pence a pound, and another quarter p̄te ᴉerof in porke or barly, or both, the barly att 4ˢ a bushell, the porke att ᵵree pound a barrell, or two pence halfe peny a pound, to be payed by the ᵳst of October next, and the remaining halfe to be payed in Indian corne att ᵵree shilling a bushell, or beife att forty shillings a barrell, or sixteen shil-ᵏgs an hundred, or rye att three shillinges and six pence a bushell, or pease ᵗ three shillings a bushell, or tarr att eight shillings and six pence a barrell ; ᵎ any or all of these ; and this payment to be payed by the first of Aprill ᵉxt ; all the aboue named sumes to be payed to the Treasurer, or where hee ᵴall appoint, prouided it be att Plymouth or Boston.

The proportions of the said sume, as it was leuied vpon the seuerall ᵂwnes, is as followeth.

Plymouth, ...	25 : 18 : 00
Duxburrow, ...	23 : 11 : 04
Scittuate, ...	42 : 07 : 00
Sandwich, ...	23 : 11 : 04
Taunton, ...	23 : 11 : 04
Yarmouth, ...	21 : 13 : 04
Barnstable, ...	25 : 18 : 00
Marshfeild, ...	21 : 13 : 04
Rehoboth, ...	25 : 07 : 00
Eastham, ...	18 : 18 : 00
Sowams, ...	10 : 10 : 00
Dartmouth, ...	14 : 00 : 00
	286 : 18 : 08

*June the fourth, 1668.

4 June.

[*39.]

T HE account giuen in by the Treasurer vnto Leiftenant Morton, Leif tenant Hunt, Leiftenant Laythorp, James Walker, John Willis, an Daniel Cole.

The Treasurer is debter to the countrey, as appeer by his } 479 : 06 : 0
account, the sume of . . . .

The Treasurer pro contra creditt vnto the countrey, by dis- } 478 : 08 : 0
bursments, as appeers by his accounts, the sume of . .

Soe that there rests due to the countrey, to ballence the } 000 : 18 :
account, ...

Debts due to the countrey by rates and fines, as followeth.

Imp\`r\`, for rates, ... 13 : 16 : 0

Item, in a mare and neate cattle, ... 11 : 15 : 0

Ralph Earle, ... 01 : 00 : 0

John Bayliffe, of Scittuate, ... 00 : 03 : 0

Item, Thomas Totman, ... 05 : 00 : 0

Item, William Barstow, his debt, ... 00 : 09 : C

Item, John Andrews, ... 00 : 13 : 0

Item, William Nicarson, ... 20 : 00 : C

Item, Joseph Hallett, ... 02 : 15 : C

Item, Arther Howland, Juni\`r\`, ... 05 : 00 : C

Item, Thomas Summers, ... 00 : 17 :

Item, Samuell Jackson, ... 00 : 03 : C

Item, Sarah Smith, of Barnstable, ... 05 : 00 : C

Item, Dinah Siluester, ... 07 : 15 :

Item, James Doughtey, ... 02 : 00 :

Itẽ, Abraham Sutliffe, by bill, ... 04 : 05 :

Itẽ, Robert Eldred, ... 20 : 00 :

Itẽ, Thomas Dellano, ... 01 : 00 :

Item, Joseph Turner, ... 05 : 03 :

Item, Joseph Bartlett, ... 00 : 03 :

Item, by Francis, the Indian sachem, ... 10 : 00 :

Item, M\`r\` Myles, ... 05 : 00 :

Item, M\`r\` Browne, ... 05 : 00 :

Item, M\`r\` Tanner, ... 01 : 00 :

Remaines due of the forty pound from the Indians, . . . 25 : 10 :

The countrey vpon old account, one barrell of powder for the countreyes ᵒcke.

John Tisdall, on a voyage to Rehoboth, ...	00 : 03 : 00
John Richmond, on the same account, ...	00 : 06 : 00
Doctor Fuller, ...	04 : 00 : 00

In reference vnto the paines and charge the Treasurer hath bin att in the ᵃntreyes busines this last yeare, as also that it rather increaseth then demin-eth, wee thinke it meet hee should be alowed the sume of twenty eight ᵃnds.

---

*Att the Court held att Plymouth in June 4ᵗʰ, Anno 1668.

WARRANTS were issued out from the Court for to leuy a rate of one hundred seauenty nine pound nine shillings and six pence, for the ʳges of the countrey, for the insueing yeare, besides the officers wages, to ᵖayed, one quarter p̃te therof in wheat or butter, the wheat att four shil-ᵗs and six pence a bushell, and the butter att six pence a pound, and an-ᵉr quarter p̃te therof in porke, att three pound a barrell, or two pence ᵉ peney a pound, to be payed by the first of October next, and the re-ᵐing halfe to be payed in Indian corne, att three shillings a bushell, or ᵉ att forty shillings a barrell, or rye att three shillinges and sixpence a ᵃell, or pease att three shillinges a bushell, or tarr att eight shillings and ᵉence a barrell, to be payed by the first of Aprill next ; all the aboue ᵉd payments to be payed to the Treasurer, or where hee shall appoint, soe ᵉ att Boston or Plymouth, by the times aboue mensioned.

The Fines of June Court, 1668.

	ll	s	d
APTAINE NATHANIEL THOMAS, fined the sume of	03	00	00
Thomas Starr, ...	00	05	00
John Mathews, ...	00	05	00
John Haddawey, ...	00	05	00
Jededia Lumbert, ...	05	00	00
Edward Gray, ...	00	10	00

1668.

4 June.

Nathaniel Soule, ...	00 : 10 :
Mary Phillips, ...	00 : 03 :
Jane Hallowey, ...	00 : 03 :
July, 1668 Richard Dwelly, fined, ...	01 : 00 :

The proportions of the rate, as it was leuied of the seuerall townes this jurisdiction, to answare in reference vnto the sume aboue expressed, followeth.

Plymouth	16 : 01 :
Duxburrow, ...	07 : 11 :
Scittuate, ...	26 : 15 :
Sandwich, ...	15 : 01 :
Taunton, ...	15 : 01 :
Yarmouth, ...	12 : 14 :
Barnstable, ...	16 : 01 :
Marshfeild, ...	12 : 14 :
Rehoboth, ...	22 : 09 :
Eastham, ...	11 : 18 :
Bridḡwater, ...	07 : 11 :
Dartmouth, ...	08 : 15 :
Swansey, ...	06 : 14

October.

[*41.]

The Fines of October Court, 1668.

M**R** JOSIAS WINSLOW, Seni**r**, ...	00 : 3
Ralph Earle, ...	00 : 5
John Cobb, of Taunton, ...	01 : 00
Abraham Sampson, Juni**r**, ...	00 : 10
Thomas Perrey, ...	01 : 00
Henery Clarke, ...	00 : 05
Sarah Barlow, ...	00 : 10
Marcye Bartlett, ...	00 : 10
Edward Crowell, ...	06 : 00
James Maker, ...	06 : 00
Richard Dwelley, forfeiture of a bond, ...	10 :

The Fines of March Court.

JAMES COLE, and Mary, his wife, fined, ... 06 : 00 : 00

James Clarke, ... 00 : 10 : 00

Phillip Dotterich, ... 00 : 10 : 00

Mary Ryder, ... 00 : 10 : 00

Hester Wormall, ... 00 : 10 : 00

John Low, ... 00 : 05 : 00

John Bryant, of Plymouth, ... 00 : 10 : 00

Christopher Blake, ... 00 : 05 : 00

Caleb Lumbert, ... 00 : 03 : 04

Wiłłam Thomas, ... 00 : 03 : 04

Samuell Arnold, Juni[r], ... 00 : 03 : 04

Richard Berrey, Seni[r], ... 00 : 05 : 00

Jededia Lumbert, ... 00 : 05 : 00

Benjamine Lumbert, ... 00 : 05 : 00

James Maker, ... 00 : 05 : 00

---

*July the 8th, 1669.

THE accoumpt giuen in by the Treasurer vnto Daniell Cole, Isacke Chittenden, William Harvey, and John Thacher, and Thomas Huckens : —

The Treasurer is debetor to the countrey, as by his account, ... } 430 : 12 : 03

The Treasurer is p̄ contra creditt to the countrey, by disburs̄ments, ... } 429 : 03 : 04

Soe ther̄ rests due to the countrey from the Treasurer, to ballence the account, ... } 01 : 08 : 11

Item, due to the countrey also in debts and corne, . . . 28 : 15 : 00

Item, more, two hatts, ... 00 : 08 : 00

Item, fines due from Ralph Earle, ... 01 : 00 : 00

From John Bayleiffe, of Scittuate, ... 00 : 03 : 04

From Thomas Totman, of Scittuate, ... 05 : 00 : 00

From Wiłłam Nicarson, ... 20 : 00 : 00

From Joseph Hallott, for p̄te of his fine, ... 02 : 15 : 00

From Arther Howland, Juni[r], ... 05 : 00 : 00

1669.

8 July.

From Samuell Jackson, of Scittuate,	00 : 03 : 04
From Robert Eldred, of Mannamoiett,	20 : 00 : 00
From Joseph Bartlett,	00 : 03 : 04
‡From Fāncis, the Indian sachem,	06 : 03 : 00
From Mr Myles,	05 : 00 : 00
From John Hathewey, of Yarmouth,	00 : 05 : 00
From Nathaniel Soule, of Duxburrow,	00 : 10 : 00
From Mary Phillips, of Taunton,	00 : 03 : 04
From Jane Hallowey, of Taunton,	00 : 03 : 04
From Mr Josias Winslow,	00 : 03 : 04
From Mr Ralph Earle,	00 : 05 : 00
From John Cobb, of Taunton,	01 : 00 : 00
From Henery Clarke, of Duxburrow,	00 : 05 : 00
From Abraham Sampson, of Duxburrow,	00 : 05 : 00
From James Cole and Mary, his wife,	06 : 00 : 00
From John Bryant, Seni^r, of Plymouth,	00 : 10 : 00
From Wiłłam Thomas, of Marshfeild,	00 : 03 : 0
From Benajah Lumbert, of Barnstable,	00 : 05 : 0
From Richard Dwelley, of Scittuate,	01 : 00 : 0
From Richard Dwelley, of Scittuate, more,	10 : 00 : 0
From Richard Berrey,	00 : 05 : 0
From Jededia Lumbert,	00 : 05 : 0

This Mr Freeman stands engaged for. The last, Mr Hinckley stands engaged for.

In reference vnto the paines and charge the Treasurer hath bine att the countreyes busineʒ this last yeare, wee thinke meet hee should be alow twenty eight pounds.

THOMAS HUCKENS.

July.
[*43.]

*July, 1669.

A RATE ordered by the Court as followeth, —

	ll oo
Item, for the Gou^r,	50 : 00 :
Item, for the majestrates,	50 : 00 :
Item, for the major,	10 : 00 :
Item, for Mistris Bradford,	12 : 00 :
Item, for the majestrates table,	30 : 00 :
Item, for Sauory,	06 : 13
	158 : 13

The Fines of October, 1669.

JOHN EWEN, ... 2 : 00 : 00
Ephraim Doan, ... 1 : 00 : 00
Gorge Russell, ... 00 : 10 : 00
Robert Laurance, ... 00 : 08 : 00
Thomas Starr, ... 02 : 00 : 00

June, 1669.

WILŁAM RANDALL fined fiue pounds to the vse of the collonie.

The Fines of March Court, 1669.

	ll	s	d
JOHN TILSON,	00	03	04

JOHN TILSON, ... 00 : 03 : 04
John Loe, ... 00 : 10 : 00
Nathaniel Fitsrandall, ... 02 : 02 : 00
Christopher Blake, ... 00 : 05 : 00

*June, 1670.

THE accoumpt giuen in by the Treasurer to Richard Bourne, James Walker, and Thomas Huckens, as followeth : —

The Treasurer was found debtor to the collonie as by his coumpt, ... } 319 : 10 : 10

The Treasurer p contra creditt, ... 288 : 14 : 01

The Treasurer is debtor to ballence the account, . . . 20 : 16 : 09

Item, more from John Bayley, of Scittuate, ... 00 : 03 : 04
Item, Thomas Totman, of Scittuate, ... 05 : 00 : 00
Item, Joseph Hollett, of Barnstable, for p̃te of his fine, . . 02 : 15 : 00

17

1670.

Item, Samuell Jackson, of Scittuate,	00 : 03 : 0
Item, John Hathewey, of Yarmouth,	00 : 05 : 0
Item, Mary Phillips, of Taunton,	00 : 03 : 0
Item, Mr Josias Winslow, of Marshfeild,	00 : 03 : 0
Item, Ralph Earle, of Dartmouth,	00 : 05 : C
Itē, John Cobb, of Taunton,	01 : 00 : C
Item, Wilłam Thomas, Marshfeild,	00 : 03 : C
Itē, Christopher Blake,	00 : 05 : C
Iť, Wilłam Randall, of Scittuate,	05 : 00 :
Itē, Richard Berrey, of Yarmouth,	00 : 05 : C

Debts behind vpon excise accoumpt.

Item, from Wilłam Swift, of Sandwich,	04 : 00 :
Item, from John Sprague, of Duxburrow,	01 : 00 :
Item, from Wilłam Harvey,	01 : 00 :
Item, from John Miller, of Yarmouth,	01 : 00 :
Item, from Edward Sturgis, of Yarmouth,	01 : 00 :
Item, from Arther Harris, of Bridḡwater,	01 : 00 :
Item, Thomas Huckens,	00 : 10 :

Due to James Walker for two journeys, one to Plymouth, and one to Mount Hope, } 01 : 04 :

And for Leifť Nash to Mount Hope,

And to Mr Treasurer for his sallary the last yeare, . . 28 : 00 :

By vs,   RICHARD BOURNE,
JAMES WALKER.

[*45.]   *The charge to be raised by rate for this psent yeare for defraying of knowne expenses.

	ll	s
Item, for the Gour and Assistants,	100 : 0 :
Item, for the Major,	10 : 0 :
Item, for nessesaries to accomodate the majestrates as Mistris Bradford did, }	12 : 0 :
Item, for the majestrates table,	30 : 0 :
Item, for the vnder marshall,	06 : 13 :
Item, for the officers wages,	40 : 0 :

Warrants were issued out from this Court to leuy a rate of one hundred a sixty pounds twelue shillings and eight pence, for the charges of the collo

r the ensueing yeare, besides the officers wages ; the aforesaid sume to be
ayed, the one halfe in wheat, barly, and butter, the wheat att four shillings
bushell, the barly att three shillings and sixpence a bushell, and the butter
t fiue pence a pound ; the other halfe, one halfe of it to be payed in Indian
orne, att three shillings a bushell, and the other halfe in rye and pease, the
e att three shillings and six pence a bushell, and the pease att three shil-
ngs a bushell ; all which payements to be good and marchantable, and to be
liuered to the Treasurer, or where hee shall appoint, soe it be att Boston or
ymouth, the first halfe by the 15th of October next, and the latter halfe by
e first of Aprill next, and the charge of transportation defrayed.

The proportions of the aboue written charge to be leuied by rate on each
wne of this jurisdiction.

	ll	s	d
Plymouth,	14	16	0
Duxburrow,	06	14	8
Bridgwater,	06	14	8
Scittuate,	24	04	0
Taunton,	13	09	4
Sandwich,	13	09	4
Yarmouth,	10	19	4
Barnstable,	14	16	0
Marshfeild,	10	19	4
Rehoboth,	20	04	00
Eastham,	10	06	00
Swansey,	06	00	00
Dartmouth,	08	00	00

The Fines of June Court, 1670.

ONATHAN HATCH, for selling liquor to the Indians, fined,	03 : 00 : 00
Samuell Chanddler, for being drunke,	00 : 05 : 00
John Sprague, for suffering Samuell Chandler to be drunke his house,	00 : 05 : 00
Thomas Pope, for villifying the minnestry,	00 : 10 : 00
Thomas Hughes, for breaking the Kinges peace,	00 : 03 : 04
Thomas Lucas, for breaking the Kinges peace,	00 : 03 : 04
Samuell Norman, for breaking the Kinges peace,	00 : 03 : 04
Lydia Tayler, for breaking the Kinges peace,	00 : 03 : 04

1 6 7 0.   *The Fines of July Court, 1670.*

July.

ELISHA HEDGE, for selling liquor to the Indians, fined,   02 : 10 : 0
Abisha Marchant, for being in bed with Mary Jones, . 02 : 00 : 0

October.   *The Fines of October Court, 1670.*
[*46.]

		ll	s
WILLAM ROGERS, ...	05 : 00 : 0
Edward Jenkens, for his daughter, ...	03 : 00 : 0
Jabez Snow and his wife, ...	10 : 00 : 0
John Cooke, ...	00 : 10 : 0
Willam Kinsman, ...	00 : 10 : 0

---

1 6 7 0-1.   *The Fines of March Court, 1670.*

March.

JOHN SUTTON, ...   02 : 00 :
James Pursevall, ... , . . .   05 : 00 :
Willam Hedge, ...   01 : 10 :
John Gray, ...   01 : 10 :
Edward Sturgis, Juni^r, ...   01 : 10 :
John Gray, more, ...   00 : 03 :
An Indian called Will, living about Yarmouth, fined, . .   01 : 00 :
Willam Griffin, ...   00 : 03 :
Richard Michell, ...   00 : 03 :
Nathaniel Tilden, ...   02 : 00 :
John Sprague, ...   00 : 05 :
Richard Tayler *Tayler*, ...   00 : 10 :

---

1 6 7 1.   *June, 1671.*

June.
[*48.]

MR TREASURERS accoumpt giuen into to Leift Morton, Ensig
Eames, Willam Paybody, and Thomas Huckens, as followeth : —
The Treasurer was found debter to the collonie as by his } ll   s
accoumpt, ... } 330 : 14 :

The Treasurer contra creditt, ...   308 : 10 : 07

The Treasurer is debter to ballence the account, ...   22 : 03 : 10

Item, more by Mr Bacon for Abraham Hedge, ...   00 : 03 : 00   June.

Item, more from John Bayley, of Scittuate, ...   000 : 03 : 04

Item, from Mary Phillipes, of Taunton, ...   000 : 03 : 04

Item, from Mr Josias Winslow, Seni^r, ...   000 : 03 : 04

Item, from Ralph Earle, of Dartmouth, ...   000 : 05 : 00

Item, from Jonathan Hatch, of Saconeeset, ...   03 : 00 : 00

Item, from Edward Jenkens, of Scittuate, for his daughter,   03 : 00 : 00

Item, from Wilłam Hinksman, of Marshfeild, ...   000 : 10 : 00

Item, from John Sutton, of Scittuate, ...   02 : 00 : 00

Item, from John Gray, of Yarmouth, ...   01 : 10 : 00

Item, from Edward Sturgis, Juni^r, ...   01 : 10 : 00

Item, from Wilłam Hedge, ...   01 : 10 : 00

Item, from John Gray, for Indian Will, ...   01 : 00 : 00

Item, from John Sprague, of Duxburrow, ...   000 : 05 : 00

Item, from Leift̄ Laythorp, 30^s, Wilłam Swift, 10^s, wid- ⎫
ɔw Barstow, 30^s, ...⎬   03 : 10 : 00
                                                      ⎭

Item, from Gorge Vaughan for excise, 20^s.

The country debtor to Mr Treasurer for his sallery last ⎫
ⸯare, ...⎬   28 : 00 : 00
                                              ⎭

To Jonathan Hatch, ...   01 : 01 : 00

To Robert Finney, ...   000 : 06 : 00

To Joseph Waterman, ...   000 : 15 : 00

To Edward Southworth, ...   000 : 15 : 00

To Mr Treasurer goeing to Mount Hope, ...   001 : 10 : 00

To Capt̄ Bradford, ...   001 : 10 : 00

To Mr Treasurer twise to Taunton, ...   02 : 00 : 00

To Ensigne Aldin, 9^s shillings or a gun, ...   00 : 09 : 00

To Thomas Huckens, ...   00 : 01 : 06

To Wilłam Witherell, ...   00 : 03 : 00

To the Gou^r and Major, 40^s, ...   02 : 00 : 00

To Mr Williams, 20^s, Gorge Vaughan, 12^s, Tho: West, 4^s,   01 : 16 : 00

EPHRAIM MORTON,
MARKE EAMES,
WILŁAM PAYBODY,
THOMAS HUCKENS.

1671.   *June, 1671.

June.
[*49.]

A TT this Court warrants were issuẽ for the leuying of 296¹¹ : 13 : 04 b͟
rate for the charges of the collonie, to be raised by rate for thi
following yeare.

Item, for the Gouʳ and Majestrates, ...	100 : 00 : 0
Item, for the Major, ...	10 : 00 : 0
Item, for nessesaries to accõmodate the majestrates, . . .	12 : 00 : 0
Item, for the majestrates table, ...	30 : 00 : 0
Item, for the vnder marshall, ...	06 : 13 : 0
Item, for the officers sallery, ...	40 : 00 : 0
Iť, for the charges of the comissioners theire sitting this yeare att Plymouth, ... }	80 : 00 : 0
Iť, for the printing of the booke of lawes, ...	20 : 00 : 0
Item, for monys to provide bread for the goeing forth on the expedition against the Indians, ... }	10 : 00 : 0

308 : 13 :

The abouesaid sumẽ (soe much of it as concerned the treasure) is to b
payed tõ thirds therof in wheat, and barly, and butter, or mony; the whe͟
att fiue shillings a bushell, the barly att three shillings 6ᵈ a bushell, the butte
att fiue pence a pound; the other third pᵗᵉ in Indian corne, rye, and pease
the pease and rye att three shillings six pence a bushell, the Indian att thre
shillings a bushell. The first payment to be payed att or before the first o
October next; the second by the first of Aprill next.

The proportions leuied on the seuerall townes.

	To the Treasurer.		To the Officer
	ll s		Sallerys.
Plymouth, ...	24 : 10	. . . .	03 : 14 : 0
Duxburrow, . . .	11 : 09	. . . .	01 : 13 : (
Bridg̃water, ...	11 : 09	. . . .	01 : 13 : (
Scittuate, ...	40 : 16	. . . .	06 : 01 : (
Taunton, ...	22 : 17	. . . .	03 : 07 : (
Sandwich, ...	22 : 17	. . . .	03 : 07 :
Yarmouth, . . .	18 : 10	. . . .	02 : 17 :
Barnstable, ...	24 : 10	. . . .	03 : 14 :
Marshfeild, ...	18 : 17	. . . .	02 : 17 : (
Rehoboth, ...	33 : 16	. . . .	05 : 01 :

Eastham,	. . . . 16 : 10	. . . .	02 : 14 : 00
Swansey,	. . . . 11 : 09	. . . .	01 : 10 : 00
Dartmouth,	. . . . 14 : 12	. . . .	02 : 00 : 00
Middleber,	. . . . 06 : 12	. . . .	00 : 00 : 00

1671.

June.

$$278 : 14$$
$$42 : 13$$
$$236 : 01$$

*The Fines of June Court, 1671.

[*50.]

JOHN GRAY, for swearing prophanly, fined, ... 00 : 05 : 00

Samuell Mathewes, for sayleing from Yarmouth to Boston, n y^e Lords day, ... } 01 : 10 : 00

Nathaniell Soule, being detected for telling seuerall lyes, ned, ... } 00 : 00 : 00

James Cole, Seni^r, for being drunke the second time, fined, 00 : 10 : 00

Joseph Ramsden, for being found drunke the second time, ned, ... } 00 : 10 : 00

Willam Walker, for telling a lye, fined, ... 00 : 10 : 00

Walter Winser, for selling liquors to the Indians, fined, . 01 : 10 : 00

The Fines of October Court, 1671.

October.

CYLES RICKARD, Seni^r, for selling syder to the Indians, 00 : 10 : 00

‡John Ottis, for selling syder without order from the ourt, or to appeer to answare for the same att the Court, . } 02 : 00 : 00‡

John Bucke, for comiting fornication with Mary Attkin- n, fined, ... } 10 : 00 : 00

Mary Attkinson, for comitting fornication with John Buck, 10 : 00 : 00

1671-2. *The Fines of March Court, 1671.*

March.

SAMUELL ARNOLD, Juni^r, for comitting fornication with ⎫
Holmes, before marriage, ... ⎬ 05 : 00 : 00
. . . . ⎭

Holmes, for comitting fornication with Samuel Ar- ⎫
nold, Juni^r, ... ⎬ 05 : 00 : 00
. . . . ⎭

Josias Palmer, for speaking opprobriously of Mr Wither- ⎫
ley's church, ... ⎬ 00 : 10 : 00
. . . . ⎭

John Loe, for prophaning the Lords day, fined, ... 02 : 00 : 00

Samuell Packer, Seni^r, for selling liqoor and syder to the ⎫
Indians, ... ⎬ 01 : 00 : 00
. . . . ⎭

James Walker, Seni^r, for braking order about a stray horse, 01 : 00 : 00

Joseph Harding, for abusing the constable of Eastham, in ⎫
the execution of his office, fined, ... ⎬ 00 : 10 : 00
. . . . ⎭

1672. **June the 7th, 1672.*

7 June.
[*52.]

MR TREASURERS accoumpt giuen in to Leiftenant Morton, Daniel
Smith, Thomas Huckens, and John Tompson.

The Treasurer was found debter to the collonie by his ⎫
accoumpt, ... ⎬ 485 : 07 : 07
. . . . ⎭

The Treasurer p contra, creditt, ... 482 : 08 : 05

The Treasurer debtor to ballence, ... 02 : 19 : 1

Due to the contry.

By p̃te of Swanseys rate, ... 03 : 16 : 0

Item, by p̃te of Barnstable rate, when Mr Thomas Allin ⎫
was constable, ... ⎬ 01 : 08 : 0
. . . . ⎭

Item, by 21 bushells of Indian corne, ... 03 : 03 : 0

Item, by Mr Bacon, for Abraham Hedge, ... 00 : 03 : 0

Item, from John Bayley, of Scittuate, ... 00 : 03 : 0

Item, from Mr Josias Winslow, Seni^r, ... 00 : 03 : 0

Item, from Jonathan Hatch, besides his goeing to Taunton, 01 : 19 : 0

Item, from John Sutton, of Scittuate, ... 02 : 00 : 0

Item, from Nathaniel Soule, ... 03 : 19 : 0

Item, from John Loe, ... 01 : 00 : 00
Item, Samuell Packer, Seni^r, of Bridgwater, ... 01 : 00 : 00
Item, by p̃te of Dartmouth rate, ... 00 : 15 : 00
The countrey debtor to Mr Treasurer for his sallery the } ll 30 :
st yeare, ...

1 6 7 2.

7 . June.

June the 7th, 1672.

RDERED by the deputies that the Gou^r, the major, and Mr Hinckley, shall have, for theire care, paines, and charge, about p^rusing and vising our lawes, the sume of fifty shillings for each of them ; and more to Hinckly, for transcribing the lawes, thirty fiue shillings ; and to M^r nckley, for goeing to Rhode Iland, twenty shillinges ; and to Mr Southworth, the same journey, the same sume of twenty shillinges, to be payed out of treasury.

*The Fines of June Court, 1672.

[*53.]

ARY CHURCHILL, for comitting fornication, fined, . 06 : 00 : 00
‡Dorcas Billington, for comitting fornication, fined, } 05 : 00 : 00‡
e was whipt,‖ . . . .
Susannah Turner, for comitting fornication, fined, . . . 08 : 00 : 00
Daniel Cole, son of Job Cole, for cursing, fined, . . . 00 : 10 : 00

July.
[*54.]

*July, 1672.

ARRANTS were issued out to the seuerall plantations of this gou^rment to leuy the charges to be raised by rate for this p^rsen^t e as followeth : —

Item, for the Gou^r and Assistants, ... 100 : 00 : 00
Item, for the Major, 10^{ll}, and for the Treasurer 30^{ll}, . . 40 : 00 : 00
Item, for nessesaries to accomodate to majestrates table, . 12 : 00 : 00

18

1672.

July.

Item, to entertaine the comissioners, ... 80 : 00 : 0

Item, for Thomas Sauory, ... 06 : 13 : 0

Item, for the officers wages, ... 40 :

Two thirds wherof to be payed in wheat, barly, butter, or mony; the wheat att 4ˢ 6ᵈ a bushell, the barly att three shillings and six pence a bushell and the butter att fiue pence a pound. The rest in rye att three shillin and six pence a bushell, and pease att three shillinges and six pence a bushell the Indian corne att three shillings a bushell.

The proportions to be payed by the seuerall Townes.

	ll	s		To the Office Wages. ll	
Plymouth, ...	24 : 10		. . . .	03 : 14 :
Duxberry, ...	11 : 09		. . . .	01 : 13 :
Bridgwater,. . . .	11 : 09		. . . .	01 : 13 :
Scittuate, ...	40 : 16		. . . .	06 : 01 :
Taunton, ...	22 : 17		. . . .	03 : 07 :
Sandwich, ...	22 : 17		. . . .	03 : 07 :
Yarmouth, ...	18 : 10		. . . .	02 : 17 :
Barnstable, ...	24 : 10		. . . .	03 : 14 :
Marshfeild, ...	18 : 12		. . . .	02 : 17 :
Rehoboth, ...	33 : 16		. . . .	05 : 01 :
Eastham, ...	16 : 10		. . . .	02 : 14 :
Swansey, ...	11 : 09		. . . .	01 : 10 :
Dartmouth, ...	14 : 12		. . . .	02 : 00 :
Middleberry, . . .	06 : 12		. . . .	
	278 : 09				

The first payment to be payed to the Treasurer att or before the first October next, the latter by the first of Aprill next.

October.

[*55.]

The Fines of October Court, 1672.

WILŁAM MAKEPEACE, for selling liqoor to the Indians, fined fiue pounds, ... } ll 5 : 00

Jabeze Lumbard, for selling liquor to the Indians, fined
fifty shillings, ... } 2 : 10

Thomas Jones, for being drunke the second time, fined ten illinges, ... } 00 : 10 :

Edward Coleman, for cursing, fined fiue shillings, . . . 00 : 5 :

The Fines of March Court, 1672.

	ll	s	d
BRAHAM HEDGE, ...	05	00	00
Abisha Marchant and his wife, ...	10	00	00
Allexander Kanudah, ...	00	03	04
Francis Curtice, ...	02	10	00
Gorge Russell, of Duxburrow, ...	00	10	00
Thomas Nicolls, ...	00	10	00
Robert Sanford, ...	00	05	00

---

*June the 7th, 1673.

THE Treasurers accoumpt taken by vs whose names are vnderwritten, ordered therto by the Court : —

The Treasurer was found debter to the collonie by the acmpt, ... } 476 : 19 : 7

The Treasurer p contra creditt, ... 429 : 08 : 11

The Treasurer debter to ballence, ... 47 : 10 : 08

The collonie debtor to the Treasurer for his sallery, as wee ceiue, ... } 030 : 00 : 00

To ballence, ... 17 : 10 : 8

More, in debts vngathered.

As by bill from ⌃ Richmond, of Taunton, of lips fine, ... } 39 : 0 : 00

More, in Fines due to the Collonie.

By Daniell Cole, Junir, ... 00 : 10 : 00

By Wilłam Makepeace, ... 05 : 00 : 00

1673.

By Jabez Lumbert, ... 02 : 10 : 0

By Thomas Jones, of Taunton, ... 00 : 04 : 0

By Francis Curtice, ... 02 : 10 : 0

By Mr Bacon for Abraham Hedge, ... 00 : 03 : 0

By Thomas Packer, of Bridgwater, ... 01 : 00 : 0

By the Squa Sachem, of Saconett, ... 50 : 00 : 0

The totall sume due to the collonie, ... 118 : 14 :

> JOHN FREEMAN,
> EPHRAIM MORTON,
> MARKE EAMES,
> JOHN TOMPSON,
> THOMAS HOWES.

The Fines of June Court, 1673.

ISACK NEGERS, for breach of peace, fined, ... 00 : 03 :

Wilłam Bassett, for breach of peace, in striking 2 ladds, fined, ... } 00 : 05 :

The Fines of October Court, 1673.

JOHN KNOWLMAN, for being drunke, fined, ... 00 : 05 :

Benjamine Chettenden, for being drunke, fined, . . . 00 : 05 :

Humprey Johnson, for coming into this gouᵗment, and erecting a house in the township of Scittuate, som time this sumer, and dwelling in the said house, contrary to law, fined, } 00 : 10 :

1673-4.

March, 1673.

HUMPHREY JOHNSON, for cutting downe a land marke, and therby breakeing the law of this gouᵗment, fined, . } 05 : 00 :

June the 7th, 1674.

THE Treasurers accoumpt taken by vs whose names are vnderwritten, being appointed heervnto by the Court : —

The Treasurer was found debtor to the collonie, ... 325 : 12 : 00

Pr contra creditt, ... 303 : 07 : 06

The Treasurer debtor to ballence the accoumpt, ... 22 : 04 : 00

Item, more in fines not yett gathered.

Pr Daniell Cole, Junir, ... 00 : 10 : 00

Pr Willam Makepeace, ... 05 : 00 : 00

Pr Thomas Jones, of Taunton, ... 00 : 04 : 00

Pr Francis Curtice, ... 02 : 00 : 06

Pr John Bayley, of Scittuatt, ... 00 : 03 : 04

                     07 : 17 : 07

Due to the worshipfull Treasurer, as wee apprehend, for his llery, 30ll, hee haueing had more labour and trouble last yeare en ordinary, ... } 30 : 00 : 00

> JOHN FREEMAN,
> EDMOND HAWES,
> WILLAM CLARKE,
> DANIELL SMITH.

June, 1674.

THE townes proportions to the rates leuied by order of the Court, held att Plymouth the fourth of June, 1674.

Plymouths proportion is, ... 16 : 10 : 7½

Duxburrows proportion is, ... 07 : 15 : 2½

Bridgwaters proportion is, ... 07 : 15 : 2½

Scittuates proportion is, ... 27 : 11 : 06½

Tauntons proportion is, ... 15 : 08 : 11½

Sandw proportion, ... 15 : 08 : 11½

Yarmouthes proportion is, ... 12 : 09 : 03½

1674.

June.

Barnstables proportion is, ...	16 : 10 : 07
Marshfeilds proportion is, ...	12 : 11 : 04
Rehoboths proportion is, ...	22 : 16 : 06
Easthams proportion is, ...	11 : 02 : 09
Swanseys proportion is, ...	07 : 16 : 06
Dartmouths proportion is, ...	09 : 19 : 02
Middleberrys proportion is, ...	04 : 19 : 01
The totall, ...	188 : 15 : 1C

These proportions were ordered to be payed in barley, and wheat, ar
butter, or siluer ; the wheat att four shillings a bushell, the barlye att thr
shillings and six pence a bushell, and the butter att four pence a poun
viz$\S$, two thirds thereof ; and the other third in Indian corne and rye ; t
rye att three shillings and six pence a bushell, and the Indian att three sh
lings a bushell, all good and marchantable, to be deliuer^d to the Treasurer,
his order, either att Boston or Plymouth, and the charge of transportati
defrayed ; the first payment by the first of October next, and the lat
payment by the first of Aprill next, ensuing the date heerof.

The Fines of June Court, 1674.

ITEM, Josias Holmes, for selling liquors to the Indians, fined,   02 : 00 :
William Randall, Seni^r, for breakeing the Kings peace, fined,   00 : 03 :

July.

The Fines of July Court.

ITEM, William Maycomber, for breach of the Sabbath, fined,   02 : 00 :
John Rickard, Juni^r, son of John Rickard, for breaking
the King's peace, fined, ... } 00 : 03

Samuell Dunham, Juni^r, for breaking the King's peace,
fined, ... } 00 : 03

The Fines of October Court, 1674.

EORGE DAUSON, for Sabbath breakeing, fined, . . . 02 : 00 :

John Chase, for comiting fornication, fined, ... 05 : 00 :

Dorethy, the wife of Wiłłam Tubbs, for breaking the } 00 : 3 : 4
inges peace, ... }

Joseph Colston, for disorder about drinking, ... 00 : 05 :

7 : 08 : 8

‡The wife of Gyles Leich, Senʳ, for breakeing the Kings } 00 : 03 : 04‡
ace, ... }

*The Fines of March Court, 1674.

OHN MATHEWES, for filthy speech, ... 05 : 00 :

The wife of Gyles Leich, for breaking the Kinges peace, 00 : 03 : 04

e Treasurers accoumpt taken by the subscribers herof, appointed thervnto by the honored Court, &c̃.

	ll	s
The Treasurer was found debtor, ...	283 : 13 :	½
Pʳ contra creditt, ...	233 : 11 : 11	
The Treasurers sallery, ...	030 : 00 : 00	
Remaines due to ballence the accoumpt, ...	020 : 01 : 01	

Still due to the country by fines.

From Daniell Cole, Juniʳ, ...	000 : 10 : 00
From Wiłłam Makepeace, ...	005 : 00 : 00
From Francis Curtice, ...	02 : 00 : 00
From John Bayley, of Scittuate, ...	00 : 03 : 04
From Josiah Holmes, of Duxburrow, ...	001 : 00 : 00
From Gorḡe Dauson, of Middleberrey, ...	002 : 00 : 00
More, due by bond, for Indian Hoken, sold, ...	08 : 00 : 00

18 : 13 : 04

MARKE EAMES,
DANIELL SMITH,
BARNABAS LAYTHORP.

*June the 10th, 1675.

THE rate proportioned to the seuerall townes as they are to be payed i
to the worshipfull Treasurer.

		ll
Plymouth,	. . . .	16 : 10 : 0
Duxburrow,	. . . .	07 : 15 : 0
Bridḡwater,	. . . .	07 : 15 : 0
Scittuate,	. . . .	27 : 11 : C
Taunton,	. . . .	15 : 08 : 1
Sandwich,	. . . .	15 : 08 : 1
Yarmouth,	. . . .	12 : 09 : (
Barnstable,	. . . .	16 : 10 : (
Marshfeild,	. . . .	12 : 11 : (
Rehoboth,	. . . .	22 : 16 : (
Eastham,	. . . .	11 : 02 : (
Swansey,	. . . .	07 : 16 : (
Dartmouth,	. . . .	09 : 19 : (
Middleberry,	. . . .	04 : 19 : (
	Suma totalis, ...	188 : 15 :
More to be payed to the officers wages,	. . . .	040 : 00 :

These proportions were ordered to be payed in barly, wheat, butter,
siluer ; the wheat att four shings and six pence a bushell, the barly att th
shillings and six pence a bushell, and the butter att fiue pence a pound, t
thirds therof ; and the other third in Indian corne, rye, and peases ; the rye
three shillings and six pence a bushell, the pease att three shillings a bush
and the Indian att three shillings a bushell, all good and marchantable, to
deliuered to the Treasurer, or his order, and the charge of transportation
frayed ; the first payment by the first of October next, and the latter p
ment by the first of Aprill next.

*The Fines of June Court, 1675.

		ll	s
ROBERT CROSMAN,	. . . .	02 : 00 :	
James Burt, of Taunton,	. . . .	00 : 10 :	
Nathaniell Hall,	. . . .	05 : 00	
Ephraim Tinkham,	. . . .	02 : 00	
Samuell Wood,	. . . .	05 : 00	

June the 9th, 1676

THE honored Treasurer gaue in his accoumpt to vs, the subscribers, which is as followeth, viz⸗ : —

	ll	s	d
The Treasurer was found debtor, ...	1082	04	07
Pr contra creditt, ...	1142	00	10
Remaines to ballence the accoumpt, ...	059	16	03

More in debts owing by the collonie.

Item, to the honored Gour Winslow, as pte of his sallery,	02 : 17 : 00
Item, to Mr James Browne, his whole sallery, ...	07 : 03 : 00

Debts due to the collonie.

By Tauntons rate in June, 1675, ...	15 : 03 : 11
Item, by their second rate in December, ...	13 : 00 : 00
Item, moř, by a barrell of powder, Wiłłam Harvey and John ⸗hmond had, from Rehoboth, ... }	05 : 00 : 00
By rates in June, (75,)	22 : 16 : 06
By December rate, ...	15 : 00 : 00
By Mr Nathaniel Thomas, by bill, ...	15 : 00 : 00
By Mr Hinckley, for a muskett his son had of the Gour, .	01 : 00 : 00
By Capt Freeman, for a gun, ...	01 : 00 : 00
By Leift Ellice, three guns, & ten pound of powder, and 12 ⸗nd of bulletts, ... }	03 : 15 : 00
By Scittuate, for 14 guns and a barrell of powder, . . .	19 : 00 : 00
By Plymouth, eight guns, ...	08 : 00 : 00
By Duxburrow, fiue guns, ...	05 : 00 : 00
By Marshfeild, 21 guns, ...	21 : 00 : 00
By Francis Barker, ...	01 : 01 : 00

By old fines.

Daniell Cole, Junir, ...	00 : 10 : 00
By Wiłłam Makepeace, ...	05 : 00 : 00
By Francis Curtice, ...	02 : 00 : 00
By John Bayley, ...	00 : 03 : 04
By Josias Holmes, ...	01 : 00 : 00
By Gorğe Dauson, ...	02 : 00 : 00
The Treasurers sallery not yett payed, which is	30ll : 00 : 00

THOMAS HOWES,
JOSEPH LAYTHORPE,
DANIELL SMITH.

1676.

8 June.
[*68.]

THE rate for the publicke charges of the collonie proportioned to th̄ seuerall townes of this jurisdiction, as they are to be payed to th̄ Treasurer.

	ll	s
Plymouth, ...	19 : 08 : (
Duxburrow, ...	08 : 16 : (
Bridḡwater, ...	08 : 16 : (
Scittuate, ...	31 : 19 : (
Taunton, ...	18 : 04 :]
Sandwich, ...	18 : 04 :]
Yarmouth, ...	14 : 16 : (
Barnstable, ...	19 : 08 : (
Marshfeild, ...	14 : 16 : (
Rehoboth, ...	27 : 03 : (
Eastham, ...	12 : 13 : (
	194 : 07 :

These proportions were to ˄ payed, two p̄tes of three therof in whe and barly, and butter, or siluer; the wheat att 4ˢ 6ᵈ a bushell, the barly three shillings and six pence a bushell; and the butter att fiue pence a poun this first payment to be made att or before the first of October next af the date heerof; and the other third p̄te to be payed in Indian corne and r̄ the Indian corne att three shillings a bushell; the rye att three shillinges a six pence a bushell. This latter payment to be payed att or before the fī of Aprill next after the date heerof, all good and marchantable, to be deliuᵉᵈ the Treasurer, or where hee shall appoint, prouided it be att Plymouth Boston, and the charge of transportation defrayed.

1677.

13 July.
[*70.]

OUR honored Treasurer gaue in his accompt, which is as follow viz͗ : —

	ll	s
The Treasurer was found debtor, ...	815 : 08 :
Pʳ contra creditt with the Treasurer's sallery, ...	792 : 06 :
There is due to the collonie to ballen͂, ...	23 : 02 :

The collonies debts.

By Taunton mony rate, (76,)	016 : 00 : 0
By theire corne rate, ...	018 : 04 : 11
By Marshall Pratts sallery, pay to him by the Treasurer, ue from Taunton, ...	03 : 13 : 2
By Rehoboth mony rate, ...	016 : 00 : 00
By Marshall Nashes rate, payed by the Treasurer, . . .	05 : 10 : 3

13 July.

Due to the collonie in fines.

From Makepeace, ...	05 : 0 : 0
By John Bayley, ...	00 : 03 : 4
By Gorḡ Dauson, ...	02 : 00 : 0

DANIEL SMITH,
BARNABAS LAYTHORP,
JOHN MILLER.

July 7th.

7 July.

NICHOLAS WHITE, of Taunton, fined, ...	030 : 00 : 0
If payed in siluer, then, ...	15 : 00 : 0
The rate leuied this yeers for the publicke charges of the untry was, ...	162 : 15 : 06
Besides the officers wages, which is, ...	40 : 00 : 00

The Fines of October Court, 1677.

October.

[*72.]

	ll	s	d
ANN ANNIBLE, of Barnstable, widdow, fined, . . .	01	00	00
Joseph Burge, fined, ...	00	10	00

1 6 7 7-8.   *March, 1677.*

March.

SAMUELL JENNEY, ...   00 : 05 : 0
  Joseph Dunham, ...   01 : 00 : 0
  Ruhamah, the wife of Joseph Nicarson, or to be whipt, . 02 : 00 : 0
  The wife of Nathaniel Cauell, fined, or to be whipt, . . 02 : 00 : 0
  Edward Cottle, and his wife, each 40ˢ, or to be whipt, . . 04 : 00 : 0
  Samuell Nicarson, but hath libertie to appeer before the ⎫
Court to make his defence, haueing not yett been heard, . . ⎬ 02 : 00 : 0
                                                            ⎭
  Teage Jones, ...   00 : 10 : 0

---

1 6 7 8.   **June the 6ᵗʰ, 1678.*

6 June.
[*74.]

THE Treasurer's accoumpt taken by vs, subscribers, which is as follow
    eth, viz∫ : —
  The Treasurer is found debtor to the collonie, . . . 306 : 17 : 0
  Pʳ contra, ... 302 : 15 :
  To the Treasurers sallery, ... 30 : 000 : 0
  Rests still due to ballence, ... 25 : 17 :

An accoumpt of the money that was receiued for Showamett lands, togeth
    with a smale p̃sell of other lands, viz∫ : —
  The Treasurer is debtor, ... 810 : 10 : 0
  Pʳ contra creditt, ... 810 : 10 :

The towne of Taunton were found creditors

  By the com̃ittee, ... 739 : 10 : 0
  The towne of Taunton are debtors as followeth, viz : īem, ⎫
theire proportion of charges to the late warr, ... ⎬ 409 : 17 :
                                                            ⎭
    Item, to the 3 countrey rates not payed, ... 53 : 17 :
    Item, to seuerall p̃ticulare psons, payed by the Treasurer, 35 : 15 :
    Item, to goods the souldiers tooke vp of the com̃issioners, 38 : 09 :
    Item, to Assonett Necke, ... 150 : 00 :
    Item, by Bridḡwater, ... 12 : 13 :

Item, to stray cattle, ...	05 : 06 : 00	**1678.**
Item, to eighty two sheep and lambes, ...	33 : 11 : 00	
		6 June.
	739 : 10 : 00	

DANIELL SMITH,
BARNABAS LOTHORPE,
JOSEPH HOWLAND.

June the 7th, 1678.

THE rates of the seuerall townes are according to the seuerall proportions, viz⟨ : —

Barnstable, ...	29 : 03 : 00
Marshfeild, ...	22 : 16 : 08
Plymouth, ...	23 : 06 : 08
Duxburrow, ...	13 : 17 : 00
Bridḡwater, ...	13 : 17 : 00
Scittuate, ...	37 : 02 : 00
Taunton, ... · .	20 : 05 : 04
Sandwich, ...	28 : 00 : 06
Yarmouth, ...	22 : 16 : 08
Eastham, ...	19 : 15 : 04
Swansey, ...	06 : 14 : 00
Rehoboth, ...	14 : 05 : 04
	251 : 19 : 06

The seuerall kinds or specues in which the said sume is to be payed to
Treasurer.

In wheat, barly, or mony.

Plymouth, ...	15 : 13 : 04
Duxburrow, ...	08 : 00 : 00
Bridḡwater, ...	08 : 07 : 00
Scittuate, ...	24 : 02 : 00
Taunton, ...	14 : 05 : 04
Sandwich, ...	21 : 00 : 06
Yarmouth, ...	17 : 06 : 08
Barnstable, ...	22 : 13 : 00

1 6 7 8.

7 June.

Marshfeild, ... 14 : 16 :
Eastham, ... 14 : 05 :
Swansey, ... 04 : 04 :
Rehoboth, ... 08 : 05 :

June.

[*78.]

*June, 1678.

TO be payed to the Treasurer in Indian corne att 2ˢ 6ᵈ a bushell, or rye
three shillings a bushell.

Plymouth, ... 03 : 13 :
Duxburrey, ... 02 : 10 :
Bridwater, ... 02 : 10 :
Scittuat, ... 07 : 00 :
Taunton, ... 02 : 10 :
Sandwich, ... 03 : 00
Yarmouth, ... 02 : 10
Barnstable, ... 02 : 10
Marshfeild, ... 05 : 00
Eastham, ... 02 : 10
Swansey, ... 02 : 10
Rehoboth, ... 03 : 10

The officers wages to be payed in Indian corne att three shill
a bushell.

Plymouth, ... 04 : 00
Duxburrow, ... 03 : 07
Bridḡwater, ... 03 : 00
Scittuate, ... 06 : 00
Taunton, ... 03 : 10
Sandwich, ... 04 : 00
Barnstable, ... 04 : 00
Marshfeild, ... 03 : 00
Eastham, ... 03 : 00
Rehoboth, ...   ^   ^
Yarmouth, ... 03 : 00

Memoᵣ̆. Ten shillings which belonged to Marshall Nash was on
and not payed the last yeer of Yarmouth pay — the officers sallery.

The Fines of June and July Courts, 1678.

	ll	s	d	

EDWARD WANTON, ... 10 : 00 : 00‡   June and July.

   Nathaniel Fitsrandall, ... 20 : 00 : 00   [*79.]

Richard Siluester, of Milton, ... 05 : 00 : 00   Payed.

If not heerafter marryed to her with whom hee comitted }

ᵢication, ... } 5 : 00 :

ᵉ to be payd.

---

‡.*March the eight, 16⁷⁸⁄₉.*‡

	ll	

THOMAS BURMAN, of Barnstable, fined, ... 05 : 00 : 00   8 March.

  The condition of a bond giuen by Wilłam Randall, of }

ᵗuate, for and on the accoumpt of Isacke Hanmor, to pay, . } 05 : 00 : 00

Samuell Shiffericke, of Taunton, this siluer, for abusive }

ᵢages. This was deliuered to Mʳ Alden, ... } 00 : 15 : 00

Due to the country from   ^   ‡

---

‡.*March the eight, 16⁷⁸⁄₉.*‡

	ll	s	d

THOMAS BURMAN, of Barnstable, fined, ... 10 : 00 : 00

  The condition of a bond giuen by Wilłam Randall, of }

ᵘate, for and on the accoumpt of Isacke Hanmore, to pay } 05 : 00 : 00

pound, ... }

Samuell Shiffericke, for abusiue carriages, ... 00 : 15 : 00

This to be payed in siluer, deliuered to Mʳ Aldin.‡

---

‡*June the third, 1679.*‡

	ll	s	d

ATT this Court Joseph Thorne, of Scittuate, for playing }

  att cards twise, fined, ... } 01 : 00 : 00   3 June.

Joseph Peirse, for playing att cards once, ... 00 : 10 : 00

James Benitt, for playing att cards seuerall times, fined, . 01 : 00 : 00

John Holbrooke, for playing att cards, once in the woods, once himself, haueing comand there, ... } 01 : 00 :

Item, his man Patrick, att the same time, ... 00 : 10 :

Item, himselfe, once in Gannetts chamber,. . . . . . 00 : 10 :

Item, himselfe, once in the barne, ... 00 : 10 :

Item, his man, once in the barne, ... 00 : 10 :

This was abated.

John Holbrooks fine, ... 03 : 00 :

[Robert Latham,] for being drunke twise, fined, ... 00 : 10 :

[Thomas Jenkens,] for breaking the Sabboth, fined, . . . 02 : 00 :

Thirty shillings of this fine remitted.‡

---

*1678.   Fines due to the Country.

ll   s

ITEM, from Edward Wanton, for marrying himselfe, . . . 10 : 00 :

Item, from Thomas Burman, for marrying himselfe, . . 05 : 00 :

Item, from Samuell Blaake, comitting fornication, . . . 02 : 00 :

March, 1678.

THE condition of a bond from Randall in the behalfe of Isack Hanmore, ... } 05 : 00

Samuell Shiffericke, in siluer, ... 00 : 15

June, 1679.

JOSEPH THORNE, for playing att cards, 2 seuerall times, 001 : 00

Joseph Peirse, ... 00 : 10

James Benitt, ... 01 : 00

John Holbrooke, ... 01 : 00

Item, his man Patrick, ... 00 : 10

Item, the said Holbrooke, once in Gannetts chamber, . . 00 : 10

Item, himselfe, once in the barne, ...	00 : 10 : 00
Item, his man, once in the barne, ...	^ ^ ^

1679.

June.

03 : 00 : 00

Of John Holbrookes fines remitted 10ˢ.

Robert Latham, for being drunke, 2 seuerall times, fined, .   00 : 10 : 00

Thomas Jenkens, for breaking the Sabbath, fined, . . .   00 : 10 : 00

Att the Adjournment, July 1679.   July.

⌐T was ordered that the proffitts of the Cape fishing, annᵒ 1678, shalbe demaunded off Cornett Studson and Mʳ Nathaniel Thomas, in the be-lfe of the country.

Jonathan Higgens, for comitting fornication, fined, . . .   10 : 00 : 00

Isacke Woodworth, for playing at cards, 2 seuerall times, } 01 : 00 : 00
ed, ... }

Mathew Gannett, for playing att cards, &c̃, ...   02 : 00 : 00

The third of July, 1679.   3 July.

WARRANTS were issued out from the Court for a rate of   141 : 00 : 00 besides the officers sallery.

Which 141 was ordered to be payed att two seuerall payments, the for-r att or before the first of October, 1679, to be payed in wheate and barley, siluer ; the wheat att 4ˢ a bushell, the barly att 3ˢ a bushell. The latter ment to be payed in Indian corne and rye ; the Indian corne att 2ˢ 6ᵈ a shell, and the rye att three shillings a bushell ; to be payed att or before first of Aprill, 1680, all good and marchantable, to be deliuered to the easurer, or where hee shall appoint, soe it be att Plymouth or Boston, and charge of transportation defrayed.

*1679. The officers wages to be payed in Indian, 3ˢ a bushell, good,   [*82.] rchantable, transportation defrayed.

	ll s d
Plymouth, ...	04 : 00 : 00
Duxburrow, ...	03 : 00 : 00

20

1 6 7 9.

3 July.

Bridḡwater, ...	02 : 15 : 0
Scittuate, ...	06 : 00 : 0
Taunton, ...	03 : 10 : 0
Sandwich, ...	04 : 00 : 0
Yarmouth, ...	03 : 10 : 0
Barnstable, ...	04 : 00 : 0
Marshfeild, ...	03 : 00 : 0
Rehoboth, ...	03 : 05 : 0
Eastham, ...	03 : 00 : 0

1679-80.

March.

The Fines of March Court, 1679–80.

GEORḠ SAMPSON, and Elizabeth, his wife, for comiting fornication before marriage, fined, ... } 05 : 00 : 0

Wilłam Parker, of Scittuate, and Mary, his wife, for selling rum by retaile, fined, ... } 05 : 00 : 0

Isacke Negus, and Hannah, his wife, of Taunton, for comitting fornication before marriage, fined, ... } 04 : 00 : 0

Mannoah Ellis, and Mary, his wife, of Sandwich, for fornication before his marriage, fined, ... } 05 : 00 : 0

Wilłam Hunter, and Rebeckah, his wife, of Sandwich, for fornication before marriage, fined, ... } 05 : 00 : 0

1680.

4 June.

[*84.]

*June the 4th, 1680.

THE accompts taken of the Treasurer is as followeth : —

The collonie is found debtor, ...	408 : 08 : 0
Contrary creditt, ...	502 : 11 : 0
The ballence due to the contry in the Treasurers hands, .	94 : 02 : 0
Item, due to the country in Mr Hinckleys hand, . . .	01 : 12 : 0
Item, due from Rehoboth of theire last yeers rate, . .	01 : 03 : 0
Item, due from Middleberry, ...	‡02 : 00 : 00
Item, due from Manamoy, ...	01 : 00 : 00
Item, from the Freemens lands, ...	‡01 : 00 : 00

Item, from Accord Pond, ...	01 : 10 : 00	1680.
Item, Benjamine Leanard, on a bond due, ...	03 : 00 : 00	4 June.
Item, Jeremiah Hatch and Barstow, by obligation, . .	05 : 00 : 00	
Item, Leift Nash and John Soule, for Sampson, . . .	05 : 00 : 00	
It, Parker, of Scittuate, ...	05 : 00 : 00	
Item, Benitt, of Scittuate, ...	01 : 00 : 00	
Item, Woodward, of Taunton, ...	00 : 05 : 00	
Item, Josiah Smith, ...	10 : 00 : 00	
Item, Nonoquoquitt Necke, their last yeer rate, . . .	00 : 10 : 00	

EPHRAIM MORTON,
BARNABAS LAYTHORP,
JOHN THACHER,
THOMAS LEANARD,
JONATHAN BANGES.

The Fines of June Court, 1680.

TIMOTHY WHITE, fined, ...	010 : 00 : 00
Joseph White, ...	00 : 10 : 00
James Briggs, ...	00 : 10 : 00
John Cowin, ...	00 : 10 : 00
Thomas Wade, ...	^ ^ ^

*July the 10th, 1680.

FOR the Gour and Majestrates sallery, ...	100 : 00 : 00
For the officers wages, ...	40 : 00 : 00
For the Treasurers sallery, ...	20 : 00 : 00
	160 : 00 : 00

The proportions of the townes.

Plymouth, ...	16 : 10 : 00
Duxburrow, ...	07 : 15 : 00

10 July.

Bridg̃water,	. . . .	07 : 15 : 0
Sittuate,	. . . .	26 : 00 : 0
Taunton,	. . . .	16 : 10 : 0
Sandwich,	. . . .	16 : 10 : 0
Yarmouth,	. . . .	12 : 10 : 0
Barnstable,	. . . .	16 : 10 : 0
Marr̃feild,	. . . .	12 : 10 : 0
Rehoboth,	. . . .	14 : 00 : 0
Eastham,	. . . .	11 : 00 : 0
Swansey,	. . . .	07 : 00 : 0
Dartmouth,	. . . .	07 : 00 : 0
Middleberry,	. . . .	02 : 00 : 0
Mannamoÿ,	. . . .	02 : 00 : 0
		175 : 10 : 0

The freemens lands att Taunton Riuer,	. . . .	02 : 10 : 0
Accord Pond shares,	. . . .	01 : 10 : 0
Nannaquaquett Necke,	. . . .	00 : 10 : 0
		04 : 10 : 0

These were to be payed in wheat and barly, viz : two p̃tes of thre
therr̃of, wheat att 4ˢ a bushell, barly att 3 shillings a bushell; this   ×   ×
thirds therr̃of.

The 2ᶜᵒⁿᵈ payment, which was the remaining   ×   ×   ×,   in Indian corr
and rye; the Indian corne att   ×   ×   ×,   the rye att 3ˢ a bushell; times c
payment   ×   ×   ×   ×

[*87.]

		ll
*To the country charges,	. . . .	15 : 08 :
To the officer,	. . . .	03 : 05 :

[*88.]

*1680.   The officers wages proportioned on the townes.

		ll s
Plymouth,	. . . .	04 : 00 : 0
Duxburrow,	. . . .	03 : 00 : 0
Bridg̃water,	. . . .	02 : 15 : 0
Scittuate,	. . . .	06 : 00 : 0
Taunton,	. . . .	03 : 10 : 0
Sandwich,	. . . .	04 : 00 : 0
Yarmouth,	. . . .	03 : 10 : 0
Barnstable,	. . . .	04 : 00 : 0
Marshfeild,	. . . .	03 : 00 : 0

Rehoboth, ... 03 : 05 : 00   **1 6 8 0.**

Eastham, ... 03 : 00 : 00

10 July.

40 : 00 : 00

This was to be payed in Indian corne att 3ˢ pʳ bushell.

*The Fines of October Court, 1680.

RICHARD BENITT, of Rehoboth, for being drunke, fined, ... } 00 : 05 : 00

| ll | s | d |

Teage Jones, for being drunke the second time, ... 00 : 10 : 00

Samuell Packer, for disturbing the church att Bridg̃water, d, ... } 01 : 00 : 00

Isacke Harris, for disturbing the church att Bridg̃water, . 01 : 00 : 00

Robert Ransome, for selling rum by retaile, without order, d, ... } 05 : 00 : 00

The Fines of March Court, 168¾.

ITEM, Phillip Dexter, fined, ... 02 : 10 : 00

Item, Cornett Studson, ... 00 : 05 : 00

The Fines of July Session Court, 1681.

WILLAM GRIFFITH and Richard Michell for theire neglegence in not attending the publicke worship of God on the Lords day, were each ten shillings, to the vse of the collonie.

Robert Ransom, for revilling the minnestry, fined ten shillings.

Hannah Linnitt, for her light behauior with Job Randall, fined fiue and ty shillings, or be whipt.

Zacheriah Allin, for selling liquors to the Indians, fined fiue and twenty pounds; but in case hee pay the one halfe therof, in siluer mony, th but the one halfe, which is twelue pounds ten shillings in siluer mony.

James Mayo, for vnsiuell lying on a bed with *with* Martha Harding, I was fined twenty shillings.

Ralph Allin, of Sandwich, for revilling the gospell minnesters, fin ten shillings.

Nathaniel Warren, for prophaning the Sabbath, fined thirty shillings.

John Randall, for revilling Mr Mihell, preacher of Gods word Scittuate, fined ten shillings.

× Dunham, for selling strong liquors to the Indians, fined, 5 :

The 8th of July, 1681.

THE proportion of the rates of the seuerall townes : —

Plymouth,	22 : 00 :
Duxburrow,	010 : 06 :
Bridgwater,	10 : 06 :
Scittuate,	34 : 13 :
Taunton,	22 : 00 :
Sandwich,	22 : 00 :
Yarmouth,	16 : 13 :
Barnstable,	22 : 00 :
Marshfeild,	16 : 13 :
Rehoboth,	18 : 13 :
Eastham,	14 : 13 :
Swansey,	10 : 00
Dartmouth,	09 : 06
Middleberry,	03 : 00
Mannamoie,	02 : 10
Freemens Lands,	02 : 10
Saconett,	01 : 10 :
Accord Pond shares,	02 : 00
Nunnaquaqett Necke,	00 : 15
Punckateesett propriators and inhabitants,	03 : 10
Sume totall,	245 : 00

The Gou[r] and Majestrates sallery, ...	100 : 00 : 00	**1681.**
For the officers wages, ...	40 : 00 : 00	
To the Treasurers sallery, ...	20 : 00 : 00	8 July.
To the majestrates table, in siluer mony, ...	52 : 00 : 00	
To the comissioners, ...	10 : 00 : 00	
	222 : 00 : 00	

The p[r]ticulars of the officers sallery, 1681.

Plymouth, ...	01 : 00 : 0
Duxburrow, ...	03 : 00 : 0
Bridḡwater, ...	02 : 15 : 0
Scittuate, ...	06 : 00 : 0
Taunton, ...	03 : 10 : 0
Sandwich, ...	04 : 00 : 0
Yarmouth, ...	03 : 10 : 0
Barnstable, ...	04 : 00 : 0
Marshfeild, ...	× × ×
Rehoboth, ...	× × ×
Eastham, ...	× × ×

---

*July the 13th, 1682.

1682.

13 July.
[*92.]

THE proportion of the rates of the seuerall townes are as followeth, viz : —

Plymouth, ...	22 : 00 : 0
Duxburrow, ...	10 : 06 : 0
Bridḡwater, ...	10 : 06 : 0
Scittuate, ...	34 : 14 : 04
Taunton, ...	22 : 00 : 00
Sandwich, ...	22 : 00 : 00
Yarmouth, ...	16 : 13 : 04
Barnstable, ...	22 : 00 : 00
Marshfeild, ...	16 : 13 : 04
Rehoboth, ...	18 : 13 : 04
Eastham, ...	14 : 13 : 04
Swansey, ...	10 : 00 : 00

1682.

13 July.

Dartmouth, ...	09 : 06 : 0
Middlbery, ...	03 : 00 : 0
Mannamoyett, ...	02 : 10 : 0
Freemens Lands, ...	02 : 10 : 0
Little Compton, ...	02 : 10 : 0
Accord Ponds shares, ...	01 : 05 : 0
Nannaquaquat Necke, ...	00 : 15 : 0
Punckateesett inhabitants or propriators, ...	03 : 00 : 0
The inhabitants att Foards Farme, ...	00 : 15 : 0
	244 : 11 :

1682.   The officers sallery taken out of that aboue.

Plymouth, ...	04 : 00 :
Duxburrow, ...	03 : 00 :
Bridgwater, ...	02 : 15 :
Scittuate, ...	06 : 00 :
Taunton, ...	03 : 10 :
Sandwich, ...	04 : 00 :
Yarmouth, ...	03 : 10 :
Barnstable, ...	04 : 00 :
Marshfeild, ...	03 : 00 :
Rehoboth, ...	03 : 05 :
Eastham, ...	03 : 00 :
	40 : 00 :

[*93.]   *July the 13, 1682.

THE accoumpt taken of the Treasurer is as followeth, viz : —

	ll s
The Treasurer is found debter, ...	139 : 02 :
Pr contra creadit, ...	113 : 14 :
Rests still due to the country, ...	25 : 07 :

1681.   1681.   In debts still due to the collonie, as followeth : —

From Accord Pond for the yeer 1681, ...	01 : 10 :
From Benitt, of Scituate, ...	01 : 00 :
From Woodward, of Taunton, ...	00 : 10 :

From Nannquaquat Necke, ... 01 : 00 : 00 **1682.**

From Manamoy, due, ... 01 : 04 : 00

13 July.

From Yarmouth, for oyle, ... 01 : 08 : 00

From Wiłłam Gray, of Yarmouth, ... 01 : 00 : 00

From Simmons, due by bill, ... 05 : 00 : 00

From Eliezer Crocker, ... 02 : 10 : 00

From Callender, of Swansey, ... 00 : 10 : 00

From young White, of Bristoll, ... 00 : 10 : 00

From Zacheriah Allin, of Sandwich, ... 20 : 00 : 00

From the Freemens Land, ... 00 : 10 : 00

From Saconett, ... 01 : 10 : 00

From Accord Pond, ... 02 : 00 : 00

From Nunnaquaqett Necke, ... 00 : 15 : 00

From Pocassett, ... 03 : 00 : 00

Suma tota, ... 43 : 17 : 00

From Wiłłam Nelson, ... 02 : 10 : 00

From Abraham Hedge, ... 01 : 00 : 00

From Steuen Atwood, ... 01 : 00 : 00

M^m, the two Courts in this month of July, 1682, allredye accoumpted with the Treasurer.

DANIELL SMITH,

BARNABAS LAYTHORP,

EPHRAIM MORTON,

WIŁŁAM PAYBODY,

JOHN CUSHEN.

*The sume of thirty shillings receiued of Captaine Freeman for a fine of [*94.]
ꝺert Nicarson, of Mannamoiett.

June the 8, 1683. **1683.**

ꟿHE propositions of the rates of the seuerall townes for the yeer 8 June.
  1683. [*95.]

Plymouth, ... 18 : 14 : 00

Duxburrow, ... 08 : 15 : 00

Briꝺwater, ... 08 : 15 : 00

1683.

8 June.

Scittuate, ...	30 : 02 :
Sandwich, ...	18 : 14 :
Taunton, ...	18 : 14 :
Yarmouth, ...	14 : 03 :
Barnstabł, ...	18 : 14 :
Marshfeild, ...	14 : 03 :
Rehoboth, ...	14 : 03 :
Eastham, ...	12 :.03 :
Swansey, ...	08 : 10 :
Dartmouth, ...	08 : 00 :
Middleberry, ...	02 : 11 :
Mannamoy, ...	02 : 04 :
Freemens Land, ...	02 : 04 :
Little Compton, ...	02 : 04 :
Acord Pond shares, ...	01 : 02 :
Nunnaquaqutt Necke, ...	00 : 13 :
Punckateest inhabytants or propriators, ...	01 : 18 :
The inhabitants of Foard Farm, ...	00 : 13 :
	209 : 01 :

[*96.]

*1683. The Treasurers accoumpt is as followeth, viz : —

The Treasurer was found debter to the collonie, ...	275 : 12 :
P^r contra creditt, ...	258 : 03 :
Still due to the collonie, ...	017 : 08 :

In debts due to the collonie.

From Elisha Hedge, of Yarmouth, ...	08 : 00 :
From Accord Pond shares, for acrees, the totall is, . . .	05 : 10 :
From Bennitt, of Scittuatt, ...	01 : 00 :
From Woodworth, of Taunton, ...	01 : 10 :
From Nanquaquatt, due by rates, for foure yeer last past, besides what was due in the late ware, ... }	02 : 10 :
From Simons, due by bill, ...	04 : 00
From Pocassett and Punchateest, ...	05 : 00
Suma totall, ...	26 : 10

A record of the seuerall utinsels payed for by the Treasurer, which are as followeth.

A table, a cubbert, and a bedsteed, and a small table, all of
:m cost, ... } 04 : 08 : 0

More, 8 chairs, and two stooles, 10 cushens, and a carpet, 08 : 06 : 6

Item, 1 fier shouell, a great paire of tonges, and two paire
tramells, ... } 01 : 03 : 00

> DANIELL SMITH,
> JOHN THACHER,
> EPHRAIM MORTON.
> NATHANIEL THOMAS,
> JONATHAN SPARROW.

June the sixt, 1684.

¶HE Treasurers accoumpt was then taken and is as followeth, viz : —

The Treasurer was found debtor to the collonie, . . . 206 : 06 : 10

P^r contra creditt, ... 230 : 12 : 04

Rests to ballence, and is due to the Treasurer, ... 25 : 05 : 06

Which said 25 : 05 : 06 was the same sixt of June payed to the said
asurer, by the collonie.

Debts still due to the collonie are as followeth : —

Imprimis, from Accord Pond shares not yet payed, . . 06 : 12 : 00

From Nunnaquaquatt Neck, ... 00 : 13 : 00

From Pocassett and Punkateest, ... 05 : 00 : 00

From Foard Farm, ... 00 : 07 : 00

From Nunnaquaqutt, for former rates not yett payed, . . 02 : 10 : 00

From Woodworth, of Taunton, ... 00 : 10 : 00

From Simmons, ... 04 : 00 : 00

From Pocassett, ... 01 : 10 : 00

From Isacke Allin, of Rehoboth, ... 02 : 10 : 00

From Saunders, of Sandwich,. . . . . 02 : 10 : 00

From Sutton, of Scittuate, ... 07 : 00 : 00

> DANIELL SMITH,
> BARNABAS LAYTHORP,
> EPHRAIM MORTON, Seni^r,
> JOHN MILLER.

1684.   **June the sixt, 1684.*

6 June.

[*100.]

THE proportions of the rates of the seuerall townes are as follo
eth : —

		ll	s
Imp^r, Plymouth, ...		18 : 14 :	
Duxburrow, ...		08 : 15 :	
Bridḡwater, ...		08 : 15 :	
Scittuaᵗ, ...		30 : 02 :	
Sandwich, ...		18 : 14 :	
Taunton, ...		18 : 04 :	
Yarmouth, ...		14 : 03 :	
Barnstable, ...		18 : 14 :	
Marshfeild, ...		14 : 03 :	
Rehoboth, ...		15 : 17 :	
Eastham, ...		12 : 09 :	
Swansey, ...		08 : 10 :	
Dartmouth, ...		08 : 00 :	
Middleberry, ...		02 : 11 :	
Mannamoy, ...		02 : 04 :	
The Freemens Land, ...		02 : 04 :	
Little Compton, ...		02 : 14 :	
Accord Pond sharrers, ...		01 : 02 :	
Nunnaquaquat Necke, ...		00 : 13 :	
Punckateest propriators, ...		01 : 18 :	
The inhabytants of Foards Farm, ...		00 : 13 :	
		209 : 01 :	

1685.   **Jun: 12th, 1685.*

12 June.

[*103.]

THE Treasurer is D^r to the colony : —

	ll	s
To the rates from the seuerall towns, ...	169 : 01 :	
To Accord Pond, ...	004 : 00 :	
To Fords Farme, ...	000 : 07 :	
To Zachariah Allen, of Rehoboth, ...	02 : 10 :	
To Henry Sanders, 2 : 10 : yᵉ Gouer^r had 2 : 2, ...	00 : 08 :	
To Sutton, of Scituate, ...	07 : 00 :	
To Capᵗ Thatcher, for a fine, ...	00 : 05 :	

To the Gouer^r for a fine, ... 01 : 00 : 00   **1685.**

To Caleb Hopkins, of Eastham, for a fine, ... 01 : 00 : 00

To Ambross Fish, of Sandwich, for a fine, ... 00 : 08 : 00   12 June.

To a fine receued at Tānton, ... 00 : 03 : 00

Of John Briggs, of Scituate, ... 00 : 05 : 00

To Caleb Cooke, for a fine, ... 01 : 10 : 00

At Duxbury, for a fine, ... 00 : 03 : 00

To William Pallmer, for a fine, ... 05 : 00 : 00

To Scituate, for a fine, ... 05 : 00 : 00

To John Washbourn, for a fine, ... 04 : 15 : 00

William Gray, of Yarmouth, for a fine, ... 00 : 03 : 00

To Mr Barnabas Lothropp, for a fine, ... 00 : 05 : 00

To the Priuatteers, for a fine, ... 05 : 19 : 00

To receued from Barnstable, p^r acc^{tt} of a whale, ... 00 : 12 : 00

By a mistake in the account, the last June, 1684, . . . 05 : 00 : 00

To short of Mount Hope mony, ... 19 : 00 : 00

To mony from the Cape, ... 06 : 10 : 00

Totall, ... 240 : 04 : 04

*June, 1685.   P^r contra, Cr^d.   [*104.]

	ll	s	d

To the Gouer^r & Magistrats, ... 100 ; 00 : 00

To Mr William Clarke, for their table, ... 45 : 00 : 00

To the Treasurer, ... 20 : 00 : 00

To the vnder marshall, ... 06 : 13 : 04

To witneses & entertainm^{tt} about the Indian squaw, . . . 01 : 10 : 00

To the Gouer^{rs} goeing to Swansey, ... 01 : 10 : 00

To drinke for the soldiers at the proclamation of Kinge } 01 : 05 : 00
mes the Second, at, ... }

To the jayler for imprisoning the Indian squaw, ... 00 : 15 : 00

To a wolfe, ... 00 : 05 : 00

To keeping the Gouer^{rs} horse at March Court, ... 00 : 04 : 00

To charges to a man & horses to send upon one of the } 06 : 00 : 00
misioners to Coñetticut, ... }

To the vnder marshall for whipping & imprisoning, . . . 00 : 07 : 00

To the smith for irons for the prisoner, ... 00 : 05 : 00

To the Indian marshall, ... 00 : 05 : 00

To Breett, ... 00 : 02 : 00

To Mr Michell for election sermon, ... 01 : 00 : 00

1685.

12 June.

To charges for the Indian squaw,	. . . .	01 : 05 : 00
To Capt Jacobbs,	. . . .	03 : 00 : 00
To the Freemens Lands, not receued,	. . . .	02 : 04 : 00
To Acord Pond, not receued,	. . . .	01 : 02 : 00
To Nonaquackett Neck, not receued,	. . . .	00 : 13 : 00
To Punkatest, not paid,	. . . .	01 : 18 : 00
To charges about the priuateers,	. . . .	00 : 05 : 00

194 : 03 : 0

BARNABAS LOTHROPP,
JONATHAN SPARROW,
ISAAC LITLE.

June.

[*106.]

Ju͠n 1685.

MONY to be raised to defray the charge of this colony for this year, s far as at present apears, & for what was expended extraordinary the yeare past.

ll   s

For the Gouer^r & Magistrats salery,	. . . .	100 : 00 : 0
For the Treasurers salery,	. . . .	020 : 00 : 0
For officers sallery,	. . . .	35 : 00 : 0
For the magistrats table,	. . . .	45 : 00 : 0
For Nathaniell Hall, in siluer 30; in prouission 6,	. . .	36 : 00 : 0
For William Clarke, for seuerall disbursm^{tts} as p^r note of perticulars apears, siluer, ...	}	48 : 00 : 0
For the Gouer^{rs} man & horse, to comission,	. . . . .	04 : 00 : 0
For the secretary for writting ouer the new lawes, for paper & wax for the comisions, & for writting 10 or 12 dayes for the Courte, ...	}	03 : 10 : 0
Towards printing the lawes,	. . . .	30 : 00 : 0
For the comittee that spent a months time about reuiueing the lawes, ...	}	20 : 00 : 0
For a barell of powder spent when King James the 2 was proclaimed, ...	}	05 : 00 : 0

Totall, ... 346 : 10 : 0

*June 6th, 1685.

THE proportions of the rats of the seuerall towns are as followeth : —

Plimouth, ...	31 : 00 : 00
Duxbury, ...	14 : 10 : 00
Bridḡwater, ...	14 : 19 : 00
Scittuate, ...	49 : 18 : 06
Sandwich, ...	31 : 01 : 00
Taũton, ...	30 : 03 : 00
Yarmouth, ...	23 : 09 : 06
Barnstable, ...	31 : 00 : 00
Marshfeild, ...	23 : 19 : 06
Rehoboth, ...	26 : 04 : 06
Eastham, ...	21 : 12 : 06
Swansey, ...	14 : 01 : 00
Dartmouth, ...	13 : 03 : 06
Midlebery, ...	04 : 03 : 06
Manomoy, ...	03 : 12 : 08
Free town, ...	03 : 12 : 08
Litle Compton, ...	03 : 12 : 08
Accord Pond, ...	01 : 16 : 06
Nanaquakett, ...	01 : 01 : 08
Punkatest proprietors, ...	02 : 06 : 08
Fords Farme, ...	01 : 01 : 08
Totall, ...	346 : 10 : 00

*June ye 5th, 1686.

THE Generall Court made choyce of Barnabas Lothrop, Esqr, Capt Joseph Lothrop, Capt Jonathan [Sparrow], and Leivtt Isaac Little, to ke the Treasurers [accompt].

*June ye 5th, 1686. Pr contra.

	ll	s	d
To the Governr & Magistrates, ...	100 : 00 : 00
To Mr Clarke for their table, ...	045 : 00 : 00

1686.

To the Treasurers salliry, ...	020 : 00 : 00
To the under marshall, ...	006 : 13 : 04
To Nathaniel Hall, ...	036 : 00 : 00
For the comittee, ...	020 : 00 : 00
To the Govern', man & horse, ...	004 : 00 : 00
For a barrel of powder expended at the proclamation of ⎱ King James, ... ⎰	005 : 00 : 00
For printing yᵉ law books, 36ˡˡ, ...	036 : 07 : 00
For bringing home the law books, ...	000 : 07 : 00
To William Voabes, pʳ order of the Court, ...	001 : 05 : 00
To Samˡ Sprague, ...	000 : 05 : 0
To the under marshall for whipping, ...	000 : 10 : 0
For repairing irons for the prisoners, ...	000 : 03 : 0
To Mʳ Russell, ...	001 : 00 : 0
For the officers salliry, ...	035 : 00 : 0
To Mʳ William Clarke, ...	048 : 00 : 0
To the secretary for writing paper & wax, ...	003 : 10 : 0
For the rates of Accord Pond, remitted, ...	001 : 16 : 0
For the rates of Anaquakett Neck, not paid, ...	001 : 01 : 0
For the rates of Puncateast, not paid, ...	002 : 06 : 0
For yᵉ rates of Foords Farme, not paid, ...	001 : 01 : 0
For Simeon Stoddard, warr accompt, due to Mʳ Smith, . .	006 : 06 : 0
Sum̄, ...	375 : 13 : 0
The ballance due from the Treasurer, ...	037 : 03 : 0
	412 : 17 : 0

This accompt taken by us.

BARNABAS LOTHROP,
JOSEPH LOTHROP,
JONATHAN SPARROW,
ISAAC LITTLE.

June y' 5ᵗʰ, 1686.

THE proportions of the rates of the severall towns are as followeth : —

		ll	s	d
Imprᵐis,	Plimouth,	19	17	06
	Duxborough,	09	08	03
	Bridgewater,	09	17	09
	Scituate,	31	19	08
	Sandwich,	19	17	06
	Taunton,	19	06	06
	Yarmouth,	15	00	10
	Barnstable,	19	17	06
	Marshfield,	15	09	10
	Rehoboth,	16	06	01
	Eastham,	13	04	04
	Swansey,	09	00	00
	Dartmouth,	08	10	00
	Middleborough,	02	13	09
	Monnamoyet,	02	06	09
	Little Compton,	02	06	09
	Freetowne,	02	06	09
	Nanaquaket Neck,	00	14	00
	Punkateast,	02	00	06
	Foords Farme,	00	13	09
		215	18	00

Inspexi, anno 1716.

22

LISTS OF FREEMEN

AND OTHERS.

PLYMOUTH RECORDS.

LISTS OF THE NAMES OF FREEMEN AND OTHERS TAKEN AT VARIOUS TIMES.

[The following lists contain the names of those who were admitted to the freedom of the colony of New Plymouth, together with those who took the oath of fidelity, and those who were able to bear arms, in the year 1643. Nothing is given to denote what the list on page *44 is intended to represent; but there is internal evidence that it is a list of freemen taken about the year 1658. This portion of the records is contained in the same manuscript volume in which the Conveyances of Lands by the Indians are recorded, and the Treasurer's accounts preserved. Originally they were written in a separate volume of very small dimensions, and by various persons. As persons died or removed from the colony, their names were cancelled in the lists.]

The Names of the Freemen of eich Towne. Plymouth.

Mᴿ WILLIAM BRADFORD, Goũnʳ,

‡Mʳ Thomas Prence,‡
‡Mʳ John Browne,‡
‡Mʳ John Alden,‡
‡Capt̃ Miles Standish,‡   } ‡Assistants, 1633.‡
‡Mʳ Wilłm Collyer,‡
‡Mʳ Tymothy Hatherley,‡
‡Mʳ John Jenney,‡ ‖dead,‖

‡Mʳ Edward Winslowe,‡
‡Mʳ Wilłm Brewster,‡ ‖dead,‖
‡Mʳ John Atwood,‡ ‖dead,‖
‡Mʳ Steephen Hopkins,‡ ‖dead,‖
‡Mʳ Raph Smyth,‡
‡Mʳ Isaack Alerton,‡
‡Mʳ Wilłm Thomas,‡
 Mʳ John Reynor,
 Mʳ John Howland,

‡Mʳ John Done,‡
‡Robͭe Heeks,‡ ‖dead,‖
 Manasseth Kempton,
‡Mʳ John Combe,‡ Disfranchised for being drunke.
 John Winslow,
‡Kenelme Winslow,‡
‡Josias Winslow,‡
 Francis Cooke,
‡Nathaniell Sowther,‡

(173)

John Shaw,

James Hurst,

John Dunhame,

Wil‡m Pontus,

Josuah Pratt,

‡Phineas Pratt,‡ ‖goñ,‖

‡Georḡ Soule,‡

Edward Dotey,

Thomas Clarke,

Thomas Cushman,

Wil‡m Paddy,

[*2.]　*Richard Sparrow,

‡Edward Banges,‡

‡Nicholas Snow,‡

John Cooke, Juñ,

Thomas Willett,

George Watson,

John Faunce,

John Barnes,

John Holmes,

‡Anthony Savory,‡ ‖dead,‖

Roᵬte Bartlett,

Richard Church,

‡Abrahame Pearse,‡

‡Raph Wallen,‡ ‖dead,‖

Samuell Eedy,

James Cole,

Wil‡m Hodgkine,

‡Richard Higgens,‡

‡Richard Clough,‡

‡Thomas Atkinson,‡

‡John Jenkine,‡

‡Josias Cooke,‡

Roᵬte Lee,

Nathaniell Morton,

‡Georḡ Bower,‡

‡Thomas Hill,‡

‡Mʳ Thom: Burne,‡

‡Mʳ Charles Chauncey,‡

Gabriell Fallowell,

Gyles Rickett,

‡Samuell Hicks,‡

‡John Smaley,‡

Edmond Tilson,

John Dunham, Junʳ,

‡Mʳ Wil‡m Hanbury,‡

Thomas Southwood,

‡Robert Waterman,‡

Mʳ John Combe,

John Finney,

Richard Wright,

Andrew Ring.

Freemen of Duxborrow.

Mʳ Wil‡m Collyer,

Mʳ John Alden,

Capᵗ Miles Standish,

Mʳ Raph Partrich,

Jonathan Brewster,

‡Steephen Tracye,‡

Wil‡m Bassett,

‡Leiftennᵗ Wᵐ Holmes,‡

Edmond Chaundlor,

Christopher Waddesworth,

Henry Howland,

Loue Brewster,

Experience Michelle,

Roger Chaundlor,

‡Joseph Rogers,‡

Samuell Nash,

Phillip Delanoy,

Abraham Pearse,

Moyses Symonson,

Henry Sampson,

Constant Southwood,

John Paybody,

Wilłm Tubbs,

Francis Sprague,

Mᵣ Comfort Starr,

‡Mʳ Wilłm Kempe,‡   DUXBURY.

‡Job Cole,‡

‡Mʳ Thomas Besbeech,‡

Georḡ Sowle,

‡John Tisdall,‡

Georḡ Partrich,

Wilłm Brett,

John Washbourne,

Tho: Heyward.

---

*Freemen of Scituate.   SCITUATE.
[*4.]

Mʳ Tymothy Hatherley,

Mʳ John Lathrope,

‡Wilłm Gilson,‡ ‖dead,‖

Mʳ Charles Chauncey,

‡Anthony Annable,‡

Humfrey Turner,

Wilłm Hatch,

Georḡ Kennerick,

‡James Cudworth,‡

Samuell Fuller,

‡Isaack Robinson,‡

‡Henry Rowley,‡

‡John Cooper,‡

‡Henry Cobb,‡

Samuell House,

‡Edward Foster,‡ ‖dead,‖

‡Georḡ Lewes,‡

‡Barnard Lumbert,‡

‡Henry Bourne,‡

‡Mʳ Thom̃ Besbeech,‡

Samuell Hinckley,

John Lewes,

Richard Sillis,

‡Edward Fitzrandle,‡

John Williams,

‡John Twisden,‡ ‖depᵗᵉᵈ yᵉ gouᵐment.‖

Thomas Chambers,

John Hewes,

Walter Woodward,

Edmond Eddenden,

Thomas Clapp,

Edward Jenkin,

John Allen,

---

*Freemen of Sandweech.   SANDWICH.
[*5.]

Mʳ Edmond Freeman,

Mʳ Wilłm Leuerich,

Mʳ John Vincent,

Richard Burne,

SANDWICH.

‡Thomas Armitage,‡
Mᣴ Wilłm Wood,
Gorḡ Allen,
Thoᣴ Tupper,

Thoᣴ Burges,
Wilłm Newland,
Mᣴ Henry Feake,
James Skiffe.

COHANNET
[*6.]

*Freemen of Cohannett, ‖now called Taunton.‖

Captaine Wilłm Poole,
Mᣴ John Gilbert, Sen.,
Mᣴ Henry Andrewes,
‡John Stronge,‡
John Deane,
Walter Deane,
7 Edward Case,
Wilłm Parker,

‡John Parker,‡
‡Mᣴ John Bushop,‡
Wilłm Halloway,
‡Wilłm Hailstone,‡
Richard Williams,
George Hall,
Oliuer Purchase.

YARMOUTH.
[*7.]

*Freemen of Yarmouth.

Thomas Payne,
‡Phillip Tabor,‡
Mᣴ Anthony Thacher,
Mᣴ John Crowe,
Wᵐ Palmer,
‡Wilłm Nicholson,‡
Mᣴ Marmaduke Mathews,
Thoᣴ Falland,

Richard Hore,
Emanuell White,
James Mathewes,
Richard Prichard,
Edmond Hawes,
Daniell Cole,
Job Cole,
Thomas Howes.

BARNSTABLE.
[*8.]

*Freemen of Barnestable.

‡Mᣴ Joseph Hull,‡
Mᣴ Lathrope,
Mᣴ Thomas Dimmack,

Wilłm Caseley,
Mᣴ Roᖯte Linnett,
Mᣴ John Mayo,

Anthony Annable,
‡James Cudworth,‡
Isaack Robinson,
Henry Rowley,
John Cooper,
Henry Cobb,
Barnard Lumbert,
Henry Bourne,

Samuell Hinckley,
Edward Fitzrandle,
Georg̃ Lewes,
Samuell Jackson,
James Hamlene,
Thomas Hinckley,
Nathaniell Bacon,
Dolor Davis.

BARNSTABLE.

---

*Marshfeild.

MARSHFIELD.
[*9.]

Mʳ Edward Winslow,
Mʳ Wᵐ Thomas,
Josias Winslow,
Kanelme Winslow,
Mʳ Thomas Burne,
Mʳ Edw: Buckley,

Robᵗᵉ Waterman,
John Dingley,
Thom̃ Shillingsworth,
John Russell,
Mʳ Nathaniell Thomas.

---

*Rehoboth.

REHOBOTH.
[*10.]

Steven Paine,
Wil⊦m Carpenter,

Walter Palmer,
Mʳ Sam: Newman.

---

*Nawsett.

NAWSETT.
[*11.]

Mʳ Thomas Prence,
Mʳ John Done,
Edward Bangs,
Nicolas Snow,
John Jenkine,
23

Josias Cooke,
Sam: Hickes,
John Smaleley,
Joseph Rogers,
Rich: Higgenson.

The Names of such as haue taken the Oath of Fidelitie of the Towne of Marshfeild in the Yeare 1657.

Thomas Doghed,
John Adames,
Samuell Baker,
Robert Latham,
Josepth Rose,
Edward Bumpas, Juni^r,
John Branch,
James Doughtey,
Robert Parker,
John Howland, Juni^r,
Mr Edmond Hincksman,
Richard Siluester,
Thomas Tilden,
Francis Crocker,

John Dooth,
John Thomas,
Abraham Jackson,
John Thomas,
John Rogers, Juni^r,
John Walker,
Gorge Vaughan,
Wiłłam Foard, Juni^r,
Grigory Flecnam,
Wiłłam Maycomber,
Richard French,
Ralph Chapman,
John Bumpas.

The Names of such as haue taken the Oath of Fidelitie in the Towne of Rehoboth in the Yeare 1657.

Robert Abell,

1658.

Abraham Martin,
John Mathewes,
John Miller, Seni^r,
Tho: Cooper, Seni^r,
Phillip Walker,
Wiłłam Buckland,
Edward Hall,
Rob: Wheaton,
John Miller,
John Woodcocke,
Anthony Perry,
Rob: Fuller,
Roger Annadowne,
Jonas Palmer,
Richard Bullocke,

Obadiah Bowin,
John Butterworth,
Jonathan Bosworth,
Tho: Wilmott,
Rob: Joanes,
Josepth Pecke,
John Pecke,
Stephen Paine, Juni^r,
John Miller, Juni^r,
James Riddawey,
Gorg̃ Kenericke,
Gorg̃ Robinson,
Wiłłam Carpenter, Juni^r,
John Reed,
John Perren,

John Phitte,

Rise Leanard,

Jonathan Blisse,

Henery Smith,

John Doghead,

Samuell Newm̃, Juni[r].

Josepth Peck, Juni[r],

Rob: Morton,

Richard Bowin, Juni[r],

Francis Steuens,

Josepth Carpenter.

REHOBOTH.

1662.

---

*The *Names of such as haue taken the Oath of Fidelitie of the Towne of Barnstable in the Yeare 1657.*   BARNSTABLE. [*15.]

Barnabas Laythorpe,

Peter Blossome,

Moses Rowley,

Nicolas Dauis,

Jonathan Hatch,

Elisha Parker,

M[r] John Bursley,

Thomas Shawe,

Thomas Lewis,

James Cleghorne,

James Lewis,

Gorg̃ Haward,

Thomas Lumbert, Seni[r],

Thomas Lumbert, Juni[r],

Ralph Joanes,

Josepth Lumbert,

John Hathawey,

M[r] Thomas Dexter, Seni[r],

Dauid Linnitt,

Richard C ,

John Dauis,

Henery Tayler,

Josias Hallott,

Samuell Bacon,

Wilłam Dexter,

Richard Foxwell,

Caleb Lumbert.

---

*The *Names of such as haue taken the Oath of Fidelitie att Sandwich in the Yeare 1657.*   SANDWICH. [*16.]

Henery Sanders,

Wilłam Swift,

Myles Blacke,

Thomas Gibbs,

Thomas Burgis,

Ezra Perrey,

John Burgis,

Jeremiah Whitney,

Henery Vincent,

Nathaniell Fish,

John Fish,

Benjamin Nye,

SANDWICH.

Gorge Bewitt,	Richard Smith,
John Green,	Gorḡ Barlow,
Steuen Winge,	Lodowick Hawkes,
Thomas Tobey,	Thomas Tupper,
Henery Dillingham,	Jacob Burgis,
Mr Edmond Freeman, Junir,	Steuen Skiffe.

SCITUATE.

[*17.]

The Names of such of the Towne of Scittuate as haue taken the Oath of Fidelitie in the Yeare 1657.

John Palmer, Senir,	Richard Standlocke,
John Palmer, Junir,	Steuen Tilden,
John Turner, Senir,	Jonas Pickle,
John Turner, Junir,	Samuell Vtley,
Thomas Turner,	John Durand,
Daniell Turner,	Robert Whetcombe,
Thomas Oldum,	Abraham Sutliffe,
Nathaniell Rawlins,	Jeremiah Hatch,
Steuen Vinall,	Mathew Gannett,
Gorge Pitcoke,	John Whiston,
Daniell Hickes,	John Sutton,
Wiłłam Randall,	Obadiah Winter,
Wiłłam Brookes,	Thomas Hatch,
Walter Hatch,	Thomas Hiland,
Wiłłam Curtis,	Steuen Tilden,
Thomas Ingham,	John Cowin.

In the yeare 1662.

John Otis.

1668.

Charles Stockbridḡ,	John Allin,
Experience Leichfeild,	Nathaniell Turner,
Samuell Clapp,	Israell Cudworth,
Thomas Kinge, Junir,	Henery Chettenden.

*The Names of such as haue taken the Oath of Fidellyty.
Plymouth.

Thomas Whitney,
‡Allexander Higgens,‡
‡Humphry Hewett,‡
‡Wiłłm Dennis,‡
Steephen Wood,
Gabriell Fallowell,
‡Wiłłm Fallowell,‡
Thom̃ Pope,
Thom̃ Williams,

Edmond Tilson,
‡John Allen,‡
John Wood,
‡Raph Hill,‡
Francis Billington,
Francis Goulder,
John Finney,
M͏ʳ John Groome.

h of the Towne of Plymouth as haue taken the Oath of Fidelitie
in the Yeare 1657.

Arther Hathewey,
Ephraim Tinkham,
Hugh Cole,
John Jourdaine,
Edward Gray,
John Smith, Seniʳ,
James Cole, Juniʳ,
Wiłłam Browne,
Gorge Bonum,
Josepth Dunham,
John Haward,
Nicolas Hodgis,

Samuell Cutbert,
John Holmes,
Samuell Rider, Juniʳ,
Josepth Warren,
John Moses,
Benjamine Eaton,
Josepth Billington,
Robert Ransom,
John Smith, Juniʳ,
Wiłłam Nelson,
Josepth Ramsden.

Names of those that haue taken the Oath of Fidelitie at Duxborrow, in the Yeare 1657.

Josepth Andrewes,
Thomas Bonney,
Zoeth Howland,
John Robins,
Nathaniell Bassett,

Thomas Butler,
Samuell Chandeler,
Roger Glasse,
John Harmon.

DUXBURY.
[*20.]

*Of Duxborrow that haue taken the Oath of Fidelitie.

‡Mr Willm Wetherrell,‡
Thomas Heyward,
‡Thomas Weyburne,‡
Edward Hall,
John Washburne, Senior,
‡Edmond Hawes,‡
Robte Mendame,
Willm Sherman,
John Mynor,
John Rowe,
Thomas Bonney,
‡Mr Willm Kemp,‡
‡Robte Waterman,‡
‡Dolord Davis,‡
‡Abraham Blush,‡
John Willis,
Edmond Hunt,
‡John Barker,‡
‡Robte Barker,‡
‡Joseph Biddle,‡

John Rogers,
Georg̃ Partrich,
Edward Bumpasse,
John Tisdall,
‡Rowland Leyhorne,‡
John Carew,
John Vobes,
Wm Merick,
Maurice Trevant,
Abraham Sampson,
Richard Beare,
John Browne,
‡Robte Carver,‡
Wm Renolds,
John Phillips,
James Lindell,
Edmond Weston,
Samuell Tompkins.
Arthur Harrison,
‡Raph Chapman.‡

1668.

Josepth Wadsworth.

SCITUATE.
[*21.]

*Of Scituate that haue taken the Oath of Fidelitie.

Mr William Vassell,
Henry Ewell,
Willm Crocker,
Robert Shelly,
John Crocker,
Joseph Coleman,
Nicholas Wade,
Willm Parker,
Georg̃ Willerd,

Thom̃ Hyland,
Thom̃ Pinson,
Thom̃ Pryor,
Isaack Wells,
Willm Holmes, Señ,
Edmond Eddenden,
Henry Merick,
Thom̃ Chittenden,
Willm Perry,

Roᵇte Linnell,
Josias Checkett,
1 John Stockbridᵍ,
Richard Foxwell,
Isaack Stedman,
Thomas Kinge,
Thomas Byrd,
John Winter,
Samuell Jackson,
Abraham Preble,
John Hollet,
James Cochman,

Richard Bankes,
Wilłm Willes,
Thomas Tart,
Robert Steedson,
Thoᵐ Hinckley, } now of Barnestable.
Henry Coggen,
John Woodfeild,
John Emerson,
John Dammen,
Radulphus Elmes,
Joseph Tilden.

SCITUATE.

*At Scittuate, Januar. 15ᵗʰ, 1644. [*22.]

Resolued White,
Edward Jenkine,
John Hoare,
John Whetstone,
Richard Mann,
Ephraim Kempton, Junʳ,
Hercules Hills,
John Bryan,
John Whitcombe,
Thomas Ensine,
Peter Collymer,
Wilłm Hatch, Juʳ,
Roᵇte Hamond,
John Rogers,
Isaack Chittenden,
John Hewes,

Henry Aduerd,
John Weatherden,
Thomas Hick,
Isaack Buck,
Elisha Besbye,
Georᵍ Russell,
Wilłm Randle,
Thomas Clapp,
Christopher Winter,
Wilłm Peakes,
Jeremiah Burrowes,
Walter Briggs,
Ephraim Kempton, Señ,
George Sutton,
Symon Sutton,
Thomas Robinson.

---

*Of Sandwich that haue taken the Oath of Fidelitie.

SANDWICH.
[*23.]

Edward Dillinghame,
Richard Chadwell,

John Carman,
Thomas Burges,

SANDWICH.

John Briggs,	John Ruckman,
James Skiffe,	Andrew Hellott,
Mr John Stukeley,	Wiłłm Hurst,
John Dingley,	John Joyce,
Richard Kerby,	Anthony Wright,
Michaell Turner,	28 John Didcutt,
George Blisse,	Mr Vincent Potter,
Georg̃ Knott,	Mr Wiłłm Edge,
Joseph Winsor,	Mr Henry Feake,
Thom̃ Shillingworth,	Wm Almy,
Mr John Blakemore,	Thom̃ Tupper,
Nathaniell Willis,	Peter Gaunt,
Peter Wright,	Robte Badfish,
Thom̃ Launder,	Anthony Bessy,
Wiłłm Harlow,	Georg̃ Slawson,
Thom̃ Boardman,	Wiłłm Newland,
John Fish,	Joseph Hollye,
Jonathan Fish,	John Blackwell.

John Gibbs took this oath 14th of August, 1671.

EASTHAM.
[*24.]

*The Names of such of the Towne of Eastham as haue taken
the Oath of Fidelitie in the Yeare 1657.

Ralph Smith,	Thomas Paine,
Josepth Harding,	Gorg̃ Crispe,
John Done,	✳ John Younge,
Jonathan Sparrow,	John Mantah,
John Banges,	Jonathan Higgens.
John Mayo,	

This 29th of the tweluth, 1670.

John Rogers,	John Cole.

James Rogers tooke the oath of fidelitie before Mr Freeman ; like
Ephraim Done.

Nathaniell Mayo, 1678.   Daniell Smith.

The Names of those that haue taken the Oath of Fidelitie of the BRIDGEWATER.
Towne of Bridgwater in the Yeare 1657.

Samuell Edson,	Marke Laythorpe,
Lawrance Willis,	Thomas Haward,
Francis Godfrey,	Wiłłam Snow,
John Ames,	John Haward.
Guido Bayley,	

---

*Of Yarmouth that haue taken the Oath of Fidellytye. YARMOUTH.
[*25.]

Mr Nicholas Symkins,	Wiłłm Twineing,
Mr William Lumpkin,	Robte Dennis,
Mr Marmaduk Mathewes,	Emanuell White,
Mr John Crowe,	Richard Sares,
Mr Anthony Thacher,	William Clarke,
Mr Thom̄ Howes,	James Mathewe,
Wm Chase,	Richard Prichard,
Wiłłm Palmer,	Thomas Falland,
Yeluerton Crowe,	Edward Sturges,
Hugh Tillie, als Hillier,	Richard Templer,
Peter Worden,	Wiłłm Nickerson,
John Miller,	James Cade,
Samuell Rider,	Wiłłm Northcoate,
Thomas Hatch,	Thom̄ Flawne,
Giles Hopkins,	Thom̄ Bray,
Gabriell Wheldon,	Richard Hore,
James Brussells,	Thom̄ Starr,
John Clary,	Francis Baker,
Josuah Barnes,	Mr Andrew Hellott.

*he Names of such of Yarmouth as tooke the Oath of Fidelitie in
the Yeare 1657.*

Samuell Rider, Senir,	Robert Eldred,
Richard Tayler,	*John Winge,	[*26.]

YARMOUTH.

Wiłłam Chase,	Richard Berrey,
Robert Nicarson,	Thomas Phillipes,
Dauid Okillia, Irishman,	John Dillingham,
Nicolas Nicarson,	Thomas Gage,
John Whilden,	Paule Seares,
John Miller,	Wiłłam Eldred,
Richard Lake,	Thomas Howes,
Thomas Crow,	Rich: Tayler,
Samuell Hall,	John Bell.

1669.   Shuball Dimake tooke the oath of fidelitie.

COHANNETT.
[*27.]

Of Cohannett that haue taken the Oath of Fidellytie.

Mr Richard Smyth,	Richard Paul,
Mr Nicholas Street,	Wiłłm Harvey,
Thomas Gilbert,	Hughe Rocester,
Thoᵯ Corke,	Franč Streete,
John Richmond,	Wiłłm Scadding,
Hezekiah Hore,	12 John Gungill,

TAUNTON.

The Names of such of Taunton as haue taken the Oath of Fidelit
in the Yeare 1657.

Francis Street,	Edw: Bobbitt,
Phillip Leanard,	Jonas Austine,
John Cobb,	Tho: Casswell,
Henery Andrewes,	Daniel Mokene,
Christopher Thrasher,	Edw: Cobb,
Gorg̃ Macye,	John Bryant,
James Bell,	John Briggs,
Thomas Lincon,	Josepth Wilbore,
James Phillips,	Sadrach Wilbore,
Peter Pitts,	John Cloy,
Aron Knapp,	Jonas Burt,

Thomas Cilton,
Richard Burt,
Will: Shepherd,
John Hathewey,
Richard Stacye,
Thomas Joanes,
John Cobb,
John Maycomber,
Peter Stakenbery,
*Jeremiah Newland,
John Hall,
Thomas Brayman
John Turner,
James Lennett,

Thomas Willington,
James Bell,
Jabesh Hackett,
Edward Rew,
Wiłłam Eavance,
Gyles Gilbert,
Josepth Gilbert,
Francis Smith,
Nicolas White,
Wiłłam Wetherell,
Jonas Austine,
Robert Crossman,
Timothy Hallowey,
Jonathan Briggs.

TAUNTON

[*28.]

---

*August, 1643. The Names of all the Males that are able to beare Armes from xvj. Yeares old to 60 Yeares, w*th*in the sev*r*all Towne-shipps.*

PLYMOUTH.

[*29.]

Plymouth.

+ M*r* Wiłłm Hanbury,
+ Raph Joanes,
+ ‡John Jenkine,‡
+ Charles Thurstone,
  Roḃte Eldred, 1,
  Roḃte Wickson, 2,
+ George Crips,
  John Howland, Señ, 3,
  John Howland, Juñ, 4,
‡Francis Cooke,‡
  Jacob Cooke, 5,
+ John Cooke, Ju*r*, his boy, 6,
+ Samuell Eaton,
  Wiłłm Spooner, 7,
+ Phineas Pratt,
+ ‡George Clarke,‡
  Francis Billington, 8,

  Benjamin Eaton, 9,
  ‡Abraham Pearse, the blackamore,‡
+ Mathew Fuller,
+ John Bundy,
  Thurston Clarke, Jun*r*, 10,
  ‡Gregory Armestrong,‡
+ Roḃte Lee,
  Nicholas Hodges, 11,
  Thomas Gray, 12,
+ ‡John Shawe, Señ,‡
  James Shawe, 13,
  John Shawe, Ju*r*,
  ‡Stephen Bryan,‡
  John Harman, 14,
  John Winslow, 15,
  Samuell Kinge, 16,
+ Edward Dotey,

PLYMOUTH.

[*30.]

Wil̶m Snowe, 17,
John Holmes, 18,
Wil̶m Hoskine, 19,
‡James Hurst,‡
‖George Lewes,‖
‡Mʳ John Atwood,‡
Wil̶m Crowe,
*Thomas Southwood,
+ Mʳ John Done,
James Cole, Señ,
James Cole, Juñ,
Heugh Cole,
Thomas Lettis,
John Grome,
₹ Brick,
Thomas Willet,
‡John Cooke, Señ,‡
+ Samuell Hicks,
Ephraim Hicks,
+ Richard Knowles,
+ James Renell,
‡James Adams,‡
John Yeonge,
Edward Holman,
‡Caleb Hopkins,‡
John Heyward,
Wil̶m Baker,
Richard Bashop,
+ John Gorame,
Mʳ Wᵐ Paddy,
Henry Atkins,
Mʳ Bradford,
John Bradford,
Samuell Stertevant,
Samuell Cutbert,
+ Mʳ Thomas Prence,
Thom̃ Roberts,
Wil̶m Nelson,
John Smyth,

+ Nathˡ Sowther,
Mʳ John Reynor,
Samuell Fuller,
Samuel Eddy,
Richard Sparrow,
+ John Kerby,
‡John Jenney, Sen.,‡
‡Samuell Jenney,‡
+ John Jenney, Juʳ,
Richard Smyth,
+ Josias Cooke,
John Wood,
Henry Wood,
Steephen Wood,
Ro̶te Paddock,
Josuah Pratt,
Richard Wright,
Andrew Ringe,
Gabriell Fallowell,
Thomas Cushman,
Thom̃ Sauory,
John Finney,
‡Webb Addey,‡
Thomas Pope,
Giles Rickett, Señ,
John Rickett,
Giles Rickett, Junʳ,
Georg̃ Watson,
John Barnes,
‡Edward Edwards,‡
+ John Jordaine,
John Dunhame,
Thom̃ Dunhame,
Samuell Dunhame,
Edmond Tilson,
+ John Smaley,
‡Francis Goulder,‡
Thomas Whitney,
+ Ezra Couell,

+ Anthony Snow,
+ Richard Higgens,
+ John Jenkine,
Nathaniell Morton,
Manasseth Kempton,
John Morton,
Ephraim Morton,
James Glasse,
+ Edward Banges,
Joseph Ramsden,
+ Jeremiah Whitney,
+ Nicholas Snow,
+ Marke Snow,
‡Wiłłm Fallowell,‡
Roḃte Finney,
John Smith, Senʳ,
Thoɱ Clarke,
Georḡ Bonum,

‡Wiłłm Shercliffe,‡
John Churchell,
Joseph Greene,
Thomas Morton,
+ Thomas Williams,
John Faunce,
Richard Church,
‡Gabriell Royle,‡
Nathaniell Warren,
Joseph Warren,
Roḃte Bartlett,
Thoɱ Shreeue,
+ Thoɱ Little,
John Tompson,
Ephraim Tinkham,
‡Wiłłm Browne,‡
+ Thomas Tiley,
‡Wᵐ Hartopp.‡

147

Duxborrow, 1643.

Moyses Symons,
Samuell Tompkins,
James Lyndall,
Thoɱ Ouldame,
Edmond Weston,
Wiłłm Hillier,
Wᵐ Foard,
Francis West,
Francis Godfrey,
Solomon Lenner,
John Irish,
Phillip Delanoy,
Mʳ John Alden, Señ,
John Alden, Juñ,
Jos: Alden,‖
Morris Truant,

John Vobes,
+ Wiłłm Sherman,
Samuell Nash,
Abraham Sampson,
Georḡ Soule,
Zachary Soule,
Wᵐ Maycumber,
Wᵐ Tubbs,
Wᵐ Paybody,
Experience Michell,
Henry Howland,
Henry Sampson,
John Browne,
Edmond Hunt,
Wiłłm Brett,
John Phillips,

DUXBURY.

Thomas Gannett,
Wm Mullens,
John Tisdale,
Nathanell Chaundor,
+ John Harding,
John Aymes,
+ Francis Goole,
John Wsborne, Señ,
John Washbore, Juñ,
Phillip Washborne,
Wm Bassett, Señ,
Wm Bassett, Juñ,
Francis Sprague,
Wiltm Laurance,
John Willis,
Jonathan Brewster,
+ Wiltm Brewster,
Loue Brewster,
Constant Southworth
Capt Standish,
Alexander Standish,
John Heyward,
John Farneseed,

Yong Jo: Brewster,
Haden

Thoñ Bonney,
Robte Hussey,
Richard Wilson,
Thoñ Heyward, Señ,
Thoñ Heyward, Juñ,
Th: Robins,
Arthur Harris,
Edward Hall,
Christopher Waddesworth,
+ Wiltm Clarke,
+ Mr Comfort Starr,
John Starr,
Daniell Turner,
Georg Partrich,
+ John Maynard,
+ Steephen Bryan,
John Roger,
+ Joseph Rogers,
Joseph Pryor,
+ Benjamin Reade,
Abraham Pearse,
Wm Merick,
Will: Hartub. 76.

Sam: Chanler.

SCITUATE.
[*32.]

*1643.   Scittuate.

Mr Charles Chauncey,
Thomas Hanford,
Robert Haward,
Raph Clemes,
Nathaniell Mote,
Henry Advard,
Wiltm Parker,
John Hollett,

Gowen White,
Wiltm Perrie,
Wiltm Holmes,
Thomas Ensigne,
Georg Willerd,
Richard
Walter Briggs,
John Hore,

John Wadfeild,
Thomas Allen,
John Hewes,
James Cudworth,
John Whistons,
Nicholas Wade,
John Tilton,
Thomas Symons,
‡Edward Foster,‡
Thomas Rawlins, Señ,
Thomas Rawlins, Juñ,
Roᵇte Brelles,
John Witherden,
John Beamont,
Richard Toute,
Georḡ   ^
Thomas Tarte,
John Dammon,
John Hammon,
Christopher Winter,
Henry Merrite,
John Merrite,
Isaack Chittenden,
Joseph Collman,
John Whitcombe,
Thomas Lapham,
Edmond Eddenden,
Thomas Hyland,
John Rogers,
Thomas Chambers,
Richard Curtis,
Willm Curtis,
Joseph Tilden,
Thoñ Tilden,
Edward Tarte,
Georḡ Sutton,
2 Symon Sutton,
*Thomas Pynson,
Richard Gannett,

Willm Randle,
Willm Hatch,
John Lewes,
Thomas Wyborne,
John Winter,
Humfrey Turner,
John Turner,
John Turner,
John Hewes,
John Williams, Señ,
John Williams, Juñ,
Edward Williams,
James Cushman,
‡James Till,‡
Jeremie ^
Peter Collemore,
Willm Wills,
Samuell Fuller,
Isaack Buck,
Willm Hatch,
Walter Hatch,
Harke Luse,
Thomas Clay,
Goodman Read,
Thomas Robinson,
Edward   ^
‡Ephraim Kempton, Señ,‡
Ephraim Kempton, Juʳ,
Walter Woodworth,
Isaack Stedman,
Georḡ Russell,
Georḡ Moore,
Mʳ Willm Vassell,
John Vassell,
Resolued White,
Willm Pakes,
Jacob ^
Thomas King,
Mʳ Weatherell,

[*33.]

SCITUATE.

Thomas Byrd,
Edward Jenkins,
Georg̃ Kennerick,
Mᴿ Garrat,
Henry Mason,
Elisha Besbeach,

John Bryant,
John Hatch,
John Stockbridg̃,
48 Robte Stutson,
   ^ Glasse. 100.

SANDWICH.

[*34.]

1643.   Sandwitch.

Henry Feake,
Daniell Wing,
Peter Gaunt,
Thomas Johnson,
Miles Black,
Nicholas Wright,
Edward Dillinghame,
John Fish,
Richard Kerby,
Thomas Launder,
Henry Saunderson,
John Winge,
Willm Wood,
John Ellis,
Thomas Nichols,
Anthony Bessy,
Joseph Winsor,
Nathaniell Willis,
Anthony Wright,
‡Richard Chadwell,‡
Jonathan Fish,
Samuell Arnold,
Georg̃ Allen,
Richard Burges,
Henry Cole,
Joseph Holly,

Thom̃ Burges, Senʳ,
Thomas Burges, Junʳ,
Thomas Tuper,
Hẽry Dillingham,
Henry Sephen,
Thomas Butler,
James Skiffe,
Laurance Willis,
John Presbury,
John Freeman,
Edmond Clarke,
Willm Swyft,
Michaell Turner,
Peter Wright,
Stephen Winge,
Thomas Bordman,
Raph Allen,
Francis Allen,
Thomas Gibbs,
Edmond Freeman, Juʳ,
Nathaniell Fish,
Robte Botefish,
Thomas Greenfeild,
Mathew Allen,
John Johnson.   51.

[Sherjashubb Bourne, — John Nye, — tooke this oath, anno 1673.]

[*35.]

*John Bell,
Peter Hanbury,

John Greene,
Richard Burne,

SANDWICH.

‡Thomas Shillingsworth,‡
‡John Dingley,‡
John Vincent,
‡John Joyce,‡
Wilłm Newland,
Edmond Berry,
Georḡ Buitt,
John Newland,
Benjamin Noy,
Georḡ Knott,
‡John Blakemore,‡
Mr Wilłm Leuerich,
Mr Edmond Freeman, Señ.
68

---

*Barnistable. 1643.

BARNSTABLE.
[*36.]

Mr John Lathrope,
Mr John Mayo,
Thomas Dimmock,
Richard Foxwell,
Nathaniell Bacon,
Samuell Mayo,
John Scudder,
Roger Goodspeed,
Henry Cobb,
Barnard Lumbard,
Thomas Huckings,
Edward Fitzrandle,
Georḡ Lewes,
Isaack Wells,
Henry Rowley,
Thomas Lothrope,
John Hall,
Thomas Lumbard,
Robte Linnett,
Wilłm Casley,
John Bursley,
Thomas Allen,
Samuell Jackson,
Wilłm Tilly,
Samuell Hinckley,
Thomas Hinckley,
John Smyth,
25

‡James Cudworth,‡
Mr Nicholas Symkins,
James Hamblin,
Henry Coggen,
Henry Borne,
Wilłm Crocker,
Austine Bearse,
Thomas Shawe,
John Cooper,
Thomas Hatch,
Robert Shelly,
‡Wilłm Pearse,‡
Wilłm Beetes,
John Crocker,
Abraham Blush,
Henry Ewell,
Dolor Davis, & his sonns,
Laurance Lichfeild,
Thomas Boreman,
Anthony Annable,
John Casley,
46 John Russell,
*John Foxwell, [*37.]
Thomas Blossome,
Samuell Lothrope,
Joseph Lothrope,
David Linnett,

BARNSTABLE.

Nathaniell Mayo,
Richard Berry,
John Blower,
Francis Crocker,

Benjamin Lothrope,
John Davis,
Nicholas Davis, 60.

YARMOUTH.
[*38.]

Yarmouth. 1643.

Robert Dennis,
Thomas Flaune,
‡Nicholas Sympkins,‡
Willm Chase, Senr,
Willm Chase, Junr,
Anthony Thacher,
Andrew Hellot, Juñ,
Samuell Williams,
John Derbey,
Thomas Payne,
Willm Twyneing,
James Mathews,
Yelverton Crowe,
John Crowe,
Tristrame Hull,
Edward Sturges,
Anthony Berry,
Thomas Howe,
Thomas Falland,
Nicholas Wadiloue,
Samuell Hellott,
Willm Palmer,
Richard Taylor,
Willm Lumpkine,
Willm Grause,
Henry Wheildon,

Samuell Rider,
Richard Prichett,
Richard Temple,
Thomas Starre,
Benjamin Hamond,
James Bursell,
Willm Edge,
Robert Davis,
Richard Seeres,
Heugh Norman,
Peter Worden,
Willm Nicholsone,
John Burstall,
Emanuell White,
Willm Norcutt,
Mr Marmaduke Mathews,
Richard Hore,
Roger Else,
John Gray,
Andrew Hellott, Señ,
Job Cole,
Daniell Cole,
Heugh Tilly, als Hillier, 49,
John Joyce,
Wm Pearse,
  ˄ Boreman.

*Taunton. 1643.

Mr John Browne,
Mr Willm Poole,
John Browne,
James Browne,
James Walker,
Oliū Purchase,
+ Thomas Gilbert,
Richard Stacye,
Willm Hollway,
Tymothy Hollway,
Willm Parker,
Peter Pitts,
John Parker,
Willm Hailstone,
Wm Hodges,
Willm Phillips,
John Maycumber,
Thomas Coggin,
James Wyatt,
Edward Rew,
Thoū Harvey,
James Chichester,
Willm Seward,
Aron Knapp,
John Barratt,   Richard Williams,
Nichlolas Hart,
Willm Powell,

Edward Bobbett,
Richard Paule,
Anthony Slocome,
Edward Case,
Thomas Farewell,
Tobias Saunders,
Henry Andrewes,
John Gallop,
John Gilbert, Junr,
John Stronge,
Thoū Cassell,
John Deane,
Edward Abbott,
Walter Deane,
Wm Wetherrell,
Hezekiah Hore,
George Macie,
Georḡ Hall,
John Perry,
Benjamin Wilson,
Mr Street,
Richard Williams,
Willm Evans,
Christopher Thrasher,
Thomas Cooke,
Thoū Cooke, Jr,
John Gingell. 54.

---

*Freemen of Marshfeild.

Mr Edward Winslow,
Mr Willm Thomas,
Josias Winslowe,
Kenelme Winslowe,
Mr Thoū Burne,
Mr Edward Buckley,

Robte Waterman,
John Dingley,
Thoū Shillingsworth,
John Russell,
Mr Nathll Thomas.

MARSHFIELD.

[*42.]

*1643. Marshfeild.

Mr Edward Winslow,	× Russell,
John Thomas,	Kenelme Winslowe,
Roƀte Chambers,	James Adams,
Arthur Hadaway,	Arthur Howland,
Twyford West,	Wiƚƚm Halloway,
Edward Bumpas,	Edward Brough,
John Rowse,	John Barker,
Roƀte Carver,	Thomas Howell,
Leiftennant Nathaniell Thomas,	Raph Chapman,
Anthony Watters,	Roƀte Barker,
Thomas Roberts,	Wiƚƚm Barden,
Henry Draton,	Wiƚƚm Brookes,
Raph Trumle,	Gilbert Brookes,
Allexander Williams,	Nathaniell Biell,
James Pittney,	Richard Beare, 41,
John Dingley,	Jos: Winslow,
Thomas Chillingsworth,	Anthony Snow,
Mr Edward Buckley,	John Goarum,
Wiƚƚm Hayle,	Josp^{he} Bidle,
Tymothy Williams,	∧ Putle,
John Bourne,	∧ Sherman,
Wiƚƚm Launder,	John Walker,
Roger Cooke,	Mr Win: man
Roƀte Waterman,	Wm Lathame,
Josias Winslow,	∧ Laurence.
× Lillye,	

REHOBOTH.

[*43.]

*Freemen of Seacunck, als Rehoboth.

Steven Payne,	Mr Saml Newman,
Wiƚƚm Carpenter,	Tho: Read, 1673.
Walter Palmer,	

[The following appears to be a list of Freemen, and to have been taken about the year 1658.]

*First, Plymouth.

Capᵗ Thomas Willett,
Mʳ John Howland,
Leifᵗ Tho: Southworth,
Mannasses Kemton,
Mʳ Wᵐ Bradford,
Francis Cooke,
John Shaw,
‡James Hurst,‡
John Dunham, Seniʳ,
‡Edward Doty.‡
Tho: Clarke,
The Elder Cushman,
John Cooke, Juniʳ,
Gorge Watson,
‡John Barnes,‡
Robert Bartlett,
Samuell Eedy,
James Cole, Seniʳ,
Wilłam Hoskins,
Robert Lee,
Nathaniell Morton,
Gabriell Fallowell,
Gyles Rickard, Seniʳ,
Edward Tilson,
‡Leiftenant Southworth,‡
Richard Wright,
John Dunham, Juniʳ,
Andrew Ringe,
Robert Finney,
John Morton,
Serjeant Ephraim Morton,

John Wood,
Henery Wood,
Jacob Cooke,
Samuell Dunham,
Samuell Hickes,
Francis Goulder,
John Churchill,
Samuell Fuller,
Wilłam Harlow,
Wilłam Spooner,
Serjeant James Shaw,
Tho: Lettice,
Gyles Rickard, Junʳ,
*Benajah Pratt,
‡Mʳ Wilłam Bradford,‡
John Rickard, 44,
Nathaniell Warren,
Thomas Morton,
‡Serjeant   ⌃   , ‡
‡Jonathan Dunhame,‡
‡Jonathan Shaw,‡
Steuen Bryant,
Wilłam Nelson,
Wilłam Clarke,
James Clarke,
Arther Hathaway,
Gorḡ Bonum,
Joseph Dunham,
Samuell Rider,
Abraham Jackson,
Jonathan Pratt.

*2^{condly}, *Duxburrow.*

M^r Wiłłam Collyare,

Mr John Alden,

‡Mr Ralph Partrich,‡

Edmond Chandeler,

Christopher Wadsworth,

‡Henery Howland,‡

Experience Michell,

Roger Chandeler,

Leif t Samuell Nash,

Phillip Delano,

Moses Simonson,

Henery Sampson,

Constant Southworth,

Wiłłam Tubbs,

Francis Sprague,

‖John Rogers,‖

Gorge Soule,

Gorge Partrich,

Abraham Peirse,

John Washburne, Seni^r,

Mr Allexander Standish,

Mr John Alden, Juni^r,

Wiłłam Paybody,

Edmond Weston,

Wiłłam Clarke,

Zacarya Soule,

Robert Barker,

‡Stephen Bryant,‡

John Washburne, Juni^r,

Abraham Sampson,

‡Mr Josias Standish,‡

Francis West,

Benjamin Bartlett, 32,

Joseph Aldin,

Jonathan Aldin,

John Tracye,

Josepth Wadsworth,

Jonathan Shaw,

‡Jonathan Pratt.‡

---

*3dly, *Scitteatte.*

Mr Timoth Hatherley,

Cap t James Cudworth,

Humphrey Turner,

Samuell House,

John Williams, Seni^r,

Tho: Chambers,

John Hewes,

Walter Woodworth,

Edward Jenckens,

John Allen,

Samuell Jackson,

Tho: Bird,

Tho: Clapp,

Wiłłam Wills,

Robert Studson,

John Williams, Juni^r,

Isacke Chettenden,

‡Sarjē John Bryant,‡

‡Wiłłam Randall,‡

Leif t James Torrey, 20,

Henery Ewill,

Josepth Wormall,

M^r Wiłłam Witherell,

Mr Thomas Kinge,

John Turner, Seni^r,
John Turner, Juni^r,
Resolued Whicte,
Thomas Pinchen,
Stephen Vinall,
John Vinall,
Jeremiah Hatch,
Rodulphus Elmes,
Isacke Bucke,
Josepth Colman, Seni^r,
Walter Briggs,

Humphrey Johnson,
Wilłam Barstow,
John Hollett,
Wilłam Brookes,
Gilbert Brookes,
Rich: Curtis,
Wilłam Curtis,
Walter Hatch,
John Sutton,
John Hanmore,
Mathew Ganett.

*4ᵍ, Sandwich.

Mr Edmond Freeman, Seni^r,
Mr John Vincent,
Richard Burne,
Tho: Tupper,

Tho: Burgis,
‡Wilłam Newland,‡
James Skiffe,
Wilłam Bassett, Juni^r, 9.

*5ᵗ, Taunton.

Capt Wilłam Poole,
John Deane,
Walter Dean,
‡Edward Case,‡
Wilłam Parker,
‡Wilłam Hailstone,‡
Richard Williams,
Gorge Hall,
John Tisdall,

Leift James Wyate,
James Walker,
‡George Macye,‡
Wilłam Harvey, 12,
Anthony Slocom,
Wilłam Witherell,
Peter Pitts,
Tho: Linkolne.

*6^{ly}, *Yarmouth.*

Mr Anthoney Thacher,
Mr John Crow,
Mr Tho: Howes,
[Mr John Miller,]
Tho: Falland,
Richard Hoar,
Emanuell White,

James Mathews,
Mr Edmond Hawes,
Edward Sturgis,
‡Samuell Arnold,‡
Richard Sares, 11,
Mr Yelverton Crow,
Josepth Howes.

---

*7^{ly}, *Barnstable.*

‡Mr Tho: Dimacke,‡
‡Wiłłam Casley,‡
Mr Robert Linnitt,
Mr Tho: Allin,
Anthony Anable,
Wiłłam Casley,
Isacke Robinson,
Henery Rowley,
John Cooper,
Henery Cobb,
Barnard Lumbert,
Henery Bourne,
Samuell Hinckley,
Edw: Fitsrandall,
Gorḡ Lewis, Seni^r,
James Hamblen,
‡Mr Tho: Hinckley,‡
Nathaniell Bacon,
Samuell Fuller,
John Finney,
John Crocker,

John Chipman,
John Smith,
Roger Goodspeed,
John Gorum,
Trustrum Hull,
Abraham Blush,
Tho: Huckens,
Leifẗ Mathew Fuller,
Austine Bearce,
John Jenckens,
Robert Shelley,
John Scudder,
Tho: Laythorp,
Josepth Laythorp, 33,
Gorge Lewis, Juni^r,
M^r Wiłłam Sarjeant,
Mr Tho: Dexter, Seni^r,
Tho: Lewis,
James Lewis,
John Howland,
Will: Dexter.

*8^{ly}, *Marshfeild.*

‖Major ‡Captaine‡ Josias Winslowe,‖
‡Mr Josias Winslow, Seni^r,‡
 Mr Kanelme Winslow,
‖Mr Josias Winslow, Seni^r,‖
 Mr Tho: Burne,
‖Mr Samuell Arnold,‖
 John Dingley,
 John Russell,
 Capt Nathaniell Thomas,
 Robert Caruer,
 Mr Tho: Besbech,
‡Capt Josias Winslow,‡
 Anthony Snow,
 John Bourne,

 Mr John Bradford,
 Leif^t Peregrine White,
 Elisha Besbey,
 Mr Anthoney Eames,
 Ensigne Marke Eames,
‡Richard Beare,‡
 Wil^tam Foard, Seni^r, 18,
 Gor͠g Russell,
 Timothy Williamson,
 John Rouse,
 John Addams,
 Wil^tam Foard, Juni^r,
 Mo͠ris Truant,
 Wil^tam Holmes.

*9^{ly}, *Rehoboth.*

 Mr John Brown,
 Mr Samuell Newman,
 Mr Stephen Payne,
‡Wil^tam Carpenter,‡
 Walter Palmer,
 Nicolas Iyde,
 Mr Tho: Cooper,
 Richard Bowine,

 Leif^t Peter Hunt, 9,
 John Allin,
 Mr Nicolas Pecke,
 Wil^tam Sabin,
 Daniell Smith,
 Mr John Browne, Juni^r,
 Mr James Browne,
 Phillip Walker.

*10^{ly}, *Eastham.*

 Mr Thomas Prence,
 Mr John Done,
 Edward Banges,
 Nicalas Snow,

 Josias Cooke,
 John Smalley,
 Leif^tē Josepth Rogers,
 Richard Higgens,

26

EASTHAM.

Job Cole,
Daniell Cole,
Robert Vixon,
Stephen Wood,
Richard Sparrow,
Mr John Freeman,
Nathaniell Mayo,

Henery Attkins,
Wilłam Walker, 17,
Marke Snow,
Wilłam Merricke,
Samuell Freeman,
Thomas Paine.

BRIDGEWATER.
[*55.]

*11^{ly}, Bridgwater.

Wilłam Britt,
Wilłam Bassett, Seni^r,
Tho: Haward, Seni^r,
John Willis,
Samuell Tompkins, 5,

Ensigne Josias Standish,
John Carre,
Lawrance Willis,
Tho: Haward, Juni^r,
Arther Harris.

PLYMOUTH.   *List of the Names of the Freemen of the Colonie of New Plymou
[*56.]   taken by Nathaniel Morton, Secretary, the first × Anno 16⅚⅞.

Major William Bradford,
Mr John Cotton,
The Elder Mr Thomas Cushman,
Mr Thomas Clarke,
Gorge Watson,
Leift Ephraim Morton,
Gyles Rickard, Seni^r,
Richard Wright,
Nathaniel Morton,
John Dunham,
Samuell Dunham,
Mr Joseph Bradford,
Mr Samuell Fuller,
Serjeant William Harlow,
Thomas Morton,
Gyles Rickard, Juni^r,

Andrew Ringe,
Stephen Bryant,
William Clarke,
James Clarke,
Gorge Bonum,
Leift Joseph Howland,
Joseph Dunham,
Jonathan Shaw,
Samuell Ryder,
Abraham Jackson,
Jonathan Pratt,
James Cole,
Nathaniell Southworth,
George Morton,
Ephraim Tilson,
Thomas Cushman, Junier,

John Doten, Jo × × PLYMOUTH.
John Jordane, Jo × × , Senr,
Joseph Bartlett, John Rickard, son of Gyles Rickard,
Thomas Faunce, Eph × × , Juni^r,
Eliezer Churchill, Joseph ×
Baruch Jourdaine, Isack ×
Elkanan Cushman, John Morton,
Nathaniell Holmes, John Binson,
Jonathan Morey, Nathaniell Atwood,
Joseph Warren, Samuell Gardiner,
Jonathan Barnes, 48, Gyles Rickard, Juni^r.
*W × × , Senr, [*57.]

ceived & admitted as Freemen at ye Generall Court held at Plimouth the first Tuesday of June, 1689, these underwritten.

John Churchell, Caleb Cooke,
Willm Churchell, Francis Cooke,
James Warren, Jacob Cooke,
Eleazer Ring, Saml Harlow,
Willm Ring, Jonathan Shaw.
Joshua Pratt, William Harlow, Junr,
Giles Rickard, Junr, Eleazer Dunham,
Saml Lucas, Isaac Samson,
Richard Cooper, Eleazer Cushman,
Benony Lucas, Edward Dotey, Senr.

Duxborrow.

DUXBURY.

Mr John Alden, Gorge Partrich,
Mr Ichabod Wiswall, Mr Allexander Standish,
Experience Michell, Capt Josias Standish,
Moses Simonson, William Paybody,
Henery Sampson, Edmond Weston,
John Rogers, Seni^r, William Clarke,

DUXBURY.

Benjamine Bartlett,
Francis West,
Robert Barker,
John Tracye,
Leiſt Jonathan Alden,
Rodulphus Thacher,
Samuell Hunt,
Abraham Sampson,
Samuell Weston,
Joseph Wadsworth,
William Tubbs,
John Delano,

[*58.] *Francis Barker,
John Wadsworth,

Edward Southworth,
David Aldin,
John Simmonson,
Josias Holmes,
William Brewster,
Wrestling Brewster,
Peter West,
Roger Glass,
Joseph Chandler,
Thomas Dillano,
Elnathan Weston,
Stephen Samson,
Sam¹ Dillano,
Abram Pierce.

SCITUATE.

Scittuate.

[*59.] Mʳ William Witherell,
Mʳ Thomas Kinge,
Leiſt Isacke Bucke,
Cornett Robert Studson,
Edward Jenkens,
Walter Woodworth,
Thomas Clapp,
William Wills,
Capt John Williams,
Gorge Russell,
John Bryant,
Henery Ewell,
John Turner, Seniʳ,
John Turner, Juniʳ,
Thomas Pencen,
Stephen Vinall,
Jeremiah Hatch,
Rodulphus Elmes,
Walter Briggs,
Richard Curtice,
Walter Hatch, 21,

*Matthew Gannett,
Samuell Wetherell,
John Cushen,
Petter Collymore,
John Bryant, Juniʳ,
Joseph Barstow,
Joseph Siluester,
Thomas Roes,
Joseph Woodworth,
Theophilous Witherell,
John Studson,
Thomas Kinge, Juniʳ,
Thomas Wade,
Ensigne John Allin,
William Hatch,
Samuell Clapp,
Thomas Jenkens,
James Torrey,
William Torrey,
Mʳ Thomas Palmer,
Israell Chettenden,

Nathaniel Church,
John Whiston,
Israell Hubburt,
Joseph Turner,
Willm Barstow,
Joseph Willis,
William Barrell,
James Briggs,
Benjamine Studson,
Samuell Wood,

William Perrey,
Nathaniel Brookes,
Samuell Studson,
John Reed,
Thomas Jenkins,
Nathaniel Turner,
Benjamin Pierce,
Abraham Sutliff,
Stephen Otis,
Joseph Otis.

SCITUATE.

---

*Sandwich.

SANDWICH.
[*60.]

Mr Edmond Freeman,
James Skiffe, Senir,
Thomas Burge, Senir,
James Skiffe, Junir,
Thomas Tupper,
Stephen Skiffe,
Joseph Burge,
William Swift,

John Blackwell,
Willam Rollox,
Jonathan Nye,
Henery Dillingham,
Sherjashub Burne,
Shuball Smith,
William Bassett, 15.

Taunton.

TAUNTON.

Mr Gorge Shoue,
Walter Deane,
Richard Williams,
Leift Gorge Macey,
James Walker,
William Harvey,
William Witherell,
John Hathwey,
Thomas Linkolne,
Peter Pitts,
Francis Smith,

Samuell Smith,
Ensigne Thomas Leonard,
Samuell Williams,
John Bryant,
John Cobb,
Nathaniell Williams,
Joseph Williams,
John Richmond,
William Hall,
James Tisdall,
Thomas Dean,

TAUNTON.

[*61.]

James Lenard, Junir,
Richard Steuens,
*John Deane,
Joseph Deane,
Thomas Harvey, Senir,
Thomas Harvey, Junir,
Esra Dean,
Thomas Gilbert,
Richard Burt,
Joseph Wilbor,
Shadrach Wilbore,

Henery Hodgis,
John Deane,
Mr Gyles Gilbert,
John Hathwey, Junier,
Joseph Thresher,
Samuell Hall, Senir,
John Crosman,
Mr Saml Danforth,
Mr Nathl Shove,
Israel Thrasher,
Phillip King.

YARMOUTH.

Yarmouth.

Mr John Thacher,
James Mathewes,
Mr Edmond Hawes,
Mr John Vincent,
Jeremiah Howes,
Edward Sturgis, Senir,
John Miller,
Joseph Howes,
Henery Vencent,
John Hawes,
Kanelme Winslow,

Sacheriah Ryder,
Paule Saeres,
Samuell Hall,
Joseph Ryder,
John Burge,
Samuell Hall, Senir,
Ensigne Silas Sares,
Thomas Sturges,
John Rider,
Joseph Hall,
Jeremiah Howes, Junir.

BARNSTABLE.

[*62.]

**Barnstable.*

Mr Thomas Hinckley,
Mr Barnabas Laythorp,
Elder John Chipman,
Capt Joseph Laythorpe,
Ensigne Barnard Lumbert,
James Hamblen, Senir,

Will: Crocker,
Roger Goodspeed,
Abraham Blush,
Austine Bearse,
John Jenkens,
Robertt Shelley,

John Scudder,
Thomas Laythorp,
Gorge Lewis,
Leifteñ John Howland,
William Dexter,
James Cobb,
James Hamblin, Juni^r,
James Hamblin,
Thomas Lewis,
Job Crocker,
John Finney, Juni^r,
Jabez Lumbert,
Nathaniell Bacon,
Joshua Lumbert,
Edward Lewis,
Leiftenant Samuell Allen,
Mellatiah Laythorpe,
Samuell Hinckley,
John Hinckley,
John Barker,
John Dunham, Junier,

James Gorum,
William Trope,
John Hamblen,
Samuell Hinckley,
Joseph Blush,
Mr Thomas Hinckley, Juni^r,
Joseph Crocker,
Eliezer Hamblin,
John Smith,
John Robinson,
Dauid Linitt,
Saml Lewes,
Cornelius Briggs,
James Whippoo,
Benjamin Lumbert,
John Otis,
John Hinkley,
Barnabas Lothrop, Junr,
Thomas Allin,
James Paine.

BARNSTABLE.

---

*Marshfeild.

MARSHFIELD.
[*63.]

Mr Samuell Arnold,
Capt Nathaniell Thomas,
Leiftenant Peregrine White,
Elisha Besbe,
John Dingley,
Anthony Snow,
John Bourne,
John Rouse,
Morrise Truant,
William Foard, Juni^r,
John Rogers,
Samuell Sprague,
Arther Howland, Juni^r,

John Foster,
Nathaniel Winslow,
Jacob Dingley,
Michell Foard,
Francis Croker,
Ephraim Litle,
Hopestill Bestbey,
Josiah Crooker,
Leift Isacke Litle,
John Doged,
John Branch,
John Hewett,
Samuell Arnold, Juni^r,

208 PLYMOUTH COLONY RECORDS.

MARSHFIELD.

Seth Arnold,
John Sherman,
Israell Holmes,
Justus Ames,
John Barker,
Josiah Holmes,
Thomas Wood,
Jonathan Ames,
Samuell Little,
John Read,
Samuell Thomas,
Isacke Holmes,
Josias Snow,
Daniell White,
Clement Kinge,
Abraham Holmes,
Robert Stanford,
Richard Childs,
John Thomas,

Mr Isaac Winslow,
Mr Nathl Thomas, Junr,
Kenelm Baker,
Nath^{ll} Winslow, Junr,
Saml Doggett,
Saml Sherman,
John Rouse,
David Eames,
Benjamin Phillips,
Ebenezer White,
Robert Stanford,
John Foster, Junr,
John Silvester,
John Walker,
James Macall,
John Sayer, Junr,
Joseph Taylor,
William Stevens.

EASTHAM.
[*64.]

*Eastham.

Mr John Freeman,
Mr John Done,
Mr Samuell Treat,
Job Cole,
Daniel Cole,
Robert Vixon,
Steuen Wood,
Ensigne William Merrick,
Henery Atkines,
Marke Snow,
William Walker,
Samuell Freeman,
Thomas Paine,
John Done, Juni^r,
Capt Jonathan Sparrow,

John Banges,
Thomas Rogers,
Joseph Harding,
Jonathan Higens,
Stephen Snow,
John Freeman,
John Mayo,
Joshua Banges,
Stephen Hopkens,
Josiah Cooke,
Daniell Done,
John Rogers,
Thomas Williams,
Joseph Stanton,
Josiah Snow,

Mr Edmond Freeman,
Ephraim Done,
John Snow,

Samuell Paine,
Thomas Paine, Juni^r.

---

*Rehoboth.

Mr Daniell Smith,
Mr Samuell Anger,
Thomas Cooper,
John Read, Seni^r,
Capt Peter Hunt,
Leift Nicholas Pecke,
William Sabin,
Anthonie Perry,
Jonah Palmer,
John Titus, Seni^r,
Wiltam Carpenter, Seni^r,
John Perram,
Samuell Newman,
Nicholas Iyd, Seni^r,
Thomas Read,
Gilbert Brookes,
Jonathan Fuller,
John Pecke,
Samuell Pecke,
Thomas Cooper, Juni^r,
Enocke Hunt,
Jonathan Bosworth, Seni^r,
Preserued Abel,
John Ormsbey,
Jonathan Blesse,
Gorge Kinricke,

Scrj: Thomas Wilmouth,
Richard Whittacare,
Samuell Sabin,
Joseph Pecke,
Abraham Perram,
John Willmouth,
John Titus, Juni^r,
Stephen Paine,
Noah Mason,
Daniel Read,
Thomas Kenricke,
John Hunt,
Joseph Bosworth,
Samuell Robinson,
Nathaniel Chaffey,
Samuell Walker,
Samuell Bullocke,
Jonathan Wilmouth,
Nicholas Iyde,
Joshua Smith,
Gorge Robinson,
Joseph Sabin,
John Perram,
Christopher Sanders,
John Woodcock, Senr,
Phillip Walker.

27

[The following list comprises some of the names of the purchasers. The leaf containing the thirty
nine first names is lost. The full list is on the 177th page of the fourth volume of Court Orders.]

[*66.]   *Samuell Fuller,   Phillip Delanoy,

Francis Eaton,   Moyses Simonson,

William Bassett,   George Soule,

Franc͠ Sprague,   Edward Holman, 53,

The heirs of John Crackstone,   Mr James Sherley,

Edward Bumpus,   Mr Beachampe,

William Palmer,   Mr Andrews,

Peter Browne,   Mr Hatherly,

Henry Sampson,   Mr William Thomas.

Experience Mitchell,   In all 58.

Copied from the Booke of Acts and Passages of Court, from anᵒ 1640 t
anno 1651.

ꝑ SAMUEL SPRAGUE, Secretary to the Genrll Court

of New Plimouth Colony, 1686.

INDEX.

INDEX

TO

BIRTHS, MARRIAGES, DEATHS, AND BURIALS.

is Index is generally in chronological order, and frequently the names of parents are repeated; but this course
been adopted to save time in examination, which was deemed of more consequence than a strictly alphabetical
gement.   D. P.

BIRTHS.

BELL, DOROTHY, daughter of Preserved, Rehoboth, 16 November, 1677, . . .66

Joanna, daughter of Preserved, Rehoboth, 11 January, 1681, ... 76

Preserved, children of, ... 66, 76

s, Adames, William, son of James, Scituate, 16 May, 1647, ... 19

Anna, daughter of James, Scituate, 18 April, ... 19

Richard, son of James, Scituate, 19 April, 1651, ... 20

Mary, daughter of James, Scituate, 27 January, 1653, ... 20

James, children of, ... 19, 20

, Hannah, daughter of John, Rehoboth, 10 October, 1673, ... 52

ohn, child of, ... 52

Allin, Caleb, Sandwich, 27 June. 1648, . . 6

sther, Sandwich, 8 December, 1648, . . . 6

benezer, Sandwich, 10 February, 1649, . . 9

udah, son of George, Sandwich, 30 January, 1650, ... 11

eorge, child of, ... 11

sther, daughter of Jonah, Jun., Taunton, 3 January, 1662, ... 38

onah, Jun., child of, ... 38

Mary, daughter of Jonah, Taunton, 12 May, 1663, ... 38

arah, daughter of Jonah, Taunton, 4 November, 1665, ... 38

onah, son of Jonah, Taunton, 17 August, 1667, ... 38

onah, children of, ... 38

Allen, Isaac, son of Isaac, Rehoboth, 3 January, 1674, ... 53

Catharine, daughter of Isaac, Rehoboth, 18 January, ... 88

Isaac, children of, ... 53, 88

Elizabeth, daughter of Daniel and Mary, Swansey, 28 September, 1673, . . . 48

Christian, daughter of Daniel, Swansey, 26 January, 1674, ... 61

Daniel, children of, ... 48, 61

John, son of Gedian and Sarah, Swansey, 20 October, 1673, ... 48

Gedian, child of, ... 48

Angeir, Anger, Ames, son of Samuel, Rehoboth, 29 June, 1681, ... 76

Hannah, daughter of Samuel, Rehoboth, 10 August, 1682, ... 78

Samuel, children of, ... 76, 78

Annible, Samuel, son of Anthony and Anne, (Alcocke,) 2 January, 1646, ... 41

Ezekiel, son of Anthony and Anne, (Alcocke,) Barnstable, ... 41

Desire, daughter of Anthony and Anne, (Alcocke,) Barnstable, October, 1653, . . 41

Anthony, children of, ... 41

Armsbey, Armesbey, Armsbee, Armbey, Thomas, son of Thomas, Taunton, 23 February, 1668, ... 54

Mary, daughter of Thomas, Taunton, 3 October, 1671, ... 54

Rebekah, daughter of Thomas, Taunton, 26 May, 1672, ... 60

Judith, daughter of Thomas, Taunton, 8 January, 1673, ... 59

Thomas, children of, ... 54, 59, 60
</table>

(213)

Armsbey, see Ormsbey.
Arnoll, Samuel, son of Samuel, Yarmouth, 9 May,
    1649, ... 9
  Samuel, child of, ... 9
Atkins, Mary, daughter of Henry, Plymouth, 13
    March, 1647, ... 5
  Samuel, son of Henry, Plymouth, 24 Febru-
    ary, 1651, ... 13
  Henry, children of, ... 13
  Isaac, son of Henry, Eastham, 14 June, 1657, 30
  Henry, child of, ... 30
Austine, John, son of Jonah, Taunton, 1 July, 1671, 54
  Jonah, son of, ... 54

MARRIAGES.

Adams, James, and Frances Varssell, Scituate,
    16 July, 1646, ... 19
Alcocke, Anne, and Anthony Annible, Barnstable,
    1 March, 1645, ... 41
Allen, Allin, William and Priscilla Browne, Sand-
    wich, 21 March, 1649, ... 9
  Isaac, and Mary Bowin, Rehoboth, 30 May,
    1673, ... 52
  Joseph, and Hannah Sabin, Rehoboth, 10 No-
    vember, 1673, ... 52
  Jonah, Sen., and Frances Hill, (of Unketey,)
    Taunton, 14 December, 1667, ... 38
Andrewes, Hannah, and Isaac Negus, Taunton,
    7 April, 1679, ... 83
  Sarah, and Garett Talbutt, Taunton, 1 April,
    1664, ... 38
Annible, Anthony, and Anne Alcocke, Barnstable,
    1 March, 1645, ... 41
  Hannah, and Thomas Burman, Barnstable,
    1 March, 1645, ... 41
  Susanna, and William Hatch, Scituate, 13
    May, 1652, ... 28
Ansell, Mary, and Joseph Laythorp, Barnstable,
    11 December, 1660, ... 46
Atwood, Mary, and John Holmes, Plymouth, 11
    December, 1661, ... 23
Auger, Thomas, and Elizabeth Packer, (of Bridge-
    water,) Taunton, 14 November, 1665, 30, 38
Austin, Esther, and Anthony Newland, Taunton,
    16 December, 1682, ... 86

DEATHS AND BURIALS.

Adams, Adames, Richard, son of James, Scituate,
    died 25 July, 1651, ... 20, 21
  James, child of, ... 20, 21
Allen, George, Sen., Sandwich, buried 2 May, 1648, 6
Allin, Constant, wife of Jonah, Sen., Taunton,
    died 22 April, 1667, ... 38

Allin, Jonah, Sen., wife of, ...
  Nehemiah, Swansey, buried, 24 June, 1675, .
Annadowne, Roger, Rehoboth, buried 13 Novem-
    ber, 1673, ...
Annible, Jane, wife of Anthony, Barnstable, buried,
    December, 1643, ...
  Anthony, wife of, ...
Armstrong, Gregory, Plymouth, died 5 Novem-
    ber, 1650, ...
Atkins, Mary, daughter of Henry, Plymouth, died
    15 June, 1649, ...
  Henry, child of, ...
Atwood, Ann, Plymouth, died 1 June, ...
Austin, Austine, Jonah, Taunton, died 10 May,
    1676, ...
  Jonah, Sen., Taunton, died 30 July, 1683, .

BIRTHS.

BACON, SAMUEL, son of Samuel and Mar-
    tha, (Foxwell,) Barnstable, 9 March,
    1659—1660, ...
  Martha, daughter of Samuel and Martha,
    (Foxwell,) Barnstable, 6 January, 1661,
  Samuel, children of, ...
  Hannah, daughter of Nathaniel and Hannah,
    (Mayo,) Barnstable, 4 September, 1643,
  Nathaniel, son of Nathaniel and Hannah,
    (Mayo,) Barnstable, 5 February, 1645, .
  Mary, daughter of Nathaniel and Hannah,
    (Mayo,) Barnstable, 12 August, 1648, .
  Samuel, son of Nathaniel and Hannah,
    (Mayo,) Barnstable, 25 February, 1650,
  Elizabeth, daughter of Nathaniel and Han-
    nah, (Mayo,) Barnstable, 28 January,
    1653, ...
  Jeremiah, son of Nathaniel and Hannah,
    (Mayo,) Barnstable, 8 May, 1657, . .
  Mercy, daughter of Nathaniel and Hannah,
    (Mayo,) Barnstable, 8 February, 1659, .
  Nathaniel, children of, ...
Baker, Samuel, son of Francis, Yarmouth, first of
    May, 1648, ...
  Francis, child of, ...
  Daniel, Yarmouth, 2 September, 1650, .
Banges, Bethiah, daughter of Edward, Eastham,
    28 May, 1650, ...
  Mercy, daughter of Edward, Eastham, 15 Oc-
    tober, 1651, ...
  Apphiah, daughter of Edward, Eastham, 1
    October, 1651, ...
  Edward, children of, ...
  Edward, son of Jonathan, Eastham, 30 Sep-
    tember, 1665, ...
  Rebekah, daughter of Jonathan, Eastham,
    1 February, 1667, ...

ges, Jonathan, son of Jonathan, Eastham, 11
May, 1670, ... 56
Jonathan, children of, ... 56
nes, Lydia, daughter of John, Plymouth, 24
April, 1647, ... 4
John, child of, ... 4
Elizabeth, daughter of Thomas, Swansey, 14
February, 1674, ... 61
Thomas, child of, ... 61
ow, Eliezer, son of Robert, Plymouth, 15 Sep-
tember, 1669, ... 32
Robert, son of, ... 32
let, Lydia, daughter of Robert, Plymouth, 8
June, 1647, ... 4
Mercy, daughter of Robert, Plymouth, 10
March, 1650, ... 11
Robert, children of, ... 11
, Benjamin, son of Robert, Rehoboth, 6 June,
1674, ... 53
Robert, child of, ... 53
se, Mary, daughter of Austine, Barnstable,
1640, ... 41
Martha, daughter of Austine, Barnstable, 1642, 41
Priscilla, daughter of Austine, Barnstable, 10
March, 1643, ... 41
Sarah, daughter of Austine, Barnstable, 28
March, 1646, ... 42
Abigail, daughter of Austine, Barnstable, 18
December, 1647, ... 42
Hannah, daughter of Austine, Barnstable, 16
November, 1649, ... 42
Joseph, son of Austine, Barnstable, 25 Janu-
ary, 1651, ... 42
Esther, daughter of Austine, Barnstable, 2 Oc-
tober, 1653, ... 42
Lydia, daughter of Austine, Barnstable, Sep-
tember, 1655, ... 42
Rebekah, daughter of Austine, Barnstable,
September 26, 1657, ... 42
James, son of Austine, Barnstable, July, 1660, 42
Austine, children of, ... 41, 42
Jane, daughter of James, Taunton, 4 April,
1658, ... 40
ohn, son of James, Taunton, 15 August, 1660, 40
ames, son of James, Taunton, 10 July, 1663, 40
Nathaniel, son of James, Taunton, 7 January,
1664, ... 40
Sarah, daughter of James, Taunton, 15 Sep-
tember, 1666, ... 40
Elizabeth, daughter of James, Taunton, 15
November, 1668, ... 40
Mary, daughter of James, Taunton, 7 July,
1669, ... 40
oseph, son of James, Taunton, 27 June, 1670, 55
Esther, daughter of James, Taunton, 15 August, 1672, ... 55

Bell, James, children of, ... 40, 55
Benjamine, Joseph, ... 41
Berstow, Deborah, daughter of William, Scituate,
August, 1650, ... 18
William, son of William, Scituate, Septem-
ber, 1652, ... 18
William, children of, ... 18
Besbey, Martha, daughter of John, Marshfield, 13
October, 1688, ... 89
John, son of John, Marshfield, 15 Septem-
ber, 1690, ... 89
Elijah, son of John, Marshfield, 29 January,
1691-2, ... 89
Mary, daughter of John, Marshfield, 28
March, 1693, ... 89
Moses, son of John, Marshfield, 20 October,
1695, ... 89
Elisha, son of John, Marshfield, 3 May, 1698, 89
John, children of, ... 89
Bessey, David, Sandwich, 23 May, 1649, . . . 9
Billington, Rebecca, daughter of Francis, Plym-
outh, 8 June, 1647, ... 4
——, daughter of Francis, Plymouth, 25
February, 1651, ... 13
Francis, children of, ... 4, 13
Blackwell, Michael, Sandwich, first of June, 1648, 6
Michael, son of John, Sandwich, 16 Novem-
ber, 1676, ... 64
John, child of, ... 64
Blanding, Blandinge, Samuel, son of William, Re-
hoboth, 11 April, 1680, ... 73
Obadiah, son of William, Rehoboth, 14 April, 87
William, children of, ... 73, 87
Blush, Sarah, daughter of Abraham and Anne,
Barnstable, 2 December, 1641, ... 41
Joseph, son of Abraham and Anne, Barnsta-
ble, 5 April, 1648, ... 41
Abraham, son of Abraham and Hannah, (Bar-
ker,) Barnstable, 16 October, 1654, . . 41
Abraham, children of, ... 41
Boatfish, Botfish, ——, Sandwich, 27 March, 1648, 5
Joseph, son of Robert, Sandwich, 3 April,
1651, ... 13
Robert, child of, ... 13
Bobbit, Bobbitt, Edward, son of Edward, Taunton,
15 July, 1655, ... 40
Sarah, daughter of Edward, Taunton, 20
March, 1657, ... 40
Hannah, daughter of Edward, Taunton, 9
March, 1660, ... 40
Damaris, daughter of Edward, Taunton, 15
September, 1663, ... 40
Elkana, daughter of Edward, Taunton, 15
December, 1665, ... 40
Dorcas, daughter of Edward, Taunton, 20
January, 1666, ... 40

ryant, Sarah, daughter of John, Scituate, 29
September, 1648, ... 18
Mary, daughter of John, Scituate, 24 February, 1649, ... 18
Martha, daughter of John, Scituate, 26 February, 1651, ... 18
Samuel, son of John, Scituate, 6 February, 1653, ... 18
John, children of, ... 18, 19
John, son of Stephen, Plymouth, 7 April, 1650, 10
Mary, daughter of Stephen, Plymouth, 29
May, 1654, ... 22
Stephen, son of Stephen, Plymouth, 2 February, 1657, ... 22
Sarah, daughter of Stephen, Plymouth, 28
November, 1659, ... 22
Lydia, daughter of Stephen, Plymouth, 23
October, 1662, ... 23
Elizabeth, daughter of Stephen, Plymouth, 17
October, 1665, ... 26
Stephen, children of, ... 10, 22, 23, 26
uckland, Matthew, son of Joseph, Rehoboth, 16
September, 1674, ... 53
Nehemiah, son of Joseph, Rehoboth, 31
March, 1678, ... 70
Lydia, daughter of Joseph, Rehoboth, 5 September, 1680, ... 73
Joseph, children of, ... 53, 70, 73
David, son of Benjamin, Rehoboth, 22 March, 1675, ... 62
Benjamin, son of, ... 62
ullocke, Mary, daughter of Samuel, Rehoboth, 5
October, 1674, ... 53
Thankful, daughter of Samuel, Rehoboth, 1681, ... 77
Samuel, children of, ... 53, 77
ampas, Lydia, daughter of Joseph, Plymouth, 2 August, 1669, ... 33, 34
Wybra, daughter of Joseph, Plymouth, 15
May, 1672, ... 34
Joseph, children of, ... 33, 34
andy, Bundey, James, son of John, Taunton, 29
December, 1664, ... 36
Sarah, daughter of John, Taunton, 4 March, 1668, ... 35
John, son of John, Taunton, 6 October, 1677, 70
Joseph, son of John, Taunton, 1 January, 1679, ... 82
Edward, son of John, Taunton, 13 August, 1681, ... 85
John, children of, ... 35, 36, 70, 82, 85
Samuel, son of Samuel, Taunton, 4 October, 1670, ... 39
Samuel, child of, ... 39
rman, Hannah, daughter of Thomas and Hannah, (Annible,) Barnstable, May, 1646, 41

Burman, Thomas, son of Thomas and Hannah, (Annible,) Barnstable, 1648, ... 41
Samuel, son of Thomas and Hannah, (Annible,) Barnstable, July, 1651, ... 41
Desire, daughter of Thomas and Hannah, (Annible,) Barnstable, May, 1654, ... 41
Mary, daughter of Thomas and Hannah, (Annible,) Barnstable, March, 1656, . . . 41
Mehitabel, daughter of Thomas and Hannah, (Annible,) Barnstable, September, 1658, 41
Trustrum, son of Thomas and Hannah, (Annible,) Barnstable, August, 1661, . . . 41
Thomas, children of, ... 41
Butler, Patience, born at Sandwich, 14 August, 1648, ... 6
Dorothy, daughter of Thomas, Sandwich, 23
January, 1650, ... 11
Thomas, child of, ... 11
Butterworth, Mary, daughter of John, Rehoboth, 20 March, 1677, ... 66
John, son of John, Rehoboth, 7 May, 1679, . 86
Elizabeth, daughter of John, Rehoboth, 15
January, 1682, ... 78
John, children of, ... 66, 78, 86

MARRIAGES.

Bacon, Samuel, and Martha Foxwell, Barnstable, 9 May, 1659, ... 41
Nathaniel, and Hannah Mayo, Barnstable, 4 December, 1642, ... 42
Banges, Rebecca, and Jonathan Sparrow, Eastham, 26 October, 1654, ... 15
Joshua, and Hannah Scudder, Eastham, 1 December, 1669, ... 58
John, and Hannah Smalley, Eastham, 23 January, 1660, ... 28
Jonathan, and Mary Mayo, Eastham, 16 July, 1664, ... 56
Mercy, and Stephen Merricke, Eastham, 28
December, 1670, ... 57
Apphiah, and John Knowles, Eastham, 28
December, 1670, ... 57
Baker, Mary, and Stephen Vinall, Scituate, 26 February, 1661, ... 29
Mercy, and Zechariah Eedey, Jun., Swansey, 13 February, 1683, ... 84
Barker, Hannah, and Abraham Blush, Barnstable, 41
Isaac, and Judith Prence, Plymouth, 28 December, 1665, ... 31
Barnes, Hester, and John Rickard, Plymouth, 31
October, 1651, ... 13
Mary, and Robert Marshall, Plymouth, . . 22
Jonathan, and Elizabeth Hedge, Plymouth, 4 January, 1665, ... 31

28

rgis, Thomas, and Elizabeth Basset, Sandwich, 8 November, 1648, ... 6

rman, Thomas, and Hannah Annible, Barnstable, 1 March, 1645, ... 41

rph, Stephen, and Elizabeth Perry, Rehoboth, 29 May, 1674, ... 53

tterworth, John, and Hannah Wheaten, Rehoboth, 4 September, 1674, ... 53

DEATHS AND BURIALS.

nges, Jonathan, son of Jonathan, died 11 May, 1670, ... 56

Jonathan, child of, ... 56

rnes, John, son of John, Plymouth, died 25 December, 1648, ... 5

Mary, wife of John, Plymouth, died 2 June, 1651, ... 13

John, child of, ... 5

John, wife of, ... 13

rrow, Eliezer, son of Robert, Plymouth, died 13 December, 1669, ... 32

Robert, child of, ... 32

ares, Robert, Rehoboth, 29 March, 1676, . . 63

ckmore, William, Scituate, died 21 April, 1676, 50

ckston, Sarah, wife of William, Rehoboth, buried June, 1673, ... 52

William, wife of, ... 52

sh, Anne, wife of Abraham, Barnstable, buried 16 May, 1651, ... 41

Hannah, wife of Abraham, Barnstable, buried March, 1658, ... 41

Abraham, wives of, ... 41

bbitt, Dorcas, daughter of Edward, Taunton, died 9 April, 1674, ... 55

Edward, child of, ... 55

num, Sarah, daughter of George, Plymouth, died 1649, ... 8

George, child of, 1649, ... 8

sworth, Elizabeth, wife of Nathaniel, Jun., of Nantasket, died 6 April, 1673, . . . 34

Nathaniel, Jun., wife of, ... 34

vine, Richard, Sen., Rehoboth, buried 4 February, 1674, ... 54

Richard, widow of, buried 1675, ... 63

dford, Alice, Sen., Plymouth, died 26 March, 1670, ... 33

Alice, Jun., Plymouth, died 12 December, 1671, ... 33

ggs, Sarah, wife of William, Taunton, died 20 March, 1680, ... 81

William, wife of, ... 81

wne, Dorothy, wife of John, Sen., Swansey, 27 January, 1673, ... 48

John, Sen., wife of, ... 48

Bryant, Mary, daughter of John, died, Scituate, 8 April, 1652, ... 19

Mary, wife of John, Scituate, died 2 July, 1655, ... 49

John, child of, ... 19

John, wife of, ... 49

Buckland, Buckline, Nehemiah, son of Joseph, Rehoboth, buried May, 1677, ... 64

Joseph, son of, ... 64

John, Rehoboth, buried 20 June, 1677, . . 67

Nehemiah, Rehoboth, buried 19 May, 1677, . 67

William, Rehoboth, buried 1 September, . 88

Bullocke, Mary, wife of Samuel, Swansey, died 4 October, 1674, ... 51

Samuel, wife of, ... 51

Bundy, Bundey, Patience, daughter of John, died, Taunton, 27 March, 1665, ... 30, 36

Martha, wife of John, Taunton, died 1 May, 1674, ... 55

John, child of, ... 30, 36

John, wife of, ... 55

Burt, Anna, wife of James, Taunton, died 17 August, 1665, ... 39

James, wife of, ... 39

BIRTHS.

CARPENTER, MIRIAM, daughter of William, Rehoboth, 16 October, 1674, . . 53

Obadiah, son of William, Rehoboth, 12 March, 1678, ... 70

Ephraim, son of William, Rehoboth, 25 April, 1681, ... 76

William, children of, ... 53, 70, 76

David, son of Samuel, Rehoboth, 17 April, 1675, ... 62

Solomon, son of Samuel, Rehoboth, 23 December, 1677, ... 66

Zechariah, son of Samuel, Rehoboth, 1 July, 1680, ... 73

Abraham, son of Samuel, Rehoboth, 20 September, 1682, ... 78

Samuel, children of, ... 62, 66, 73, 78

Amos, son of John, Rehoboth, 19 November, 1677, ... 67

Eliphalet, son of John, Rehoboth, 17 April, 1679, ... 86

Priscilla, daughter of John, Rehoboth, 20 January, 1680, ... 73

Dorothy, daughter of John, Rehoboth, 9 February, ——, ... 88

John, children of, ... 67, 73, 86, 88

Margaret, daughter of Joseph, Swansey, 4 May, 1675, ... 61

Joseph, child of, ... 61

Carpenter, Jotham, son of Benjamin, Swansey,
1 June, 1682, ... 80
Benjamin, child of, ... 80
Caswell, Casewell, Stephen, son of Thomas, Taun-
ton, 15 February, 1648, ... 36
Thomas, son of Thomas, Taunton, 22 Febru-
ary, 1650, ... 37
Peter, son of Thomas, Taunton, October,
1652, ... 37
Mary, daughter of Thomas, Taunton, Au-
gust, 1654, ... 37
John, son of Thomas, Taunton, July, 1656, . 37
Sarah, daughter of Thomas, Taunton, Novem-
ber, 1658, ... 37
William, son of Thomas, Taunton, 15 Sep-
tember, 1660, ... 37
Samuel, son of Thomas, Taunton, 26 January,
1662, ... 35
Elizabeth, daughter of Thomas, Taunton, 10
January, 1664, ... 35
Abigail, daughter of Thomas, Taunton, 27 Oc-
tober, 1666, ... 36
Esther, daughter of Thomas, Taunton, 4 June,
1669, ... 39
Thomas, children of, ... 35—37, 39
Stephen, son of Stephen, Taunton, 11 Decem-
ber, 1673, ... 59
Joseph, son of Stephen, Taunton, 18 May,
1678, ... 80
Stephen, children of, ... 59, 80
Cettle, Cetill, Mary, daughter of Edward, Taun-
ton, 5 April, 1683, ... 86
Edward, child of, ... 86
Chaffey, Chaffee, Chafey, Thomas, son of Nathaniel,
Swansey, 19 October, 1672, ... 49
Rachel, daughter of Nathaniel, Swansey, 7
September, 1673, ... 51
Nathaniel, son of Nathaniel, Rehoboth, 8 Feb-
ruary, 1675, ... 62
Jonathan, son of Nathaniel, Rehoboth, 7
April, 1678, ... 71
David, son of Nathaniel, Rehoboth, 22 Au-
gust, 1680, ... 73
Experience, daughter of Nathaniel, Rehoboth,
24 March, ... 87
Nathaniel, children of, . . 49, 51, 62, 71, 73, 87
John, son of Joseph, Swansey, 16 Septem-
ber, 1673, ... 51
Dorothy, daughter of Joseph, Swansey, 4 Sep-
tember, 1682, ... 80
Joseph, children of, ... 51, 80
Chandeler, Samuel, son of Benjamin, Scituate, 30
November, 1674, ... 50
Benjamin, son of, ... 50
Chettenden, Sarah, daughter of Isaac, Scituate, 25
February, 1646, ... 28

Chettenden, Rebecca, daughter of Isaac, Scituate,
25 February, 1646, ... 2
Mary, daughter of Isaac, Scituate, 17 August,
1648, ... 2
Israel, son of Isaac, Scituate, 10 October, 1651, 2
Stephen, son of Isaac, Scituate, 5 November,
1654, ... 2
Elizabeth, daughter of Isaac, Scituate, 9 Sep-
tember, 1658, ... 2
Isaac, son of Isaac, Scituate, 30 September,
1663, ... 2
Isaac, children of, ... 28, 2
Child, Jeremiah, son of Jeremiah and Martha,
Swansey, 2 September, 1683, ... 8
Jeremiah, child of, ... 8
Chipman, Elizabeth, daughter of John, Plymouth,
24 June, 1647, ...
John, child of,
Hope, daughter of John, Barnstable, 13 Au-
gust, 1652, ... 4
Lydia, daughter of John, Barnstable, 25 De-
cember, 1654, ... 4
John, son of John, Barnstable, 2 March,
1656—7, ... 4
Hannah, daughter of John, Barnstable, 14
January, 1658, ... 4
Samuel, son of John, Barnstable, 15 April,
1662, ... 4
John, children of, ... 42, 4
Church, Abigail, daughter of Richard, Plymouth,
22 June, 1647, ...
Richard, child of, ...
Churchill, Hannah, daughter of John, Plymouth,
12 November, 1649, ...
Eliezer, son of John, Plymouth, 20 April,
1652, ...
Mary, daughter of John, Plymouth, 1 Au-
gust, 1654, ...
John, children of, ... 7, 14, 1
Hannah, daughter of Eliezer, Plymouth, 23
August, 1676, ... (
Joanna, daughter of Eliezer, Plymouth, 25
November, 1678, ... (
Eliezer, children of, ... (
John, son of Joseph, Plymouth, 22 July,
1678, ... (
Joseph, child of, ... (
Clapp, Abigail, daughter of Thomas, Scituate, 29
January, 1659, ...
Thomas, child of, ...
Cleaguehorne, James, son of James and Abigail,
(Lumbert,) Barnstable, 29 January, 1654,
Mary, daughter of James and Abigail, (Lum-
bert,) Barnstable, 28 October, 1655, . .
Elizabeth, daughter of James and Abigail,
(Lumbert,) Barnstable, April, 1658, . .

MARRIAGES.

DEATHS AND BURIALS.

MARRIAGES.

DEATHS AND BURIALS.

Dean, John, children of, ... 39, 55
  Thomas, son of Thomas, Taunton, died 26
    February, 1670, ... 60
  Thomas, child of, ... 60
  Bethiah, daughter of Ezra, Taunton, died 27
    November, 1679, ... 83
  Samuel, son of Ezra, Taunton, died 16 Feb-
    ruary, 1682, ... 86
  Ezra, children of, ... 83, 86
Dennis, Robert, Yarmouth, son of, died 1649, . . 10
Dotey, Edward, Plymouth, died 23 August, 1655, 17
Druce, John, Swansey, buried 2 July, 1675, . . 61
Dunham, Jonathan, son of John, Plymouth, died
    26 August, 1650, ... 10
  John, child of, ... 10
  Samuel, Plymouth, twin children of, died 1651, 13
  Mercy, wife of Joseph, Plymouth, died 19
    February, 1666, ... 31
  Joseph, wife of, ... 31
Dunham, John, Sen., Plymouth, died 2 March,
    1668, ... 32

BIRTHS.

EASTERBROOKE, ELIZABETH, daughter
  of Thomas and Sarah, Swansey, 19 De-
    cember, 1673, ... 48
  Thomas, daughter of, ... 48
Eedy, Hannah, daughter of Samuel, Plymouth, 23
    June, 1647, ... 4
  Samuel, child of, ... 4
  Zechariah, son of Zechariah, Plymouth, 10
    April, 1664, ... 26, 75
  John, son of Zechariah, Plymouth, 10 Octo-
    ber, 1666, ... 31, 75
  Elizabeth, daughter of Zechariah, Plymouth,
    3 August, 1670, ... 33
  Samuel, son of Zechariah, Sen., Plymouth,
    3 (4) June, 1673, ... 34, 75
  Ebenezer, son of Zechariah, Sen., Plymouth,
    8 February, 1675, ... 75
  Caleb, son of Zechariah, Plymouth, 21 Sep-
    tember, 1678, ... 75
  Joshua, son of Zechariah, Plymouth, 21 Feb-
    ruary, 1680, ... 75
  Obadiah, son of Zechariah, Plymouth, 2 Sep-
    tember, 1683, ... 75
  Zechariah, children of, . . . 26, 31, 33, 34, 75
  Alice, daughter of Zechariah, Jun., Plymouth,
    28 November, 1684, ... 76
  Elinor, daughter of Zechariah, Jun., Plym-
    outh, 16 May, 1686, ... 76
  Zechariah, Jun., children of, ... 76
  Mary, daughter of John, Taunton, 14 March,
    1666 or '67, ... 37, 83

Eedy, Eliezer, son of John, Taunton, 16 October,
    1671, ... 85,
  Mercy, daughter of John, Taunton, 5 July,
    1673, ...
  Ebenezer, son of John, Taunton, 16 May,
    1679, ...
  John, Taunton, 19 January, 1670, ...
  Hannah, Taunton, 5 July, 1676, ...
  John, children of, ... 37, 83, 85,
  Caleb, son of Caleb and Elizabeth, Swansey,
    29 May, 1672, ...
  Samuel, son of Caleb, Swansey, 15 July, 1675,
  Zechariah, son of Caleb, Swansey, 28 Janu-
    ary, 1682, ...
  Caleb, children of, ... 49, 61,
  John, son of Obadiah, Plymouth, 22 March,
    1669, ...
  Hasadiah, daughter of Obadiah, Plymouth, 10
    April, 1672, ...
  Obadiah, children of, ...
Eldred, Ann, daughter of William, Yarmouth, De-
    cember, 1648, ...
  William, child of, ...
  Nicholas, Yarmouth, 18 August, 1650, . .
  Sarah, Yarmouth, 10 October, 1650, . .
Elles, John, son of Roger, Yarmouth, first of De-
    cember, 1648, ...
  Roger, child of, ...
  Benet, Sandwich, 27 February, 1648, . . .
  Mordecai, son of John, Sandwich, 24 March,
    1650, ...
  John, child of, ...
Elmes, Sarah, daughter of Rodulphus, Scituate,
    29 September, 1645, ...
  Mary, daughter of Rodulphus, Scituate, 9
    June, 1648, ...
  Joanna, daughter of Rodulphus, Scituate, 28
    March, 1651, ...
  Hannah, daughter of Rodulphus, Scituate,
    25 December, 1653, ...
  John, son of Rodulphus, Scituate, 6 July, 1655,
  Joseph, son of Rodulphus, Scituate, 16 March,
    1658, ...
  Waitstill, daughter of Rodulphus, Scituate,
    9 February, 1660, ...
  Rodulphus, children of, ... 28,
Evens, Richard, son of Richard, Rehoboth, 10
    August, 1681, ...
  Richard, child of. . . . .
Ewell, Ewill, Hannah, daughter of Henry, Scitu-
    ate, 22 June, 1649, ...
  Gershom, son of Henry, Scituate, 14 Novem-
    ber, 1650, ...
  Abia, daughter of Henry, Scituate, 27 Sep-
    tember, 1653, ...
  Ichabod, son of Henry, Scituate, June, 1659,

Freeman, Thomas, son of John, Eastham, September, 1653, ... 26
Edmund, son of John, Eastham, June, 1657, 26
Mercy, daughter of John, Eastham, July, 1659, ... 26
Prence, son of John, Eastham, 3 February, 1665, ... 56
Nathaniel, son of John, Eastham, 20 March, 1669, ... 56
John, children of, ... 26, 56
Apthia, daughter of Samuel, Eastham, 11 December, 1660, ... 27
Apphiah, daughter of Samuel, Eastham, 1 January, 1666, ... 57
Constant, son of Samuel, Eastham, 31 March, 1669, ... 57
Samuel, children of, ... 27, 57
French, Hannah, daughter of John, Rehoboth, 19 October, 1679, ... 86
John, son of John, Rehoboth, 13 April, 1681, 77
John, children of, ... 77, 86
Thomas, son of Joseph, Taunton, 12 December, 1680, ... 82
Ebenezer, son of Joseph, Taunton, 27 June, 1682, ... 86
Joseph, children of, ... 82, 86
Fuller, Thomas, son of Samuel, Sen., Barnstable, 18 May, 1650, ... 43
Sarah, daughter of Samuel, Sen., Barnstable, 14 December, 1654, ... 43
Samuel, Sen., Barnstable, child of, 8 February, 1658, ... 43
Samuel, Sen., children of, ... 43
Robert, son of Jonathan, Rehoboth, 2 March, 1673, ... 52
Elizabeth, daughter of Jonathan, Rehoboth, 12 May, 1678, ... 71
Sarah, daughter of Jonathan, Rehoboth, 23 April, 1680, ... 73
Mary, daughter of Jonathan, Rehoboth, 1 October, 1681, ... 76
Noah, son of Jonathan, Rehoboth, 12 February, ... 87
Jonathan, children of, . . . 52, 71, 73, 76, 87
John, son of John, Rehoboth, 8 September, 1674, ... 53
Abiel, son of John, Rehoboth, 30 December, 1676, ... 62
John, children of, ... 62

MARRIAGES.

Fairweather, John, and Elizabeth Dicksey, . . . 51
Falloway, Martha, and Samuel Dunham, Plymouth, 29 June, 1649, ... 8

Fallowell, John, and Sarah Wood, Plymouth, 13 February, 1667, ...
Faunce, Mary, and William Harlow, Plymouth, 15 July, 1658, ...
Patience, and John Holmes, Plymouth, 20 November, 1661, ...
Sarah, and Edward Doty, Plymouth, 26 February, 1662, ...
Mercy, and Nathaniel Holmes, Plymouth, 29 December, 1667, ...
Thomas, and Jane Nelson, Plymouth, 13 December, 1672, ...
Joseph, and Judith Rickard, Plymouth, 3 January, 1677, ...
Feake, Elizabeth, and John Dillingham, Sandwich, 24 March, 1650, ...
Fitch, Rebekah, and Moses Read, Rehoboth, 6 December, 1677, ...
Sarah, and Noah Mason, Rehoboth, 6 December, 1677, ...
Hannah, and Joseph Browne, Rehoboth, 10 November, 1680, ...
Foster, Richard, and Mary Bartlet, Plymouth, 10 September, 1651, ...
Mary, and Jonathan Morrey, Plymouth, 8 July, 1659, ...
Foxwell, Martha, and Samuel Bacon, Barnstable, 9 May, 1659, ...
Freeman, John, and Mercy Prence, Eastham, 13 February, 1649, ...
John, and Mary Prence, Sandwich, 14 February, 1649, ...
David, and Margaret Ingraham, (of Swansey,) 4 April, ...
French, Nathaniel, and Mary Tisdell, Taunton, 9 January, 1676, ...
John, and Mary Palmer, Rehoboth, 27 November, 1678, ...
Fuller, Mary, and Ralph James, Plymouth, 17 April, 1650, ...
Elizabeth, and Moses Rowley, Barnstable, 22 April, 1652, ...
Hannah, and Nicholas Bonham, Barnstable, 1 January, 1658, ...
Samuel, and Mary Iyde, Rehoboth, 12 December, 1673, ...
John, and Abigail Titus, Rehoboth, 25 April, 1673, ...
Abigail, and Thomas Cushman, Rehoboth, 16 October, 1679, ...

DEATHS AND BURIALS.

Fall, John, Swansey, buried 24 June, 1675, . .
Fallowell, Gabriel, Plymouth, died 28 Dec., 1667,

Gray, Susanna, daughter of Edward, Plymouth, 15 October, 1668, ... 32

Edward, children of, ... 12, 15, 22, 31, 32

Samuel, ... 22

Mehitabel, daughter of Joseph Gray, Taunton, 21 February, 1668, ... 80

Ephraim, son of Joseph, Taunton, 20 June, 1673, 59

Joseph, son of Joseph, Taunton, 31 December, 1673, ... 58, 59

Joseph, children of, ... 58, 59

William, born at Yarmouth, 5 October, 1650, 12

Gylson, Nathaniel, son of James, Rehoboth, 24 January, 1674, ... 53

James, son of, ... 53

MARRIAGES.

Gaille, Elizabeth, and George Robinson, Rehoboth, 12 November, 1680, ... 72

Gallop, Esther, and Henry Hodgis, Taunton, 17 December, 1674, ... 82

Garrett, Joseph, and Ruth Bucke, Scituate, 17 January, 1676, ... 50

Gaurdiner, Samuel, and Susanna Shelley, Plymouth, 20 December, 1682, ... 75

Gilbert, Thomas, and Anna Blacke, (of Milton,) Boston, 18 December, 1676, ... 70

Glover, Mary, and Thomas Hinckley, Barnstable, 16 March, 1659–60, ... 44

Godfrey, Godfree, Jane, and Israel Woodward, Taunton, 4 August, 1670, ... 69

Richard, Jun., and Mary Richmond, Taunton, 1 January, 1679, ... 83

Susanna, and Edward Cetill, Taunton, 10 July, 1682, ... 86

Goodspeed, Roger, and Allis Layton, Barnstable, December, 1641, ... 43

Gorum, Desire, Barnstable, married 7 October, 1641, 44

Gould, John, and Mary Crossman, Taunton, 24 August, 1673, ... 70

Gray, Edward, and Mary Winslow, Plymouth, 16 January, 1650, ... 11

Edward, and Dorothy Lettice, Plymouth, 12 December, 1665, ... 31

Desire, and Nathaniel Southworth, Plymouth, 10 January, 1671, ... 33

Joseph, and Rebecca Hill, Taunton, 25 February, 1667, ... 38

DEATHS AND BURIALS.

Gage, Thomas, Yarmouth, son of, died 1650, . . 12

Glase, Hannah, daughter of James, Plymouth, died 15 June, 1648, ... 5

Glase, James, child of, ...

Gorum, Captain John, Swansey, buried 5 February, 1675, ... 6

Goulder, Catharine, Plymouth, died 16 March, 1650, ... 1

Francis, Plymouth, died 17 May, 1664, . . 2

Graunt, Thomas, of Rehoboth, child of, buried September, 1676, ... 6

Gray, Thomas, Plymouth, died 7 June, 1654, . . 1

Ephraim, son of Joseph, Taunton, died 21 June, 1675, ... 7

Rebekah, wife of Joseph, Taunton, died 13 May, 1676, ... 7

Joseph, child of, ... 7

Joseph, wife of, ... 7

BIRTHS.

HACKE, WILLIAM, son of William, Taunton, 15 November, 1663, ... ε

William, son of, ... ε

Hackett, Hatckett, John, son of Jabez, Taunton, 26 December, 1654, ... 3

Jabez, son of Jabez, Taunton, 12 September, 1656, ... 3

Mary, daughter of Jabez, Taunton, 9 January, 1659, ... 3

Sarah, daughter of Jabez, Taunton, 13 July, 1661, ... 3

Samuel, son of Jabez, Taunton, 29 July, 1664, 3

Hannah, daughter of Jabez, Taunton, 25 January, 1666, ... 3

Jabez, children of, ... 3

Haddawey, John, son of, born 1657, ...

John, son of John, August, 1658, ...

John, children of, ...

Hall, Samuel, son of Samuel, Taunton, 11 December, 1664, ...

John, son of Samuel, Taunton, 19 October, 1666,

Nicholas, son of Samuel, Taunton, 28 October, 1670, ...

Mary, daughter of Samuel, Taunton, 3 October, 1672, ...

Sarah, daughter of Samuel, Taunton, 14 October, 1674, ...

Ebenezer, son of Samuel, Taunton, 19 March, 1677, ...

George, son of Samuel, Taunton, 25 January, 1680, ...

Samuel, children of, . . . 37, 39, 55, 59, 69,

Sarah, daughter of Samuel, Sen., Taunton, 2 March, 1679, ...

Samuel, Sen., child of, ...

Benjamin, son of John, Taunton, 6 December, 1677, ...

Higgens, Jonathan, child of, ... 57
  Joshua, son of Benjamin, Eastham, 1 October, 1668, ... 58
  Lydia, daughter of Benjamin, Eastham, May, 1670, ... 58
  Benjamin, children of, ... 58
  Jonathan, son of Richard, Plymouth, July, 1637, ... 27
  Benjamin, son of Richard, Plymouth, July, 1640, ... 27
  Mary, daughter of Richard, Eastham, 27 September, 1652, ... 27
  Eliakim, son of Richard, Eastham, 20 October, 1654, ... 27
  William, son of Richard, Eastham, 15 December, 1654, ... 27
  Jadiah, son of Richard, Eastham, 5 March, 1656, ... 27
  Richard, children of, ... 27
Hillies, Deborah, daughter of Hugh and Rose, Yarmouth, 30 October, 1643, ... 45
  Samuel, son of Hugh and Rose, Yarmouth, July, 1646, ... 45
  Hugh, children of, ... 45
Hinckley, Samuel, son of Samuel, Barnstable, 4 July, 1642, ... 44
  John, son of Samuel, Barnstable, 24 May, 1644, ... 44
  Samuel, children of, ... 44
  Mary, daughter of Thomas and Mary, (Richards,) Barnstable, 3 August, 1644, . . 44
  Sarah, daughter of Thomas and Mary, (Richards,) Barnstable, 4 November, 1646, . 44
  Melatiah, daughter of Thomas and Mary, (Richards,) Barnstable, 25 December, 1648, ... 44
  Hannah, daughter of Thomas and Mary, (Richards,) Barnstable, 15 April, 1651, . . 44
  Samuel, son of Thomas and Mary, (Richards,) Barnstable, 14 February, 1652, . . 44
  Thomas, son of Thomas, and Mary, (Richards,) Barnstable, 5 December, 1654, . . . 44
  Bethshuah, daughter of Thomas and Mary, (Richards,) Barnstable, 15 May, 1657, . 44
  Mehitabel, daughter of Thomas and Mary, (Richards,) Barnstable, 24 March, 1658-9, ... 44
  Admire, daughter of Thomas and Mary, (Glover,) Barnstable, 28 January, 1661, 44
  Ebenezer, son of Thomas and Mary, (Glover,) Barnstable, 22 February, 1662, . . . 44
  Thomas, children of, ... 44
Hoar, Hoare, Hore, Mercy, daughter of Hezekiah, Taunton, January, 1654, ... 39
  Nathaniel, son of Hezekiah, Taunton, March, 1656, ... 39

Hoar, Sarah, daughter of Hezekiah, Taunton, 1 April, 1658, ... 39
  Elizabeth, daughter of Hezekiah, Taunton, 26 May, 1660, ... 39
  Edward, son of Hezekiah, Taunton, 25 September, 1663, ... 39
  Lydia, daughter of Hezekiah, Taunton, 24 March, 1665, ... 39
  Mary, daughter of Hezekiah, Taunton, 22 September, 1669, ... 39
  Hezekiah, son of Hezekiah, Taunton, 10 November, 1678, ... 83
  Hezekiah, children of, ... 39, 83
  Abigail, daughter of Nathaniel, Taunton, 2 November, 1682, ... 86
  Nathaniel, child of, ... 86
Hodges, Hodgis, Mary, daughter of Henry, Taunton, 3 February, 1675, ... 82
  Esther, daughter of Henry, Taunton, 17 February, 1677, ... 82
  William, son of Henry, Taunton, 18 March, 1680, ... 82
  Charity, daughter of Henry, Taunton, 5 April, 1682, ... 86
  Henry, children of, ... 82, 86
Holmes, John, son of John, Plymouth, 22 March, 1662, ... 23
  John, child of, ... 23
Hopkins, William, son of Giles, Eastham, 9 January, 1660, ... 28
  Giles, child of, ... 28
  Elizabeth, daughter of Stephen, Eastham, June, 1668, ... 58
  Stephen, son of Stephen, Eastham, 15 July, 1670, ... 58
  Stephen, children of, ... 58
Hoskins, William, Plymouth, child of, 30 November, 1647, ... 4
  Samuel, son of William, Plymouth, 8 August, 1654, ... 16
  William, children of, ... 4, 16
  William, son of William, Plymouth, 30 June, 1681, ... 74
  William, child of, ... 74
  Anne, daughter of William, Taunton, 14 February, 1678, ... 69
  Sarah, daughter of William, Taunton, 31 August, 1679, ... 80
  William, son of William, Taunton, 30 June, 1681, ... 80
  Henry, son of William, Taunton, 13 March, 1683, 80
  William, children of, ... 69, 80, 80
Howland, Jabez, son of Jabez, Plymouth, 15 September, (November,) 1669, ... 35, 64
  Bethiah, daughter of Jabez, Plymouth, 3 June, 1674, ... 35

DEATHS AND BURIALS.

Jones, Shuball, son of Ralph, Barnstable, 27 August, 1654, ... 45
Jedidiah, son of Ralph, Barnstable, 4 January, 1656, ... 45
John, son of Ralph, Barnstable, 14 August, 1650, ... 15
Ralph, children of. 45
Jurdaine, Baruch, son of John, Plymouth, 24 February, 1650, ... 11
John, child of, ... 11

MARRIAGES.

Jackson, Abraham, and Remember Morton, Plymouth, 18 November, 1657, ... 17
James, Ralph, and Mary Fuller, Plymouth, 17 April, 1650, ... 10
Sarah, and Robert Parker, Barnstable, 28 January, 1656, ... 47
Jenkens, John, and Mary Ewer, Barnstable, 2 February, 1652, ... 45
Jones, Anna, and John Padducke, Swansey, 21 December, 1673, ... 48
Jordaine, Jourdaine, Thomas, and Esther Hall, Rehoboth, 24 December, 1674, ... 53
Jehosabath, and John Robins, Plymouth, 14 December, 1665, ... 31

DEATHS AND BURIALS.

Jennings, Susanna, Plymouth, died 23 March, 1654, ... 16
Johnson, Rachel, daughter of John, Rehoboth, buried April, 1682, ... 79
John, child of, ... 79
Jones, John, Swansey, buried 24 June, 1675, . . 61
Robert, Swansey, buried 24 June, 1675, . . 61

BIRTHS.

K EMTON, JOANNA, daughter of Ephraim, Scituate, 29 September, 1647, ... 18
Patience, daughter of Ephraim, Scituate, 2 October, 1648, ... 18
Ephraim, son of Ephraim, Scituate, 1 October, 1649, ... 18
Manasses, son of Ephraim, Scituate, 1 January, 1651, ... 18
Ephraim, children of, ... 18
Kendrick, Kenericke, Kennericke, Jasiel, son of Thomas, Rehoboth, 23 March, 1682, . 78
Mary, daughter of Thomas, Rehoboth, 2 January, ... 88

Kendrick, Thomas, children of, ... 78, 8
King, Kinge, Rhoda, daughter of Thomas, Scituate, 11 October, 1639, ... 2
George, son of Thomas, Scituate, 24 December, 1642, ... 2
Thomas, son of Thomas, Scituate, 21 June, 1645, ... 2
Daniel, son of Thomas, Scituate, 4 February, 1647, ... 2
Sarah, daughter of Thomas, Scituate, 24 May, 1650, ... 2
John, son of Thomas, Scituate, 30 May, 1652, 2
Thomas, children of, ... 2
Samuel, son of Samuel, Plymouth, 29 August, 1649, ...
Isaac, son of Samuel, Plymouth, 24 October, 1651, ... 1
Samuel, children of, ... 7, 1
Kinsley, Mary, daughter of Eldad, Rehoboth, 7 October, 1675, ... 6
Nathaniel, son of Eldad, Rehoboth, 5 February, 1678, ... 7
Eldad, children of, ... 7
Kirbey, Increase, Sandwich, February, 1649, . .
——, Sandwich, February, 1649, ...
Knowles, Samuel, son of Richard, Plymouth, 17 September, 1651, ... 1
Mehitabel, daughter of Richard, Eastham, 20 May, 1652, ... 1
Mehitabel, daughter of Richard, Eastham, 20 May, 1653, ... 8
Barbara, daughter of Richard, Eastham, 28 September, 1656, ... 8
Richard, children of, ... 12, 15,

MARRIAGES.

Kempton, Kemton, Ephraim, and Joanna Rawlins, Scituate, 28 January, 1645, ...
Joanna, and George Morton, Plymouth, 22 December, 1664, ...
Kenricke, Thomas, and Mary Perrey, Rehoboth, 17 June, 1681, ...
King, Thomas, and Jane Hatch, Scituate, 31 March, 1653, ...
Kingsley, Kinsley, John, and Mary Maury, Rehoboth, 16 March, 1674, ...
Elizabeth, and Samuel Palmer, Rehoboth, 12 January, 1680, ...
Knapp, Elizabeth, and Nicholas Stoughton, Taunton, 17 February, 1673, ...
Knott, Martha, and Thomas Tobye, Sandwich, 18 November, 1650, ...
Knowles, John, and Apphiah Banges, Eastham, 28 December, 1670, ...

Lewis, Sarah, daughter of George, Jun., and Mary, (Lumbert,) Barnstable, 12 January, 1659, . . 45

George, Jun., children of, ... 45

James, son of Thomas and Mary, (Davis,) Barnstable, March, 1654, ... 45

Thomas, son of Thomas and Mary, (Davis,) Barnstable, 15 July, 1656, ... 45

Mary, daughter of Thomas and Mary, (Davis,) Barnstable, 2 November, 1659, . . . 45

Thomas, children of, ... 45

Samuel, son of Thomas and Hannah, Swansey, 23 April, 1673, ... 48

Hephzibah, daughter of Thomas, Swansey, 15 November, 1674, ... 51

Thomas, children of, ... 51

John, son of James and Sarah, (Lane,) Barnstable, October, 1656, ... 46

Samuel, son of James and Sarah, (Lane,) Barnstable, 10 April, 1659, ... 46

James, children of, ... 46

Nathaniel, son of Nathaniel and Mary, Swansey, 17 July, 1673, ... 48

Nathaniel, son of, ... 48

Joseph, son of Joseph and Mary, Swansey, 6 June, 1672, ... 49

Sibill, daughter of Joseph, Swansey, 18 March, 1674, ... 61

Joseph, children of, ... 49, 61

Lincoln, Lincolne, Lincon, Mary, daughter of Thomas, Taunton, 12 May, 1652, . . . 39

Sarah, daughter of Thomas, Taunton, 25 September, 1654, ... 39

Thomas, son of Thomas, Taunton, 21 April, 1656, ... 39

Samuel, son of Thomas, Taunton, 16 March, 1658, ... 40

Jonah, son of Thomas, Taunton, 7 July, 1660, 40

Hannah, daughter of Thomas, Taunton, 15 March, 1663, ... 40

Constant, daughter of Thomas, Taunton, 16 May, 1665, ... 40

Elizabeth, daughter of Thomas, Taunton, 24 April, 1669, ... 39

Marcye, daughter of Thomas, Taunton, 3 April, 1670, ... 40

Thomas, children of, ... 39, 40

John, son of John, Taunton, 11 October, 1665, ... 36

Thomas, son of John, Taunton, 15 September, 1667, ... 36

John, children of, ... 36

Samuel, son of Samuel, Taunton, 1 June, 1664, 37

Hannah, daughter of Samuel, Taunton, 24 March, 1666, ... 37

Tamisen, daughter of Samuel, Taunton, 27 October, 1667, ... 37

Lincoln, Ebenezer, son of Samuel, Taunton, 15 October, 1673, ... 6⸱

Rachel, daughter of Samuel, Taunton, 16 September, 1677, ... 6⸱

John, son of Samuel, Taunton, 15 September, 1679, ... 8⸱

Samuel, children of, ... 37, 68, 8⸱

Linnitt, Samuel, son of David and Hannah, (Shilley,) Barnstable, 15 December, 1655, . 4⸱

Elisha, son of David and Hannah, (Shilley,) Barnstable, 1 June, 1658, ... 4⸱

Hannah, daughter of David and Hannah, (Shilley,) Barnstable, 15 December, 1660, 4⸱

David, children of, ... 4⸱

Little, Ephraim, son of Thomas, Plymouth, 17 May, 1650, ... 1

Thomas, child of, ... 1

Lohun, Nathaniel, son of William, Swansey, 2 February, 1674, ... 6⸱

William, son of, ... 6⸱

Lucas, John, son of Thomas, Plymouth, 15 July, 1656, ... 2

Mary, daughter of Thomas, Plymouth, 15 March, 1658, ... 2

Benoni, son of Thomas, Plymouth, 30 October, 1659, ... 2

Samuel, son of Thomas, Plymouth, 15 September, 1661, ... 2

William, son of Thomas, Plymouth, 13 January, 1662, ... 2

Thomas, children of, ... 2

Lumbert, Martha, daughter of Barnard, Barnstable, 19 September, 1640, ... ⸱

Jabez, son of Barnard, Barnstable, 1 July, 1642, ... ⸱

Barnard, children of, ... ⸱

Abigail, daughter of Joshua and Abigail, (Linnett,) Barnstable, 6 April, 1652, . . . ⸱

Mercy, daughter of Joshua and Abigail, (Linnett,) Barnstable, 15 January, 1655, . . ⸱

Jonathan, son of Joshua and Abigail, (Linnett,) Barnstable, 28 April, 1657, . .

Joshua, son of Joshua and Abigail, (Linnett,) Barnstable, 16 January, 1660, ...

Joshua, children of, ...

Jedidiah, son of Thomas, Sen., Barnstable, . ⸱

Benjamin, son of Thomas, Sen., Barnstable, 26 August, 1642, ...

Thomas, Sen., children of, ...

Jabez, Barnstable, son of, 18 February, 1661,

Luther, Edward, son of Hezekiah, Swansey, 27 April, 1674, ...

Hezekiah, child of, ...

Experience, daughter of Samuel, Swansey, 3 March, 1674-5, ...

Samuel, child of, ...

MARRIAGES.

Lane, Sarah, and James Lewis, Barnstable, October, 1655, ... 46

Laythorp, Laythorpe, Joseph, and Mary Ansell, Barnstable, 11 December, 1650, . . . 46

Mary, Barnstable, 20 November, 1656, . . 46

Thomas, of Barnstable, daughter of, married, 46

Abigail, and James Clarke, Plymouth, 7 October, 1657, ... 17

Barnabas, and Susanna Clarke, Plymouth, 3 November, 1658, ... 22

John, and Mary Cole, Jun., Plymouth, 3 January, 1671, ... 33

Layton, Allis, and Roger Goodspeed, Barnstable, December, 1641, ... 43

Leonard, Leanard, Thomas, and Mary Watson, Plymouth, 21 August, 1662, ... 23

Mary, (Bridgewater,) and John Pollard, Taunton, 24 December, 1673, ... 55

James, Jun., (Taunton,) and Lydia Calipher, (Milton,) 29 October, 1675, ... 65

Hannah, and Isaac Dean, Taunton, 24 January, 1677, ... 70

Benjamin, and Sarah Thrasher, Taunton, 15 January, 1678, ... 83

Lee, Mary, and John Howland, Plymouth, 26 October, 1651, ... 13

Lettice, Elizabeth, and William Shirtley, Plymouth, 18 October, 1655, ... 17

Dorothy, and Edward Gray, Plymouth, 12 December, 1665, ... 31

Lewis, Mary, and John Bryant, Scituate, 14 November, 1643, ... 17

George, of Barnstable, daughter of, married, 17

Thomas, and Mary Davis, Barnstable, 15 June, 1653, ... 45

George, Jun., and Mary Lumbert, Barnstable, December, 1654, ... 45

James, and Sarah Lane, Barnstable, October, 1655, ... 46

Lincoln, Lincone, Thomas, Sen., and Elizabeth Street, Taunton, 10 December, 1665, 30, 38

Linnett, Linnitt, Lynnitt, Hannah, and John Davis, Barnstable, 15 March, 1648, ... 43

Abigail, and Joshua Lumbert, Barnstable, May, 1650, ... 46

David, and Hannah Shilley, Barnstable, 15 March, 1652, ... 46

Little, Hannah, and Stephen Tilden, Scituate, 15 January, 1661, ... 29

Ephraim, Josiah Cotton and Hannah Sturtevant married by, ... 89

Lowell, John, (Boston,) and Elizabeth Silvester, Scituate, 24 January, 1658, ... 49

Lumbert, Joshua, and Abigail Linnett, Barnstable, May, 1650, ... 46

Mary, and George Lewis, Jun., Barnstable, December, 1654, ... 45

Abigail, and James Cleaguehorne, Barnstable, 6 January, 1654, ... 42

Martha, and John Martin, Barnstable, 1 July, 1657, ... 47

Jabez, and Sarah Darbey, Barnstable, 1 December, 1660, ... 46

DEATHS AND BURIALS.

Leanard, Lenard, Hannah, daughter of James, Taunton, died 25 February, 1671, . . 55

James, son of James, Taunton, died 30 December, 1674, ... 65

James, children of, ... 55, 65

Sarah, daughter of Krie, Rehoboth, 16 March, 1676, ... 64

Krie, child of, ... 64

Lettice, Lettece, Thomas, son of Thomas, Plymouth, died 3 November, 1650, ... 11

Thomas, child of, ... 11

Lewis, Joseph, Swansey, buried 24 June, 1675, . 61

Nathaniel, Swansey, died 13 October, 1683, . 85

Lohun, William, Swansey, buried 24 June, 1675, 61

Lumbert, Jabez, first-born son of, died 18 February, 1661, ... 46

Jeremiah, Barnstable, 10 June, 1671, . . . 41

BIRTHS.

MAN, RACHEL, daughter of Thomas, Rehoboth, 15 April, 1679, ... 87

Mary, daughter of Thomas, Rehoboth, 11 January, 1680, ... 73

Bethiah, daughter of Thomas, Rehoboth, 12 March, ... 87

Thomas, children of, ... 73, 87

Marchant, Mary, daughter of John, Yarmouth, 20 May, 1648, ... 6

John, child of, ... 6

Abijah, Yarmouth, 10 January, 1650, . . . 12

Marshall, Robert, son of Robert, Plymouth, 15 August, 1663, ... 24

Robert, child of, ... 24

Martin, Marten, Martine, John, son of John and Martha, (Lumbert,) Barnstable, June, 1658, . 47

George, son of John and Martha, (Lumbert,) Barnstable, October, 1660, ... 47

John, children of, ... 47

Melatiah, son of John and Jone, Swansey, 31 August, 1673, ... 48

Morton, Ephraim, son of George, Plymouth, 12
  April, 1670, ...   74
  Joannah, daughter of George, Plymouth, 27
  June, 1673, ...   74
  Ruth, daughter of George, Plymouth, 20 De-
  cember, 1676, ...   74
  George, son of George, Plymouth, 8 July,
  1678, ...   75
  Timothy, son of George, Plymouth, 12 March,
  1681-2, ...   75
  George, children of, ... 74, 75
Myles, James, son of John, the younger, Swansey,
  26 December, 1674, ...   51
  John, the younger, child of, ...   51

MARRIAGES.

Macomber, Maycomber, Sarah, (of Marshfield,)
  and William Briggs, Taunton, 6 Novem-
  ber, 1666, ...   38
  Ursilla, (Marshfield,) and Nicholas White,
  Jun., Taunton, 9 December, 1673 . .   70
Man, Thomas, and Mary Wheaton, Rehoboth,
  9 April, 1678, ...   71
Manning, Thomas, and Rachel Blisse, Swansey,
  (Rehoboth,) 28 October, 1674, . . 51, 53
Martin, John, and Martha Lumbert, Barnstable,
  1 July, 1657, ...   47
  John, and Mercy Billington, Rehoboth, 27
  June, 1681, ...   76
Marshall, Robert, and Mary Barnes, Plymouth, .   22
  Richard, and Esther Bell, Taunton, 11 Feb-
  ruary, 1676, ...   69
Mason, Noah, and Sarah Fitch, Rehoboth, 6 De-
  cember, 1677, ...   66
  Samuel, and Elizabeth Miller, Rehoboth, 2
  March, 1682, ...   79
Maury, Mary, and John Kinsley, Rehoboth, 16
  March, 1674, ...   53
Mayo, Hannah, and Nathaniel Bacon, Barnstable,
  4 December, 1642, ...   42
  Nathaniel, and Hannah Prence, Eastham, 13
  February, 1649, ...   26
  John, and Hannah Reycraft, Eastham, 1 Jan-
  uary, 1650, ...   26
  Mary, and Jonathan Banges, Eastham, 16
  July, 1664, ...   56
Medselfe, Thomas, and Ann Paine, Rehoboth, 2
  December, 1679, ...   87
Merricke, Mary, and Stephen Hopkins, Eastham,
  23 May, 1667, ...   58
  William, and Abigail Hopkins, Eastham, 23
  May, 1667, ...   56
  Stephen, and Mercy Banges, Eastham, 28
  December, 1670, ...   57

Merritt, Katherine, and John Damman, Scituate,
  June, 1644, ...   19
  Henry, daughter of, married, ...   19
Mery, Walter, and Martha Cotterell, Taunton, 17
  February, 1682, ...   86
Michell, Mary, and James Shaw, Plymouth, 24
  December, 1652, ...   14
  Jacob, and Susanna Pope, Plymouth, 7 No-
  vember, 1666, ...   31
Miller, Sarah, and John Titus, 3 July, 1677, . .   66
  Mary, and Samuel Perry, Rehoboth, 12 De-
  cember, 1678, ...   71
  Hannah, and Daniel Thurston, Rehoboth, 16
  December, 1681, ...   76
  Samuel, and Esther Bowin, Rehoboth, 20
  July, 1682, ...   79
  Elizabeth, and Samuel Mason, Rehoboth, 2
  March, 1682, ...   79
Morrey, Jonathan, and Mary Foster, Plymouth, 8
  July, 1659, ...   22
Morton, Remember. and Abraham Jackson, Plym-
  outh, 18 November, 1657, ...   17
  George, and Joanna Kempton, Plymouth, 22
  December, 1664, ...   25
  Hannah, and Benjamin Bosworth, Plymouth,
  27 November, 1666, ...   31
  Nathaniel, of Plymouth, and Anne Templar,
  of Charlestown, 29 April, 1674, . . .   35
  Joanna, of Plymouth, and Joseph Prince, of
  Hull, 7 December, 1670, ...   33
  Elizabeth, of Plymouth, and Nathaniel Bos-
  worth, Jun., of Hull, 7 December, 1670,   33
  Mercy, and Joseph Dunham, Plymouth, 18
  November, 1657, ...   17
Murcock, Mary, and William Browne, Plymouth,
  16 July, 1649, ...   8

DEATHS AND BURIALS.

Man, Rachel, wife of Thomas, Rehoboth, June, 1676,   63
  Thomas, Rehoboth, child of, buried June,
  1676, ...   64
  Thomas, wife of, ...   63
  Thomas, child of, ...   64
Mason, Martha, wife of Noah, Rehoboth, 6 Feb-
  ruary, 1675, ...   63
  Noah, wife of, ...   63
  Sampson, Rehoboth, September, 1676, . .   63
Merritt, Henry, Scituate, died last of November,
  1653, ...   19
Miller, Elizabeth, wife of John, Sen., Rehoboth,
  buried 18 April, 1680, ...   74
  John, Sen., wife of, ...   74
Morton, John, son of John, Plymouth, died 20 De-
  cember, 1649, ...   8

31

Morton, John, child of, ... 8
  Eliezer, son of Nathaniel, Plymouth, died 16
    January, 1649, ... 8
  Nathaniel, daughter of, Plymouth, still born,
    23 November, 1650, ... 11
  Nathaniel, son of Nathaniel, Plymouth, died
    17 February, 1666, ... 31
  Nathaniel, children of, ... 8, 11, 31
  Lydia, wife of Nathaniel, Sen., Plymouth,
    died 23 September, 1673, ... 35
  Nathaniel, Sen., wife of, ... 35
  John, Sen., Middleberry, died 3 October,
    1673, ... 35
  Myles, Rev. John., Swansey, died 3 February,
    1682, ... 81

BIRTHS.

NELSON, JOANE, daughter of William,
    Plymouth, 28 February, 1650, . . . 11
  William, child of, ... 11
Newland, Mary, Sandwich, 16 April, 1649, . . . 8
  Anthony, son of Jeremiah, Taunton, 1 Au-
    gust, 1657, ... 86
  Jeremiah, child of, ... 86
Newman, Antipas, son of Samuel, Rehoboth, 29
    March, 1673, ... 51
  Samuel, child of, ... 51
  Sibell, daughter of Noah, Rehoboth, 31 March,
    1675, ... 62
  Noah, child of, ... 62
Nicherson, Joseph, son of William, Yarmouth,
    10 mo., 1647, ... 3
  William, child of, ... 3
Nye, Jonathan, Sandwich, born 20 November,
    1649, ... 9
  Bethiah, daughter of Ebenezer, Sandwich, 5
    October, 1675, ... 81
  Ebenezer, child of, ... 81

MARRIAGES.

Negus, Isaac, and Hannah Andrewes, Taunton, 7
    April, 1679, ... 83
Nelson, Martha, and John Cobb, Plymouth, 28
    April, 1658, ... 17
  John, and Sarah Wood, Plymouth, 28 Novem-
    ber, 1667, ... 31
  Jane, and Thomas Faunce, Plymouth, 13 De-
    cember, 1672, ... 33
Newland, William, and Rose Holloway, Sandwich,
    19 May, 1648, ... 6
  Elizabeth, and William Witherell, Jun., Taun-
    ton, 14 March, 1681, ... 80

Newland, Anthony, and Esther Austin, Taunton,
    16 December, 1682, ... 86
Newman, Hopestill, and George Shove, Taunton,
    12 July, 1664, ... 59
Nicarson, Elizabeth, and Robert Eldred, Yarmouth,
    October, 1649, ... 10

DEATHS AND BURIALS.

Nelson, Martha, daughter of John, Plymouth,
    died 19 February, 1675, ... 64
  Sarah, wife of John, Plymouth, 4 March,
    1675, ... 64
  John, son of John, Plymouth, 5 June, 1676, 64
  John, children of, ... 64
  John, wife of, ... 64
Newman, Antipas, son of Samuel, Rehoboth,
    buried 17 July, 1673, ... 51
  Samuel, child of, ... 5
  Sibill, daughter of Noah, Rehoboth, 24 Sep-
    tember, 1675, ... 62
  Samuel, son of Noah, Rehoboth, buried 2 Oc-
    tober, 1677, ... 6
  Noah, children of, ... 63, 6
  Rev. Noah, Rehoboth, buried 18 April, 1678, 7
Norman, Elizabeth, daughter of Hugh, Yarmouth,
    died 28 May, 1648, ...
  Hugh, daughter of, ...

BIRTHS.

OLDHAM, OLDUM, MARY, daughter of
    Thomas, Scituate, 20 August, 1658, . . 4
  Thomas, son of Thomas, Scituate, 30 Octo-
    ber, 1660, ... 2
  Thomas, children of, ... 29, 4
Ormsbey, Jeremiah, son of Thomas, Taunton, 25
    November, 1672, ...
  Hannah, daughter of Thomas, Rehoboth, 23
    September, 1678, ...
  Jacob, son of Thomas, Rehoboth, 13 Septem-
    ber, 1680, ...
  Bethya, daughter of Thomas, Rehoboth, 15
    April, 1682, ...
  Thomas, children of, ... 71, 73, 78,
  Jacob, son of Jacob, Rehoboth, 23 August,
    1674, ...
  Jacob, child of, ...
  Elizabeth, daughter of John, Rehoboth, 27
    November, 1674, ...
  Mary, daughter of John, Rehoboth, 4 April,
    1677, ...
  Jonathan, son of John, Rehoboth, 26 August,
    1678, ...

Pecke, Nathaniel, son of John, Rehoboth, 6 July,
    1680, ... 73
  Abigail, daughter of John, Rehoboth, 12
    March, ... 87
  John, children of, ... 53, 67, 73, 87
  Noah, son of Samuel, Rehoboth, 21 August,
    1678, ... 70
  Jael, daughter of Samuel, Rehoboth, 14 June,
    1680, ... 73
  Rebecca, daughter of Samuel, Rehoboth, 22
    October, 1681, ... 76
  Samuel, children of, ... 70, 73, 76
  Israel, son of Israel, Swansey, 18 December,
    1674, ... 51
  Bethiah, daughter of Israel and Bethiah, Swan-
    sey, 2 January, 1683, ... 85
  Israel, children of, ... 51, 85
  Elisha, son of Nathaniel, Swansey, 19 April,
    1675, ... 61
  Nathaniel, child of, ... 61
  Elisha, son of Nicholas, Rehoboth, 4 April, . 87
  Nicholas, child of, ... · . . . 87
Penfeild, Sarah, daughter of Thomas, Rehoboth,
    20 February, 1680, ... 73
  Thomas, child of, ... 73
  John, son of Samuel, Rehoboth, 30 May, . 87
  Samuel, child of, ... 87
Percival, see Pursuall.
Perram, Sarah, daughter of Abraham, Rehoboth,
    11 October, 1679, ... 86
  Rebekah, daughter of Abraham, Rehoboth,
    11 October, 1679, ... 86
  Abraham, children of, ... 86
  Noah, son of John, Rehoboth, 24 December,
    1679, . . · 86
  John, child of, ... 86
Perren, Peren, Mary, daughter of John, Jun., Re-
    hoboth, 16 April, 1673, ... 52
  John, Jun., child of, ... 52
  Mehitabel, daughter of John, Rehoboth, 19
    April, 1677, ... 66
  Daniel, son of John, Rehoboth, 18 March,
    1682, ... 78
  Nathaniel, son of John, Rehoboth, 9 Febru-
    ary, ... 87
  John, children of, ... 66, 78, 87
  Elizabeth, daughter of Abraham, Rehoboth,
    3 December, 1681, ... 77
  Abraham, child of, ... 77
Perry, Perrey, Mehitabel, daughter of Samuel, Re-
    hoboth, 30 April, 1680, ... 73
  Jaciel, son of Samuel, Rehoboth, 6 May, 1682, 78
  Samuel, children of, ... 73, 78
  James, son of Thomas, Scituate, 12 March,
    1673, ... 50
  Thomas, child of, ... 50

Phillips, Phillipps, James, son of James, Taunton,
    1 January, 1661, ... 4●
  Nathaniel, son of James, Taunton, 25 March,
    1664, ... 4●
  Sarah, daughter of James, Taunton, 17 March,
    1667, ... 4●
  William, son of James, Taunton, 21 August,
    1669, ... 4●
  James, children of, ... 4●
  Mehitabel, daughter of Samuel, Taunton, 9
    January, 1676, ... 7●
  Samuel, child of, ... 7
Phinney, Jonathan, son of John and Elizabeth,
    (Bayley,) Barnstable, 14 August, 1655, . 4
  Robert, son of John and Elizabeth, (Bayley,)
    Barnstable, 13 August, 1656, ... 4
  Hannah, daughter of John and Elizabeth,
    (Bayley,) Barnstable, 2 September, 1657, 4
  Elizabeth, daughter of John and Elizabeth,
    (Bayley,) Barnstable, 15 March, 1658-9, 4
  Josiah, son of John and Elizabeth, (Bayley,)
    Barnstable, 11 January, 1660, ... 4●
  John, children of, ... 4●
Pickles, Jonas, son of Jonas, Scituate, 5 February,
    1658, ... 4
  Jonas, son of, ... 4
Pinchin, Thomas, son of Thomas, Scituate, 15 May,
    1640, ... 2
  Hannah, daughter of Thomas, Scituate, 4 De-
    cember, 1642, ... 2
  Thomas, children of, ... 2
Pollard, John, son of John, Taunton, 20 March,
    1675, ... ●
  John, child of, ... ●
Pope, Seth, son of Thomas, Plymouth, 13 Janu-
    ary, 1647, ...
  Thomas, son of Thomas, Plymouth, 25 March,
    1651, ...
  John, son of Thomas, Plymouth, 15 March,
    1652, ...
  Thomas, children of, ... 5, 12,
Pratt, Prate, Abigail, daughter of Benajah, Plym-
    outh, 21 November, 1657, ...
  Benajah, child of, ...
  Abigail, daughter of Jonathan, Plymouth, 16
    June, 1665, ...
  Bathsheba, daughter of Jonathan, Plymouth,
    20 February, 1666, ...
  Jonathan, son of Jonathan, Plymouth, 20
    March, 1668, ...
  Hannah, daughter of Jonathan, Plymouth,
    28 June, 1671, ...
  Jabez, son of Jonathan, Plymouth, 1 Novem-
    ber, 1673, ...
  Meletiah, daughter of Jonathan, Plymouth,
    11 December, 1676, ...

att, Bethiah, daughter of Jonathan, Plymouth,
  8 August, 1679, ... 67
Jonathan, children of, ... 32, 33, 35, 67
rsuall, Elizabeth, daughter of James, Sandwich,
  10 September, 1675, ... 81
James, child of, ... 81

MARRIAGES.

ker, Elizabeth, (of Bridgewater,) and Thomas
  Auger, Taunton, 14 November, 1665, 30, 38
Jael, (of Bridgewater,) and John Smith, Sen.,
  Taunton, 15 November, 1672, ... 59
duck, Padducke, Padduk, Mary, and Thomas
  Roberts, Plymouth, 24 March, 1650, . 11
Alice, and Zachariah Eedey, 7 May, 1663, . 23
Susanna, (of Dartmouth,) and John Eedey,
  Taunton, last of November, 1665, . . 38
Susanna, (of Dartmouth,) and John Eedey,
  Taunton, 12 November, 1665, . . . 38, 82
John, and Anna Jones, Swansey, 21 Decem-
  ber, 1673, ... 48
e, Mary, and James Rogers, Eastham, 11 Jan-
  uary, 1670, ... 58
Rebekah, and Peter Hunt, Jun., Rehoboth, 24
  December, 1673, ... 52
Mary, and Enoch Hunt, Rehoboth, 29 Octo-
  ber, 1678, ... 71
Ann, and Thomas Medselfe, Rehoboth, 2 De-
  cember, 1679, ... 87
ner, Mary, and John French, Rehoboth, 27
  November, 1678, ... 71
Samuel, and Elizabeth Kingsley, Rehoboth,
  12 January, 1680, ... 72
er, William, and Mary Rawlins, Scituate,
  April, 1639, ... 19
William, and Mary Turner, Scituate, 13 November, 1651, ... 19
Robert, and Sarah James, Barnstable, 28 January, 1656, ... 47
Elisha, and Elizabeth Hinckley, Barnstable,
  15 July, 1657, ... 47
e, Hannah, and Daniel Reed, August 20, 1677, 66
Samuel, and Rebekah Hunt, Rehoboth, 21
  November, 1677, ... 66
Esther, and Jonathan Wilmouth, Rehoboth,
  29 December, 1680, ... 72
nan, Hannah, and John Hall, Taunton, 4 Feb-
  ruary 1667, ... 66
n, Anna, and Thomas Read, Rehoboth, 16
  June, 1675, ... 62
Abraham, and Sarah Walker, Rehoboth, 27
  December, 1677, ... 66
, Pery, Perrey, Elizabeth, and Stephen
  Burph, Rehoboth, 29 May, 1674, . . 53

Perry, Samuel, and Mary Miller, Rehoboth, 12
  December, 1678, ... 71
Mary, and Thomas Kenricke, Rehoboth, 17
  June, 1681, ... 76
Nathaniel, and Sarah Carpenter, Rehoboth,
  17 May, ... 88
Phillips, Phillipps, John, and Faith Dotey, Plym-
  outh, 14 March, 1666, ... 31
Samuel, and Widow Cobb, Taunton, 15 May,
  1676, ... 70
Phinney, John, and Abigail Coggen, Barnstable,
  10 June, 1650, ... 47
John, and Elizabeth Bayley, Barnstable, 26
  June, 1654, ... 47
Pickles, Jonas, and Alice Hallee, Scituate, 23 De-
  cember, 1657, ... 49
Pinson, Pinsen, Thomas, Jun., and Elizabeth
  White, Scituate, 18 September, 1662, . 29
Hannah, and George Young, Scituate, 15 Jan-
  uary, 1661, ... 29
Pitts, Samuel, and Sarah Bobitt, Taunton, 25
  March, 1680, ... 82
Pollard, John, Taunton, and Mary Leanard, Bridge-
  water, 24 December, 1673, ... 55
Poole, John, and Elizabeth Brenton, Taunton, 28
  March, 1672, ... 59
Pope, Susanna, and Jacob Michell, Plymouth, 7
  November, 1666, ... 31
Pratt, Prat, Hannah, and William Spooner, Plym-
  outh, 18 March, 1651, ... 13
Benajah, and Persis Dunham, Plymouth, 29
  November, 1655, ... 17
Jonathan, and Abigail Wood, Plymouth, 2
  November, 1664, ... 25
Bathsheba, and John Doged, Plymouth, 29
  August, 1667, ... 31
Prence, Mercy, and John Freeman, Eastham, 13
  February, 1649, ... 26
Mary, and John Freeman, Sandwich, 14 Feb-
  ruary, 1649, ... 9
Hannah, and Nathaniel Mayo, Eastham, 13
  February, 1649, ... 26
Jane, and Mark Snow, Eastham, 9 Jan., 1660, 28
Judith, and Isaac Barker, Plymouth, 28 De-
  cember, 1665, ... 31
Presberry, Catherine, and Richard Chadwell, Sand-
  wich, 22 July, 1649, ... 9
Prince, Joseph, of Hull, and Joanna Morton, of
  Plymouth, 7 December, 1670, . . . 33

DEATHS AND BURIALS.

Padduk, Robert, Plymouth, died 25 July, 1650, . 10
Paddy, Joseph, son of William, Plymouth, died
  18 February, 1649, ... 8

Paddy, Alice, wife of William, Plymouth, died 24
    April, 1651, ...   13
    William, child of, ...   8
    William, wife of, ...   13
Paine, Alice, Taunton, died 5 December, 1682, . 85
    Stephen, Rehoboth, buried 24 January, 1677, 67
    Stephen, Sen., Rehoboth, buried 21 August,
    1679, ...   87
Palmer, John, son of Samuel, Rehoboth, buried
    15 July, ...   88
    John, son of Samuel, Rehoboth, buried 5
    January, ...   88
    Samuel, children of, ...   88
Parker, Mary, wife of William, Scituate, died Au-
    gust, 1651, ...   21
    William, wife of, ...   21
    John, Taunton, died 14 February, 1667, . .   38
Peacocke, Margery, mother of George Shove,
    Taunton, buried 17 April, 1680, . . .   85
Pecke, Sarah, wife of Samuel, Rehoboth, buried
    27 October, 1673, ...   52
    Jael, daughter of Samuel, Rehoboth, buried
    6 July, 1680, ...   73
    Judith, daughter of Samuel, Rehoboth, buried
    20 February, 1681, ...   77
    Rebekah, daughter of Samuel, Rehoboth,
    buried 2 November, 1682, ...   79
    Samuel, wife of, ...   52
    Samuel, children of, ... 73, 77, 79
    Deliverance, wife of Nathaniel, Swansey, died
    30 April, 1675, buried 1 May, 1675,   61, 63
    Nathaniel, wife of, ...   61, 63
    Nathaniel, Rehoboth, 25 August, 1676, . .   63
    ——, child of Nicholas, Rehoboth, August,
    1676, ...   63
    Nicholas, child of, ...   63
Perram, Rebecca, daughter of Abraham, Rehoboth,
    buried 14 October, 1679, ...   87
    Abraham, child of, ...   87
Perren, Peren, John, Sen., Rehoboth, buried 13
    September, 1674, ...   54
    Nathaniel, son of John, Rehoboth, 3 Septem-
    ber, 1675, ...   63
    Nathaniel, son of John, Rehoboth, buried 24
    February, ...   88
    John, children of, ... 63, 88
Perry, Perrey, Anthony, Rehoboth, buried 1
    March, 1682–3, ...   79
    Jasiell, Rehoboth, September, 1676, . . .   63
    Mehitabel, Rehoboth, September, 1676, . .   63
Phinney, Abigail, wife of John, Barnstable, buried, 47
    John, wife of, ...   47
Pontus, William, Plymouth, died 9 February,
    1652, ...   14
Poole, Timothy, son of William, Taunton, died 15
    December, 1667, ...   38

Poole, William, child of, ...   8
Prence, Thomas, Plymouth, died 29 March, 1673, 3
Presbery, John, Sandwich, buried 19 May, 1648, .

BIRTHS.

RAMSDEN, DANIEL, son of Joseph, Plym-
    outh, 14 September, 1649, ...
    Joseph, child of, ...
Randall, Joseph, son of William, Scituate, March,
    1642, ...
    Hannah, daughter of William, Scituate, March,
    1644, ...
    William, son of William, Scituate, Decem-
    ber, 1647, ...
    John, son of William, Scituate, April, 1650,
    Elizabeth, daughter of William, Scituate, Oc-
    tober, 1652, ...
    Job, son of William, Scituate, 8 February,
    1654, ...
    William, children of, ...
Rawlins, Elizabeth, daughter of Nathaniel, Scitu-
    ate, 1 March, 1653, ...
    Ruth, daughter of Nathaniel, Scituate, 27
    September, 1655, ...
    Nathaniel, son of Nathaniel, Scituate, 7 Sep-
    tember, 1662, ...
    Nathaniel, children of, ... 20, 21,
Reed, Read, Hannah, daughter of Daniel, Reho-
    both, 30 June, 1678, ...
    Daniel, son of Daniel, Rehoboth, 20 January,
    1680, ...
    John, son of Daniel, Rehoboth, 25 February,
    1682, ...
    Daniel, children of, ... 71, 73,
    Zachariah, son of Moses, Rehoboth, 25 Octo-
    ber, 1678, ...
    Bethiah, daughter of Moses, Rehoboth, 2 No-
    vember, 1679, ...
    Zechariah, son of Moses, Rehoboth, 20 Octo-
    ber, 1681, ...
    Rebecca, daughter of Moses, Rehoboth, 14
    September, ...
    Moses, children of, ... 71, 77, 87,
    Thomas, son of Thomas, Rehoboth, 25 March,
    1678, ...
    Nathaniel, son of Thomas, Rehoboth, 30 March,
    1680, ...
    Hannah, daughter of Thomas, Rehoboth, 12
    April, 1682, ...
    Thomas, children of, ... 71, 73,
Redway, Reddaway, James, son of John, Reho-
    both, 10 January, 1678, ...
    John, son of John, Rehoboth, 10 Septem-
    ber, 1682, ...

MARRIAGES.

Reed, Read, Moses, and Rebekah Fitch, Rehoboth, 26 December, 1677, ... 66

Rachel, and Thomas Wilmoth, Rehoboth, 27 June, 1678, ... 71

Daniel, and Hannah Pecke, Rehoboth, August 20, 1677, ... 66

James, and Susanna Richmond, Taunton, 18 April, 1683, ... 86

Redding, John, and Mary Bassett, Sandwich, 22 October, 1676, ... 64

Redwey, Lydia, and John Titus, Rehoboth, 17 July, 1673, ... 52

Rew, Sarah, and James Walker, Sen., Taunton, 4 November, 1678, ... 69

Reycraft, Hannah, and John Mayo, Eastham, 1 January, 1650, ... 26

Richards, Mary, and Thomas Hinckley, Barnstable, 4 December, 1641, ... 44

Richmond, Richmon, Susanna, and James Reed, Taunton, 18 April, 1683, ... 86

Mary, and Richard Godfrey, Jun., Taunton, 1 January, 1679, ... 83

Rickard, Giles, Jun., and Hannah Dunham, Plymouth, 31 October, 1651, ... 13

John, and Hester Barnes, Plymouth, 31 October, 1651, ... 13

Gyles, Sen., and Jone Tilson, Plymouth, 20 May, 1662, ... 23

Gyles, Sen., and Hannah Churchill, Sen., Plymouth, 25 June, 1669, ... 32

Judith, and Joseph Faunce, Plymouth, 3 January, 1677, ... 68

Roberts, Thomas, and Mary Padduk, Plymouth, 24 March, 1650, ... 11

Robins, John, and Jehosabath Jourdaine, Plymouth, 14 December, 1665, ... 31

Robinson, Mary, and Thomas Wilmouth, Rehoboth, 7 June, 1674, ... 53

George, and Elizabeth Gaille, Rehoboth, 12 November, 1680, ... 72

Rockett, Joseph, and Mary Wilmouth, Rehoboth, 5 January, 1680, ... 72

Rogers, Joseph, and Susanna Deane, Eastham, 4 April, 1660, ... 27

Elizabeth, and Jonathan Higgens, Eastham, 9 January, 1660, ... 28

Hannah, Duxbury, and John Tisdall, Jun., Taunton, 23 November, 1664, ... 55

James, and Mary Paine, Eastham, 11 January, 1670, ... 58

Rouse, Thankful, and Samuel Bullocke, Rehoboth, 26 May, 1675, ... 62

Rowley, Moses, and Elizabeth Fuller, Barnstable, 22 April, 1652, ... 47

Ryder, Rider, Samuel, and Sarah Bartlett, Plymouth, 23 December, 1656, ... 17

Ryder, Samuel, and Lydia Tilden, Taunton, 14 June, 1680, ...

Elizabeth, and John Cole, Plymouth, 21 November, 1667, ...

DEATHS AND BURIALS.

Rawlins, Elizabeth, daughter of Nathaniel, Scituate, died 17 February, 1659, ...

Nathaniel, child of, ...

Nathaniel, Sen., Scituate, died 23 December, 1662, ...

Redway, James, Rehoboth, buried 28 October, 1676, ...

Reed, Read, Sarah, daughter of John, Rehoboth, January, 1675, ...

John, child of, ...

Sarah, daughter of John, Jun., Rehoboth, buried 19 July, 1673, ...

John, Jun., child of, ...

John, Jun., Rehoboth, buried April, 1676, .

John, son of Daniel, Rehoboth, buried 1 March, 1682–3, ...

Daniel, child of, ...

Zachariah, son of Moses, Rehoboth, buried January, 1678, ...

Moses, child of, ...

Elizabeth, wife of Thomas, Rehoboth, buried 23 February, 1674, ...

John, son of Thomas, Rehoboth, 4 December, 1676, ...

Thomas, wife of, ...

Thomas, child of, ...

Rew, Edward, Taunton, died 16 July, 1678, . .

Reyner, Joseph, Plymouth, died 23 November, 1652, ...

Rickard, Judith, wife of Giles, Sen., Plymouth, 6 February, 1661, ...

Giles, Sen., wife of, ...

Robinson, Nathaniel, son of George, Rehoboth, buried 9 November, 1673, ...

George, child of, ...

Rocked, Joseph, Rehoboth, buried 21 July, . .

Rogers, Sarah, daughter of Joseph, Sandwich, died 15 August, 1633, ...

Joseph, child of, ...

Joseph, Jun., Eastham, died 27 January, 1660,

Rowley, Moses, child of, 15 August, 1656, . . .

BIRTHS.

SABINE, SABIN, SABEN, MEHITABEL, daughter of William, Rehoboth, 10 May, 1673, ...

DEATHS AND BURIALS.

BIRTHS.

sdall, Sarah, wife of John, Sen., Taunton, died
December, 1676, ... 69
John, Sen., wife of, ... 69
tus, Lydia, wife of John, Rehoboth, 25 November, 1676, ... 63
John, wife of, ... 63
ompson, John, son of John, Plymouth, died 11
February, 1648, ... 5
John, son of, ... 5
pper, Thomas, Sen., Sandwich, died 28 March,
1676, ... 64
Anne, Sandwich, died 4 June, 1676, . . . 64
rner, Joseph, son of John, Sen., Scituate, died
15 January, 1647, ... 20, 21
John, Sen., child of, died, ... 20, 21
ining, William, Sen., Eastham, died 15 April,
1659, ... 28

BIRTH.

TLEY, LYDIA, daughter of Samuel, Scituate, 28 December, 1659, ... 29
Samuel, child of, ... 29

MARRIAGE.

ey, Samuel, and Hannah Hatch, Scituate, 6 December, 1648, ... 29

BIRTHS.

INALL, MARY, daughter of Stephen, Scit-
uate, 29 November, 1662, ... 29
Stephen, child of, ... 29
on, Jemineth, daughter of Robert, Eastham, 30
August, 1655, ... 27
Titus, son of Robert, Eastham, 2 December,
1657, ... 27
Elizabeth, daughter of Robert, Eastham, 29
May, 1660, ... 27
Robert, children of, ... 27

MARRIAGES.

ssall, Varssell, Judith, and Resolved White,
Scituate, 8 April, 1640, ... 19
William, daughter of, married, ... 19
Frances, and James Adams, Scituate, 16 July,
1646, ... 19
mayes, Benjamin, and Mercy Bradford, Plymouth, 21 December, 1648, ... 5
ll, Mary, and Isaac Chettenden, Scituate,
April, 1646, ... 28

Vinall, Stephen, and Mary Baker, Scituate, 26
February, 1661, ... 29
Vincent, Mary, Sandwich, married 8 November,
1648, ... 6

BIRTHS.

WALKER, JOHN, son of William, East-
ham, 24, April, 1655, ... 15
William, son of William, Eastham, 2 August,
1659, ... 27
William, children of, ... 15, 27
Ebenezer, son of Philip, Rehoboth, 15 No-
vember, 1676, ... 62
Philip, child of, ... 62
Samuel, son of Samuel, Rehoboth, 11 Novem-
ber, 1682, ... 79
Samuel, child of, ... 79
Warren, Warrin, Sarah, daughter of Nathaniel,
Plymouth, 29 August, 1649, ... 7
Hope, daughter of Nathaniel, Plymouth, 6
(7) March, 1650, (1651,) 11, 24
Jane, daughter of Nathaniel, Plymouth, 10
January, (31 December,) 1652, . . 14, 24
Elizabeth, daughter of Nathaniel, Plymouth,
15 September, 1654, ... 24
Alice, daughter of Nathaniel, Plymouth, 2
August, 1656, ... 24
Mercy, daughter of Nathaniel, Plymouth, 20
February, 1657, ... 24
Mary, daughter of Nathaniel, Plymouth, 9
March, 1660, ... 24
Nathaniel, son of Nathaniel, Plymouth, 10
March, 1661, ... 24
John, son of Nathaniel, Plymouth, 23 Octo-
ber, 1663, ... 24
James, son of Nathaniel, Plymouth, 7 No-
vember, 1665, ... 24, 25
Nathaniel, children of, ... 11, 14, 24, 25
Mercy, daughter of Joseph, Plymouth, 23
September, 1653, ... 33
Abigail, daughter of Joseph, Plymouth, 15
March, 1655, ... 34
Joseph, son of Joseph, Plymouth, 8 January,
1657, ... 34
Patience, daughter of Joseph, Plymouth, 15
March, 1660, ... 34
Elizabeth, daughter of Joseph, Plymouth, 15
August, 1662, ... 34
Benjamin, son of Joseph, Plymouth, 8 Janu-
ary, 1670, ... 34
Joseph, children of, ... 34
James, son of Richard, Plymouth, 13 Janu-
uary, 1679, ... 72
James, son of Richard, Plymouth, Jan., 1682, 75

MARRIAGES.

INDEX

TO

TOWNS, PLACES, AND CLERKS.

TOWNS AND PLACES.

CLERKS.

INDEX

TO THE

TREASURY ACCOUNTS, AND NAMES OF FREEMEN AND OTHERS.

---

(262)

Copeland, John, a Quaker, ... 95
Corke, Thomas, freeman, ... 186
Cornet, allowance to, ... 121
Cottle, Edward, and wife, fined, ... 148
Cotton, John, freeman, ... 202
Couell, Ezra, ... 188
Nathaniel, fined, ... 122
Country, the, see Plymouth Colony.
Cowin, John, ... 155
freeman, ... 180
Coxall, see Copall.
Crackstone, John, heirs of, ... 210
Crips, George, ... 187
Crispe, George, freeman, ... 184
Crocker, Croker, Eliezer, ... 161
Francis, ... 194, 207
freeman, ... 178
Job, freeman, ... 207
John, ... 193, 200
freeman, ... 182
Joseph, freeman, ... 207
Josiah, freeman, ... 207
William, ... 193
freeman, ... 182, 206
Crosman, Crossman, John, freeman, ... 206
Robert, fined, ... 144
freeman, ... 187
——, of Taunton, ... 100
Crow, Crowe, John, ... 115, 194, 200
freeman, ... 176, 185
Thomas, freeman, ... 186
William, ... 188
Yelverton, ... 194, 200
freeman, ... 185
Crowell, Edward, fined, ... 126
Cudworth, Israel, freeman, ... 180
James, ... 191, 193, 198
freeman, ... 175, 177
Mrs., ... 95, 99
Curtis, Curtice, Francis, . . . 139—141, 143, 145
Richard, ... 191, 199
freeman, ... 204
William, ... 191, 199
freeman, ... 180
Cushen, John, freeman, ... 204
on committee to take the Treasurer's account, 161
Cushenah, ... 107
Cushman, Eleazer, freeman, ... 203
Elkanan, freeman, ... 203
James, ... 191
Thomas, fined, ... 112
freeman, ... 174, 188, 202
Thomas, Jun., ... 114, 116
freeman, ... 202
the elder, ... 197
See Cochman.
Cutbert, Samuel, freeman, ... 181, 188
C——, Richard, of Barnstable, freeman, 1657, . 179

DANFORTH, SAMUEL, freeman, ... 206
Dammon, Dammen, John, ... 191
freeman, ... 183
Dartmouth, ... 137
rates, 118, 123, 126, 131, 134, 138, 142, 144, 156, 158, 160, 162, 164, 167, 169
Darison, George, ... 143, 145, 147
Davis, Dolor, freeman, ... 177, 182
and sons, ... 193
John, ... 194
freeman, ... 179
Nicholas, ... 194
freeman, ... 179
Robert, ... 194
Dean, Deane, Ezra, freeman, ... 206
John, ... 195, 199
freeman, ... 176, 206
Joseph, freeman, ... 206
Thomas, freeman, ... 205
Walter, ... 195, 199
freeman, ... 176, 205
Delano, Delanoy, Dellano, Dillano, John, freeman, 204
Philip, ... 189, 198, 210
freeman, ... 175
Samuel, freeman, ... 204
Thomas, ... 124
freeman, ... 204
and wife, ... 122
Dennis, Robert, ... 194
freeman, ... 185
William, freeman, ... 181
Derbey, John, ... 194
Dexter, Philip, ... 157
Thomas, Sen., ... 200
freeman, ... 179
William, ... 200
freeman, ... 179, 207
Didcutt, John, freeman, ... 184
Dillano, see Delano.
Dillingham, Dillinghame, Edward, ... 192
freeman, ... 183
Henry, ... 96, 98, 192
freeman, ... 180, 205
wife of, ... 103
John, freeman, ... 186
Dimmack, Dimmock, Dimacke, Dimake, Shuball, freeman, ... 186
Thomas, ... 193, 200
freeman, ... 176
Dingley, Jacob, freeman, ... 207
John, ... 121, 193, 195, 196, 201
freeman, ... 177, 184, 207

PLYMOUTH COLONY VITAL RECORDS

Transcribed from the Original Records

By George Ernest Bowman

Scattered through the first two volumes of the Plymouth Colony Court Orders we find nearly one hundred records of marriages. The earliest of these was in April, 1633, and the latest in July, 1646. Careful copies of the marriage records in these two volumes are presented in this article. In the next article will begin a transcript of the records in the volume labeled "Marriages, Births and Burials."

[Marriages in the Court Orders]

[C. O., I : 15, under the year 1633] Apr. 19 Thomas Little & Ann Warren married

[p. 27, under 1633] Septr. 12 John Barnes Married unto Mary Plumer the twelvth of September

Henry Rowly maried Ann the late wife of Tho: Blossome the 17 of October 1633.

[p. 59, under 1634] March 26 John Browne & Phebe Harding were
 • married 26th of March

William Palmer junior & Elizabeth Hodgekins were married the 27 of March.

[p. 64, under 1634] March 28 John Cooke Junior * & Saragh warren were married

[p. 66] May the   Jobe Cole and Rebecka Colier ⎫
    15 1634   Love Brewster & Sarah Collier ⎬ wer maried

June Kenelme winsloe & Elen Adames widdow wer married

[p. 68, under 1634] July Francis Billington and Christian Eaton widdow wer maried

[p. 72] november 27 . 1634 John Cooper & Precilla wright wer maried

December 11 1634 Richard Higgins & lidia Chandler wer maried

December 19 1634 Phillip Delanoe and Hester Dewsbery wer maried

[p. 75] January 6 . 1634 Edward Doten and ffayth Clarke wer maried

[p. 78] Mr Prence, & Mary Collier was maried ye first of Aprill . 1635.

[p. 81, under 1635] The . 16 . of September Josias Cooke, & Elizabeth † Dean, Widow was maried.

---

* Came in the Mayflower with his father, Francis[1]. He was called "Junior" to distinguish him from an older John Cooke, who came later.

† "Mary" was first written, but was crossed out and Elizabeth interlined.

The . 25 . of Desember Nathanell Morton, & Lidia Cooper was maried.

[p. 83, under 1635] The . 14 . Jan: Rowland laherne, and flower was maryed.

Henry Samson, and Anne Plumer, was maryed the . 6 . of feb:

[p. 92, under 1636] July . 6 Thomas Willet & Mary Browne were Married.

[p. 95, under 1636] Oct. 20 Rich More & Christian Hunt Married

Oct. 28 Joseph Beadle & Rachel Deane widow * married

Nov. 2ᵈ William Hodgekins & Sara Cushman Married

[p. 122] Thomas Pope and Anne ffallowell were marryed the xxviiiᵗʰ of July 1637 . before the Gov'nor.

[p. 131] Constant Southword † and Elizabeth Collyer married the second of novembᵣ 1637.

William Tubbs and Mercy Sprague married the ninth of novembᵣ 1637

[p. 166] William Renolds and Alis Kitson were maryed xxxᵗʰ August 1638

[p. 170, at a court held 4 September, 1638] Christopher Winter of Scituate for publishing him self in marriage wᵗʰ Jane Coop[er] contrary to order & custome of this Gov'ment is fyned xˢ

[p. 171] Georg Cleare & Abigall [‡] marryed the xxᵗʰ Septembᵣ 1638

[p. 173] Gowen White of Scituate & Elizabeth Ward were marryed the xvᵗʰ of October 1638.

John Winchester of Hinghame and Hannah Sillis of Scituate were marryed the xvᵗʰ Octobᵣ 1638.

[p. 176] Richard Paul and Margery Turner of Cohannatt were marryed the viiiᵗʰ of Novembᵣ 1638.

[p. 177] Georg Partrich and Sarah Tracy marryed the [§] of Novembᵣ 1638

John Smaley & Ann Walden married the xxixᵗʰ Novembᵣ 1638

Thomas Williams & Elizabeth Tart married the xxxᵗʰ Novembᵣ 1638

[p. 181] John Smyth and Bennett Moorecock marryed the viiᵗʰ Decembᵣ 1638

Robte Waterman & Elizabeth Bourne married the xiᵗʰ Decembᵣ 1638

William Hodgskins & Ann Hynes married the 21ᵗʰ Decembᵣ 1638

Raph Hill & Margreat Toothaker married the 21ᵗʰ Decembᵣ 1638.

Georg Clarke & Alis Martin married the xxiiᵗʰ Januar 1638.

[p. 182] Henry Ewell & Sarah Annable married the xxiiᵗʰ Novembᵣ 1638

Thomas Ensigne & Elizabeth Wilder marry 17ᵗʰ Januar 1638

[p. 185] Willm Sherman & Prudence Hill married the xxiiiᵗʰ Januar 1638

* "widow" was interlined, in a later hand.

† "Southerne" was first written, but "erne" was crossed out and "word" interlined, in the same hand.

‡ Space was left for the surname.

§ Space was left for the day.

[p. 198] William Harvey & Joane Hucker of Cohannett marryed the second of Aprill 1639.
John Rogers and Ann Churchman marryed the xvi^th of Aprill 1639
[p. 210] Thom Riddings & Ellene Pennye marryed the xx^th July 1639
Richard Knowles and Ruth Bower marryed the xv^th August . 1639.
[p. 216] Heugh Norman & Sarah White marryed the viii^th Octob^r 1639
Gyles Hopkins & Katherne Wheldon marryed the ix^th octob^r 1639
Richard Willis & Amey Glasse marryed the xi^th octob^r 1639
Samuell Tompkins & Lettis ffoster marryed the xi^th Octob^r 1639
Morris Trewant & Jane [*] marryed the 16th octob^r 1639
Anthony Snowe and Abigall Warren marryed the viii^th Novemb^r 1639
Thomas Pynson & Joane Stanley marryed the xth Novemb^r 1639
Samuell Jackson & Hester Siles † marryed the xx^th Novemb^r 1639
William Paddy of Plymouth m^rchant & Alice ffreeman of Sandwich marryed the xxiiii^th of Novemb^r 1639.
Thomas Whitton and Winyfride Harding marryed 22th Novemb^r 1639.
[p. 220] Nehemiah Smyth & Ann Burne marryed the xxi^th Januar 1639
[p. 222] ffrancis Weston & margery Reeves marryed the 27th of ffebruar 1639
[p. 226] William Hurst of Sandwich and Katherne Thickston marryed the 17th march 1639
Thomas Gilbert & Jane Rossiter of Taunton marryed the xxiii^th of March 1639.
[p. 235] Georg Pidcock & Sarah Ricard marryed the xvi^th may 1640.
John Mynard & Mary Starr marryed ‡
William ffallowell & Martha Beels marryed ‡
Benjamin Nye and Katherne Tupper marryed the xix^th october 1640
Willm Hiller and ‡
William Nelson and Martha fforde marryed the xxix^th of Octob^r 1640

[C. O., II : 20] ffrancis Baker & Isabell Twineing of Yarmouth marryed the xvii^th day of June 1641
[p. 26] Thomas Southerne and Elizabeth Reynor marryed the first of Septemb^r 1641
Robert ffinney & Phebe Ripley marryed the first of Septemb^r 1641
Mr Willm Hanbury & Hannah Sowther marryed the xxviii^th Septemb^r 1641
Henry Sirkman & Bridgitt ffuller marryed the xxx^th Septemb^r 1641
[p. 90] Henry Adford & Tomson Manson of Scituate marryed the vi^th of Octob^r 1643.
John Stockbridg and Elizabeth Sone of Scituate marryed the ix^th october 1643.

* Space was left for the surname.

† "Sealis." See Richard Sealis' will in this issue.

‡ These entries were left unfinished.

James Torrey & Ann Hatch of Scittuate marryed the second of Novemb^r 1643.

[p. 107] John Gorome and Desire * Howland marryed †

Richard Wright and Hester Cooke marryed the †

Stephen Wood and Abigall Dunhame marryed the vith Novemb^r 1644

Ephraim Morton & Ann Coop[er] marryed the xviiith Novemb^r 1644

Richard Bushop and Alis Clark marryed th 5th Decemb^r 1644

John Churchall and Hannah Pontus marryed the xviiith Decemb^r 1644

Georg Bonum and Sarah Morton marryed the xxth Decemb^r 1644

Henry Wood and Abigall Jenney the xxviiith Aprill 1644.

John Carew and Elizabeth [‡] marryed the [§] June 1644

Willm Payhody and Elizabeth Alden marryed the xxvith Decemb^r 1644

Ephraim Kempton and [||] Rauline married the †

[p. 110] Anthony Annable and Ann Elcock marryed the third of march 1644

Thomas Boreman of Barnestable & Hannah Annable marryed the third of march 1644

[p. 120] James Glasse and Mary Pontus marryed the xxxith of October 1645

[p. 125] John Turner and Mary Brewster marryed the xiith Novemb^r 1645

Nathaniell Warren & Sarah Walker marryed the xixth Novemb^r 1645.

John Washborne & Elizabeth Michell marryed the vith of Decemb^r 1645

John Tompson & Mary Cooke marryed the xxvith Decemb^r 1645.

Joseph Ramsden and Rachell Eaton marryed the second Day of march 1645.

[p. 130] Richard Smyth and Ruth Bonum marryed xxviith march 1646

Edmond ffreeman ju^r & Rebecca Prence marryed the xxiith of Aprill 1646

Andrew Ringe and Deborah Hopkins marryed the xxiiith Aprill 1646

Thomas Pope and Sarah Jenney marryed the xxixth may 1646.

[p. 144] James Addams & ffrances Vasall Married ye 15th of Julie 1646.

(*To be continued*)

---

* "Mercy" was first written, but it was crossed out and "Desire" was inter⁻ lined in the same hand and ink.

† These entries were left unfinished.

‡ Space was left for the surname.

§ The day of the month was omitted.

|| Space was left for the given name.

PLYMOUTH COLONY VITAL RECORDS

TRANSCRIBED BY GEORGE ERNEST BOWMAN

(Continued from Vol. XIII, p. 86)

THE earliest births and deaths entered on the Plymouth Colony Records are found in a volume now marked "Marriages Births Burials." This book contains also marriage records of later date than those in the Court Orders, which were printed in the first article of this series. The vital records in the volume begun in the present article were printed in 1857 by the Commonwealth of Massachusetts, and edited by Dr. Nathaniel B. Shurtleff; but the book is not accessible to many of our readers, and it contains serious errors which have caused much unfortunate confusion.

The first few pages are badly worn, and Dr. Shurtleff assigned the year 1647, instead of 1648, to the first remaining record of Plymouth births. A careful study of the system of entering these records for the first few years shows that the order of entering was as follows: Plymouth Births, Plymouth Marriages and Burials, Sandwich Births, Sandwich Marriages and Burials, Yarmouth Births, Yarmouth Marriages and Burials. If this order was not followed we must assume that there were at least twenty-six births in Plymouth in 1647, but none in 1648. The death record of Isaac Cushman also confirms the date 1648.

The third death record on the first page is badly worn, but there is no doubt that the reading "Zeb[worn]eman" is incorrect. The remaining portion of the first letter is not the bottom of "Z" but of "R" and the name recorded was undoubtedly "Rebecca Freeman."

The first Yarmouth death, on the same page, should be Hugh "Tilly", not "Tilby" as printed by Dr. Shurtleff. The record is easily read at the present time.

Dr. Shurtleff omitted pages 2 and 3 in giving the original numbers. The first two pages are now numbered 1 and 2, and pages 3 and 4 are missing.

In Dr. Shurtleff's copy the first entry of a Plymouth birth, one "Winter," was printed as if it were at the bottom of page 1, and with Yarmouth Burials, instead of at the top of the next page. On page 6 of the original, the record of the stillborn son of Peter Wright was entered before his sister Sarah, not after the birth of Benet Elles, as printed in 1857.

Errors such as printing "twenty fourth", in the birth of
Lydia Barnes, where the original reads "24th", and "20th", in
the birth of Mary Marchant, where the original reads "twen-
tieth", do not alter facts and will not be especially noted
hereafter.

[SANDWICH BURIALS, PROBABLY]

[p. 1] [worn]entyeth of November
[worn]ried the tenth of febrewary
Reb[*]eman buried the 23^d of march

1647
yarmouth Regester of the beirth of theire Children
Susanna Miller Daughter of Mr John Miller was born the 2^{cond} of May
Elizabeth hedge Daughter of Mr Willam hedge was born the twentyone
  of May
Samuell Matthews the sonn of James Matthew[s] was born the first
  of May
Jonathan hallot the sonn of Andrew hallot was born the twentyeth of
  November
Ruth Tayler the Daughter of Richard Tayler was born the 29th of
  July
Mary Rider the Daughter of Samuell Ryder was born the sixt of
  September
Sara hull the Daughter of Trustrum hull was born the 18th of October
Beniamin Staare the sonn of Tho: Staare was born the sixt of febrewary
[†] Darby the sonn of John Darby was born the last of febrewary
Josepth the sonn of Willam nicherson born the 10 month 1647

1647
yarmouth Regester for mariages & burialls
hugh Tilly * Died the twenty eight of Janu[ary] buried the the Day
  folliong
henery Wilden maried to Eed[worn] the twentyfift of Janua[ry]
Sara hull the [worn]

[PLYMOUTH BIRTHS, 1648 *]

[p. 2] Winter * [worn] was born on t[worn]
Tho: & hanna Smith the sonn & [Daughter] of Richard Smith being
  twines were born on the twentythird of aprell
Lidia Barnes the Daughter of John Barnes was born on the 24th of
  aprell

* See introductory notes.

† The given name appears to have been omitted by mistake, as no space was
left for its insertion later. The leaf is perfect at this point.

Samuell Wood the sonn of henery Wood was born the twentyfift of May

hanna Glase the Daughter of James Glase was born the 2^{cond} of June

Ann Sturtivant the Daughter of Samuell Sturtivant was born the 4th of June

Lidia Bartlet the Daughter of Robert Bartlet was born on the 8th of June

Rebekah Billington the Daughter of ffrancis Billington was born on the 8th of June

Abigaill Church the Daughter of Richard Church was born on the 22^{cond} of June

hanna Eedy the Daughter of Samuell Eedy was born on the twenty-third of June

Elizabeth Chipman the Daughter of John Chipman was born on the 24th of June

hester Willet the Daughter of Mr Tho: Willet was born on the sixt of July

Sara heward the Daughter of John heward was born on the twentyeth Day of august

[worn] Paddy the sonn of Mr Willam Paddy [was born on] the sixt of September

[worn] sonn of Willam hoskins [worn] last Day of November

[worn] John Tompson

[pages 3 and 4 are missing]

[p. 5] [worn] the Daughter of M^r [worn] was borne the 26^t of December

Seth Pope the sonn of Tho: Pope was born on the 13th of January

Elizabeth Cook the Daughter of Jakob Cook was born on the 18th of January

Samuell & Elizabeth Watson being twines the sonn & Daughter of Gorg Watson were born the 18th of January

Ephraim Morton the sonn of Ephraim Morton was born on the 27th of January

Isaak Doty the sonn of Edward Doty was born on the 8th of febrewary

Isaak Cushman the sonn of the Elder Cushman was born the 8th of febrewary

Mary Atkins the Daughter of henery Atkins was born the 13th of march

Elizabeth faunce the Daughter of John faunce was born the twenty third of march

1648

Plym Regester of mariages & burialls

Elizabeth Spooner the wife of Willam Spooner Died the twenty eight of aprell

John Wood the sonn of Steven W[ood died] the [*]th [worn]

Tho Smith the sonn of Richard S[mith worn]

* This figur appears to have been either 8 or 9.

hanna Glase the Daughter of [worn] Died the 15th of June

✳ John Young was maried unto A[worn] the 13th of December

Mr Beniamin Vermayes maried unto M^{ris} Mercy Bradford the one and twentyeth of December

John Barnes the sonn of John Barnes Died the twenty fift of December

John Smith Juni of Plym was maried unto Debora howland the 4th of January

John Tompson the sonn of John Tompson Died the eleventh of febrewary

[p. 6]   164[8]

[Sandwid]g Regester of the beirth of their Children

[worn]a Boatfish borne the 27th of march

Mary Willis was borne the 14th of aprell

Bathsheuah Skiffe born the twentyone of aprell

Meriam Wood was born the 8th of May

Ezra Bourne was born the 12th of May

Micaell Blakwell was born the first of June

Caleb Allen was born the 27th of June

Patience Butler was born the 14th of august

Susanna Turner was born the 28th of September

Debora Wing was born the tenth of October

Nathaneell fish was born the 27th of november

hester Allen was born the 8th of December

A sonn of Peeter Wright still born the 16th of December

Sara Wright was born the eleventh of febrewary

Benet Elles was born the 27th of febrewary

1648

Sandwidg Regester for mariages & burials

Willam Wright buried the 2^{cond} of may

Gorg Allen senier buried the 2^{cond} of may

Gorg Knot buried the third of may

Meream Wood buried the 9th of may

Willam Newland Maried to Rose [*] holloway the 19th of May

John Presbery buried the 19th of may

Tho Burgis maried to Elizabeth Basset the 8th of november

[worn]aried to Mary Vincent the 8th of november

[worn]ed the eleventh of October

[worn] the the eleventh of December

p me Willam Wood

1648

[Ya]rmou[th] Regester of the beirth of their Children

Hannah the Daughter of Richard Templare was borne the fift of January Ann° Dom 1642

───────────

* "Allen" was first written, but it was crossed out in the same ink, and the entry completed as printed.

Elezabeth the Daughter of Edward Sturgis was born the twentieth
of aprell
Mary the Daughter of Robert Davis the 28th of the same
Samuell the sonn of ffrancis Baker the first of may
Mary the Daughter of John Marchant the twentieth of may
Ephraim the sonn of John Wing the thirtieth of may
John the soone of Roger Elles the first of December
Ann the Daughter of Richard Tayler the 2^{cond} of the same
Beniamin the sonne of John Gray about the 7th of December
[worn]nn the Daughter of Willam Eldred about the 16th of the same
[worn]amuell the sonne of Richard Templer the 22^{cond} of January
The Daughter of Peeter worden febrewary the tenth
Mary the Daughter of m^r hedge the [worn]
[worn] the son of Richard Templ[worn] yarmouth

[p. 7]   1648
yarmouth Regester of burials
Elizabeth the Daughter of hugh Norman of the age of six y[ears]
Drowned in a well the 28th of may
Ruth the Daughter of Richard Tayler was buried
the sonne of John Winge Drowned in the snow about the eleventh of
December